THE Fn' BOOK

How the Fight, Flight, Freeze & Fawn Responses Keep Us
Bleeding, Running, Standing Still, and Apologizing in Relationships

Written and Published by

PHILLIP ANTHONY

The Fn' Book: How the Fight, Flight, Freeze & Fawn Responses Keep Us Bleeding, Running, Standing Still and Apologizing in Relationships. Copyright © 2025 by Phillip Anthony

All rights reserved. No part of this publication may be reproduced, distributed, or transmitted in any form or by any means, including photocopying, recording, or other electronic or mechanical methods, without the prior written permission of the publisher, except in the case of brief quotations embodied in critical reviews and certain other noncommercial uses permitted by copyright law.

First Edition

ISBN: 979-8-218-09030-2 (hardcover)

Cover design by Nicole Collie

theFnBook.com

Table of Contents

Dedication _____

Acknowledgments _____

Introduction _____

Part I: UNDERSTANDING THE SYSTEM

Chapter One: The Fn' Problem _____ 1

Chatper Two: The Blueprint of Survival _____ 6

Chapter Three: The Body's Alarm System _____ 24

Chapter Four: The Amygdala: Your Relationship's Amber Alert ___ 38

Chapter Five: Survival Mode as a Lifestyle _____ 50

Chapter Six: Where Are You Living?

Part II: THE IMPACT OF CONNECTION _____ 68

Chapter Seven: Love Under Fire: Relationships in Survival ___ 84

Chapter Eight: The Fight Response: When Protection Becomes Aggression _____ 97

Chapter Nine: The Flight Response: Running from Intimacy ___ 116

Chapter Ten: The Freeze Response: The Silent Killer of Connection 133

Chapter Eleven: The Fawn Response: People-Pleasing at the Cost of Self _____ 154

Chapter Twelve: The Dance of Survival: When Response Patterns Collide _____ 173

Chapter Thirteen: My Story: A Life on Alert   192

Part III: BREAKING THE LOOP _____

Chapter Fourteen: Recognizing Your Triggers: The First Step to Freedom _____ 196

Chapter Fifteen: The Nervous System Knows Before You Do _____ 216

Chapter Sixteen: Rewiring Your Nervous System: From Survival to Safety _____ 242

Chapter Seventeen: The Practice of Presence. 263

Part IV: HEALING THE CONNECTION_____

Chapter Eighteen: Parenting Without Passing the Panic _____ 280

Chapter Nineteen: Forging New Circuits: A Life Beyond Survival __ 295

Epilogue _____ 308

   Bibliography and References _____ 314

Therapy is expensive. Reading a book is not.

But therapy is a complex process administered by a trained and licensed expert, right?

As one who has been a practicing therapist for 32 years as of the publishing of this book, I would say that no one is more an expert in a given condition than the one who has lived it and overcome it. Phillip Anthony has done both. He has lived the recovery from the impact of trauma in relationships and he has chased that monster back to from whence it came.

Now, Phillip is about to become a good friend of yours. Only a good friend would talk to you this way and give you this valuable insight to help immediately change your life.

He writes:

"For the first time, I understood what it was I'd been experiencing all my life as something other than a character flaw or my own weakness. It was biology."

And with those words, Phillip Anthony turns a corner in his life and relationship history, while simultaneously inviting you to turn a corner in your own life.

And this is the exact aim of this incredibly helpful book; to help you turn a corner and find a whole new path and a whole new way to live in relationships.

I have always said that we live in a world with more than one type of logic. We have classical logic where precepts lead us to conclusions and the world is predictable.

Then we have the logic of the nervous system. This logic would seem to contradict classical logic and so at first, the behavior and emotional life of human beings seems erratic and confusing. Then, amazingly as one begins to understand the nervous system, human behavior begins to make a certain kind of sense and suddenly change is within reach.

We live in amazing times; times in which we have a deep understanding and a roadmap of our brain, and our Central Nervous System. Because we do, we are no longer subject to the mysterious impulses of a nervous system on fire. We can learn to get out of the trap and with equal importance we can learn to build the life we have been hoping for.

What we now understand about the nervous system and the various elements of brain function has allowed us to not only understand, but to re-wire the unconscious patterns of behavior.

Phillip gives you the roadmap you have been looking for your entire life. Even if you weren't looking on purpose, some part of you has been looking. He gives you the roadmap to the logic of the nervous system, and in light of this, your life will begin to make sense, and the pathway of change will become clear, evident and much more available.

If in any way, you have found yourself repeating destructive patterns in your life and relationships, this book is for you and for everyone that you love. Give yourself the gift of change and all for the price of a book.

Bob Hamp

Licensed Marriage and Family Therapist

Founder of Think Differently Academy.

This book is dedicated to my parents—the ones who brought me into this world—but also to Robb and Paul: you have been the foundational father figures in my life. To Joel, Al, Jonathan, and my close circle of friends, thank you. Finally, to my son, Avi—this is for you, and my prayer is that what I have learned herein will be a light to your path and a beacon if you veer from it.

Before we dive into the heart of this book, I want to acknowledge a few important things.

First, some of the names, timelines, and specific details in this book have been altered to protect the privacy of those involved in my story. While the core experiences and lessons are authentic, I've changed identifying information where necessary. This book is about healing, not exposing or hurting others.

Second, this book contains descriptions of trauma, abuse, and difficult emotional experiences. If at any point you find yourself becoming overwhelmed while reading, please take a break. Practice some of the regulation techniques we'll discuss. Your well-being matters more than finishing a chapter.

Third, while I've done my best to accurately represent the science behind trauma responses and healing, I am not a licensed therapist, psychologist, or medical professional. The insights I share come from my personal experience, extensive reading, and work with my own therapists over the years. If you're struggling with trauma or relationship difficulties, I strongly encourage you to seek support from qualified professionals.

Finally, to anyone who has ever felt stuck in survival mode, who has found themselves repeating relationship patterns they don't understand, or who has wondered if they'll ever feel truly safe and connected—this book is for you. Your experiences are valid. Your struggles make sense given what you've been through. And healing, while not always linear or easy, is possible.

Thank you for joining me on this journey.

Full disclosure…for those of you who didn't read the Acknowledgments page: I am not a medical professional. I am not a psychologist or psychiatrist. I am not a licensed counselor or therapist.

I am a trauma survivor.

The things I'm going to share with you in this book are due largely to my surviving trauma, my understanding of the brain, my perspective of applying neuroscience—a ton of it—and conditioning myself to live a better life based on the understanding of this science.

At an early age, I was forced into living through a life of trauma. I came from a divorced home at the age of six. I experienced several divorced homes as a child. By the time I was 15, I'd been to 8 different schools. By the time I was dropping out of high school at 18, I had lived in 9 different residences. My home life—that is, the atmosphere of my home—was filled with violence, mental and emotional abuse, and never-ending conflict.

Unfortunately for me, from an early age—due to my home environment—I was conditioned to live in fight, flight, freeze, or fawn, which lasted the better part of my childhood.

I realized that there are millions of others walking the planet who have had similar experiences.

Being a child afraid of his/her parents forces the young mind of a child into "survival mode," which is at its core, the most basic and primitive function of the Acute Stress Response.

The way a child lives under the threat of fear, subconsciously conditions them to be unseen and unheard. This is a protective measure. Again, our brain wired us to "survive." For myself, this inadvertently forced me into isolation at a very young age.

During a time that should have been full of living in harmony, peace, and joy, mine was filled with continual panic, unrest, and fear.

I never knew how my parents (or later on, step-parents) were going to react from one day to the next—and many times from one moment to the next. I never knew how my parents were going to behave, and for me all I knew was this: it is better to be unseen and unheard than it is to be in the line of fire.

My parents could absolutely not regulate their emotional lives, and this poured the foundation of what would quickly become a childhood spent in survival mode for me.

Add to this the dynamic of violence; I was driven deeper into fear and flight or freeze, while my subconscious was being conditioned to work overtime to help me survive. Sadly, it would be years before I had enough and would learn to "fight"— and as my life would later prove, it wouldn't initially be the healthy kind of "fight".

My older brother bullied me regularly while I was growing up, often inflicting physical abuse. These weren't your typical, just-two-brothers-fighting kind of incidents; there was something sadistic about my brother beating me up. He knew I was shy. He knew I never fought back and was, therefore, weak. He wanted to make me feel pain, and he wanted to hurt me—no doubt out of his pain. This not only left me in a constant state of fear when I was around my brother, but it often left me in a state of *freeze*.

Over time, I eventually retreated into isolation and tried to spend as much time as I could by myself, where I ultimately felt safe.

It was in this bubble, subconsciously created, where I learned to survive. I will reflect on this time in my life throughout this book to uncover the elements of the acute stress response.

Years later, I studied boxing, hand-to-hand combat, and Aikido while living in Okinawa, Japan, as a U.S. Marine.

Whether it was because of the violence I witnessed and experienced as a child, or just the athleticism and bravado of it, I had been fascinated with "fighting" ever since I can remember.

During the early 2000s, when mixed martial arts (MMA) began its rise, I took an interest and found a fascination in the arts therein.

Over the years, I have watched hundreds of boxing matches and MMA events, and I have learned so much—metaphorically speaking—about the acute stress response from this athletic and highly regarded entertainment media.

Years ago, I gleaned a powerful metaphor of the Acute Stress Response (*The Fn' Response*)—an intriguing crossover to learn about how the component of the brain works in our lives and is correlated in the everyday living of our psyche.

In "fight" mode, most people who are not trained will do one of two things: they will naturally fight, fearing that they are in imminent danger, or they will flee and do everything possible to run away from physical confrontation.

In MMA fighting, "fighters" are typically students of several disciplines of martial arts, which they dedicated their lives to for years.

In the "Octagon," as it is called, professional fighters—in the UFC (Ultimate Fighting Championship), for example—fight in either three or five 5-minute rounds.

If you have never witnessed these men and women in action, the fights can be quite brutal. The fighters fight with 3-ounce gloves and no headgear, and they are fighting to win by any legal means within the sport. Boxing, karate, jiu-jitsu, kickboxing, wrestling, and all other forms of martial arts disciplines can be utilized to beat their opponent.

Most of the fights end in blood, and in many of them quite a bit of it!

Fight fans around the world see talent and raw violence—the kind that your average person would do anything to avoid.

What is often overlooked by most people is the fact that these athletes who fight for a living have not only trained in various martial arts disciplines over years, but they have also trained themselves to remain calm in most situations that would cause most of us to flee (flight).

The metaphor here—as it relates to the brain—is the metaphor most of us will overlook:

These fighters have spent years training themselves to be calm in the face of real physical danger.

They have dedicated years to both throwing and receiving punches. They have felt the pain of body kicks and head kicks. They have experienced the fear of surrendering to wrestling maneuvers. They have felt the uncomfortable sensation of being choked, all the while attempting to keep from "tapping out" under the immense pain and pressure to give up.

Oddly enough, the same part of the brain that is affected by physical pain is the same part of the brain that is affected by emotional pain: insulting comments and ridicule, condescending remarks thrown their way, and any kind of emotional pain brought about by negative and otherwise abusive behavior.

On March 5, 2016, an epic MMA fight occurred between Nate Diaz and Conor McGregor. At the time, Conor McGregor was considered to be the pound-for-pound best fighter in all MMA (mixed martial arts). Nate Diaz, on the other hand, was not considered a formidable opponent. It would be his 30th professional fight, and he was beginning to look and fight like an aged athlete who'd likely seen his best fighting days behind him, at least by most fighting analysts.

Conor McGregor was known to be the most accurate and powerful boxer in the lightweight division. Nate Diaz, who was also a great striker, was considered one of the best jujitsu artists in the division.

Initially, the fight seemed to be going in Conor's direction, with him outboxing and outmaneuvering Nate in the first round. By the end of the first round, Conor had drawn blood out of Nate, but the second round proved to be a challenge and a fight that no one in the UFC would see coming.

Around the second half of the second round, Nate began finding his range and tagging Conor McGregor in the face. At one point, Conor held up his hands and shrugged his shoulders, as if to say, "OK, let's go!"

Unfortunately for him, this was more than likely a response triggered by mental fatigue. In the next 30 seconds, Nate let his hands go and began pummeling Conor with a barrage of punches.

Out of desperation, Conor attempted to tackle Nate to the canvas, which many believe was a reaction I would categorize as "flight." Within seconds, Nate applied a rear naked choke—specifically, a choke around Conor's neck—forcing him to "tap out" and ultimately lose the match.

So, what's the difference between fight, flight, and freeze in the Octagon versus everyday life, and where is the metaphor?

The professional MMA (mixed martial arts) fighter has been trained to remain calm in the most dangerous of physical confrontations; most of us have not been "trained" to endure emotional abuse and maintain our composure.

Those of us who have learned to "fight" verbally with our defensive will — whether out of conditioning to be defensive at any cost or with our wits and intellect from years of being in emotionally charged environments at home or otherwise — have paid a great price for engaging in conflict on a higher level than others.

Unfortunately, the MMA fighter who is engaged in a physical fight and the (non-MMA fighter) average human being engaging in mental warfare have one thing in common: they are both "fighting" to stay alive out of a primitive need to survive in the moment.

The intention of this Fn' Book is to raise an awareness with a spin of a different perspective by utilizing the metaphor of MMA (mixed martial arts) fighting to help us better understand how the fight, flight, freeze, and fawn response (the Fn' response) works for us or against us in our relationships. Whether in business or personal relationships, the Fn' response influences our behavior toward others in every interaction.

Neuroscience is constantly at work within each of us. It is the wiring we were all designed with, and in many ways, to this present day, it continues to be co-designed by us.

I hope that by sharing this information with you, I can help create awareness.

Thank you for taking the time to read what I am about to share.

As a legendary referee, "Big" John McCarthy of the MMA Octagon would say, "Let's get it on!"

PART I: UNDERSTANDING THE SYSTEM

CHAPTER ONE

THE Fn' PROBLEM

On a warm September morning years ago, I left my marriage with nothing more than a backpack of clothes and $900 in cash. Six years of my life, my time, my energy—six years of tiptoeing and six years of running out to the garage to escape fights—had all led up to a moment of realization: I just couldn't work hard enough to change the situation I was living in.

I wasn't just leaving a marriage. I was running away from a situation that had set off every survival response inside me for years. My nervous system was so dysregulated that I'd developed chronic health conditions. I had made being a manager of my wife's issues—alcohol and narcissism—a replacement of who I was; I had ultimately lost myself somewhere along the way. The man who was confident and sure of himself, motivated, ambitious, and full of life, had become nothing more than a creature that now jumped at the smallest sound, waiting for the next time bomb, and was simply trying to find a way out of the chaos of our home.

But—before you shake your head in empathy for me or say, "This sounds like my life"—let me stop you, because what I've shared so far is only a tiny part of the story.

The real problem was with me; the real problem was in me.

This wasn't my first unsuccessful relationship or marriage.

This was my sixth marriage — a fact I once would have been ashamed of, but now it seems to me the result of a series of desperate, subconscious carnival games, each one a colossal waste of time and money. With every relationship, the pattern was mostly the same: at first, "we" connected and hoped; then, things grew tense; eventually, one of us emotionally withdrew or physically left, and the relationship crumbled. The faces and details were different, but the dynamics involved in almost all of them had been incredibly similar.

What I didn't realize until very recently, however, was that this pattern was neither just bad luck nor simply poor choices in partners. It was a raw expression of my nervous system's survival programming—specifically, the fighting-fleeing-freezing-fawning response—that was wired into me from childhood and then perpetuated through my adult years.

This book is about that response — what scientists refer to as the Acute Stress Response and what I frequently now refer to as the Fn' problem. It's about how this archaic survival mechanism, built to defend us against physical threats, will take over our relationships, sabotage our connections, and enslave us in cycles of conflict, distance, and disconnection.

But sadly, this is not just my story. It is a human story. The survival responses that have formed my relationship patterns are at work in millions of relationships around the world. And they are likely at play in your relationships, whether you are aware of it or not. They shape how you engage with conflict, how you give and receive love, how you handle vulnerability, and how you negotiate the inevitable struggles that come with two complex human nervous systems attempting to connect.

The good news — the reason I'm writing a book about all of this instead of just crying into my pillow about my relationship disasters — is that these patterns can be identified, understood, and addressed. The nervous system wired for protection can be rewired for connection. The blind reactions that have had you bleeding out, running, or standing frozen can become conscious choices that reflect your deepest values and desires.

My personal story is at the center of this because I have lived it. Over the last 30 of my adult years, I've seen therapists, counselors, psychologists, and even psychiatrists; I've read and studied the neuroscience of trauma and attachment; and I've practiced new ways of being in relationships — with myself and with other people. When I walked out of my marriage almost two years ago, I committed to a deep, neurological exploration and a rewiring of my own nervous system. I have made deep changes, not only in terms of how I feel, but in terms of how I show up in the world and in my connections with people.

"The Deepest Well," by Nadine Burke Harris, is the book I wish I had read decades ago — a practical, science-based visit from a caring, smart friend who steers us away from our worst-case reflexes and toward responsible people and policy. It's rooted in the latest neuroscience and trauma research, but it's not an academic text. It comes from the trenches of actual relationship disputes and actual healing.

In these pages and those that follow, I will rely on two metaphors that have helped me to make sense of these complex dynamics—and they aren't what I would call your typical teachers: poker and the UFC (Ultimate Fighting Championship).

As a student of poker, I know that winning at the table is about much more than the hand you're dealt — instead, it's about how you play that hand, with your ability to read the table, manage your emotions, and make strategic bets under pressure. Similarly, in relationships, it is not the "hand" you were dealt in childhood that determines success; it is how well you can read your patterns, manage your nervous system, and make choices instead of having reactions.

As a UFC enthusiast, I've watched how fighters can train to build strength and technique but also to be able to remain present and strategic even while under attack. They learn to get hit without being thrown off balance, to see their opponent's patterns, and to respond rather than react. And metaphorically, they're all necessary for successfully dealing with the inevitable upsets and triggers that come up in close intimacy.

Whether you're in a contentious relationship, are just out of one, or are trying to build a better one, you'll learn what to do and what not to do to build lasting, healthy love and a roadmap for understanding and changing your survival responses that could be getting in the way of finding success.

The first three understandings involve fighting, running away, and flight. But the true aim of healing is not escape; it is to become capable of staying present and engaged even when your survival brain is screaming at you to fight, flee, freeze, or fawn. It's a matter of seeing when you're being triggered and deciding to respond differently. It's about creating safety in your own nervous system to have real connection with other people.

This has been my focus for many, many years, but more intensely so since that morning in September when I left the marriage. And it's the work I still do every day. And it's the work I'm asking you to join me in as we explore the Fn' problem together and uncover what is possible beyond survival.

Let's begin.

CHAPTER TWO

A PLAN FOR SURVIVAL

The first time I remember feeling true terror, I was six years old. My father was drunk at home again, and the slam of our apartment door made my heart race. I knew what was coming. The criticism. The shouting. The threats. My mother's tears.

I didn't have language for what was going on in my body then. All I knew was that my stomach would tighten, my breath would grow shallow, and I would have this downcast, end-of-the-world cosmic longing to either hide behind our couch, where our German shepherd mix, Mopey, would crawl behind until my father got him out with a belt and a cross tie, whipping that poor dog, or occasionally I would stand between my mother, doing everything I could to talk my dad out of whatever it was that he was upset about.

Fight, flight, freeze.

By age 7, I was used to these reactions, even if I didn't know what they were or why they happened for decades.

Later that year, my parents divorced. It was supposed to be a fresh start in a new home, but it was really just the starting point of a tumultuous cycle that would play out over and over during my childhood. My father married again when I was 7, and I gained a stepmother and a little brother, Eric, only to lose them a few years later when my father's abuse grew to be too much for her to endure. I'll never forget the night she and my younger stepbrother slept in the hallway of the apartment under the staircase after my father beat her.

The next day, she was gone.

To this day, I can visualize my father one summer afternoon, sitting at our kitchen table, reading her goodbye letter to me and my older brother, sobbing and sobbing and sobbing. I couldn't get close to my father in his grief. I sat there petrified and paralyzed, unable to approach this man, who had terrified our household.

What I didn't know (and no 7-year-old knows) was that these responses are not random. They are not weaknesses or personal flaws. They are components of an ancient survival mechanism wired deep in our brains, a system designed to protect us from danger in the form of predators and other possible threats to our existence — like being eaten 500 feet from shore while standing in sandbars on beaches.

And to top it off, this very system that helped our ancestors flee predators on the savanna is now turning on when your partner stops talking to you, or when your boss sends you the "we need to talk" email. Learning this system is not only fascinating science, but it's also the secret to changing your relationships.

The Original Emergency System

Let's rewind for a moment. Way back... before smartphones, before cities, before farming, in the past, humans were merely another species attempting to avoid extinction.

In that world, you needed to be immediately responsive to potential threats in order to survive. If you got a glimpse of a lion, you didn't have the luxury of weighing the pros and cons or pondering the long-term ramifications of running rather than fighting. You needed an automatic response system that could circumvent your conscious thinking and move your body — now.

That is, indeed, what evolution equipped us with: the fight-flight-freeze response. This system is controlled by a complicated relationship among brain structures, hormones, and nervous system pathways, but it comes down to three basic choices when danger is encountered:

Fight: To resist the threat and fight against it.

Flight: Get the hell out of there as quick as you can.

Freeze: Ensure that you are completely still in order to not be spotted, or be ready to be hit.

Eventually, researchers and therapists discovered a fourth response that's especially pertinent to relationships:

Fawn: Resolve the danger by pleasing and complying with others.

All of these responses had an important survival role to play when we were back in our evolutionary infancy. If the threat was smaller than you, and you had a reasonable chance of winning, fighting made sense. If the predator was a bit bigger than you, you should probably run. If you couldn't run or fight, then freezing might cause the predator to lose interest or give you time to be ready when it attacked. And in social species like humans, fawning — appeasing more dominant members of the group — could prevent aggression and help maintain crucial social bonds.

These were not conscious choices.

They were automatic, lightning-fast responses powered by primitive regions of your brain that don't give a shit about your career goals or relationship status. They only care that you are alive five minutes from now. We often forget, or don't know, that our brain was not designed to bring us happiness; it was designed to keep us alive, period.

From Predators to Partners

So how does all of this relate to your relationship issues?

In all things.

Here's the thing about evolution though: it is very slow. Really slow.

Our archaic bodies and brains are basically unchanged from 200,000 years ago. The fight-flight-freeze-fawn system, which is designed to get you away from physical predators, is the same system that gets switched on when you feel emotionally endangered.

Your brain can't tell the difference between a saber-toothed tiger and a cutting remark from your partner. They both register as threats, and they both set off the same cascade of hormones and physiological responses.

When your partner criticizes you and you either "fight" by launching into defensive arguments, or (flight) remember that important email you urgently need to send, or rack your brain to think of anything to say (freeze), or start apologizing even though you've done nothing wrong (fawn)—that's your ancient survival script kicking in.

In other words, it's not that you have these responses. The difficulty is they're being woken up in contexts where they don't actually help — and often make things worse.

My Personal Blueprint: Paralyzed with Fear

I was 10 when my father remarried for the second time, bringing in my second stepmother and my 4-year-old stepsister, Austin, who became part of our family.

The pattern continued. Even though my dad was closer to religion than ever before and became involved with the church, the monster still came out from time to time. I had no idea what his mood was going to be like at any given moment, and none of us in the house knew, so we merely survived, always on the edge of our seats.

My reaction was mostly to freeze. I was silent, invisible; I was not brave enough to speak. In addition to my father, I also had an older brother, who was a split image of my father in the way of being physically and mentally abusive. Looking at or listening to others only caused me pain, so I stopped doing so. I hid for hours, reading, or playing out of view, just trying to stay under the radar.

It was around this time that my older brother molested me. The lack of clarity surrounding the situation and the embarrassment I felt contributed to my initial horror, to the point where I didn't even know if I wanted to continue living. Looking back today, I can see how this trauma nudged me toward another response: fawning. I became a people pleaser, looking so hard for love and acceptance, searching for safety, which, if I had a birthright, that would've been it.

By the time I was fourteen, I was a pressure cooker of unspoken fears and hidden feelings. But then something happened that could have never been predicted in even Nostradamus's finest work: I discovered self-help books while attending an Amway conference with some friends from the church. The first book I ever read was "Seeds of Greatness," by Denis Waitley—and to this day, it profoundly affects me every time I read his mention of the "Man in the Glass."

In my world where I could never trust adults, the self-help books served as my lifeline and private teachers, and mentors. I was hungry for understanding, and I found some in self-help, psychology, and psychiatry books. I read the Diagnostic and Statistical Manual of Mental Disorders (DSM) for hours, searching for a way to understand my family, my own experiences, and myself.

This was not mere teenage curiosity. It was survival. I was attempting to make sense of the blueprint that was being written for me.

The Nervous System: How Your Body Sends Messages

To understand how these responses operate, we need to talk about your nervous system. Don't panic —I'm not about to go all textbook on you (not yet anyway). But we can't afford to let this stuff slide.

Here's why this is relevant: Your autonomic nervous system is divided into two parts, which you cannot ignore if you want to understand why the fight-flight-freeze-fawn responses are a thing to be studied.

The Sympathetic Nervous System: This is your body's accelerator. It revs you up, gets you going, and gets you ready for action. This is the engine that turns on during fight-or-flight responses.

The Parasympathetic Nervous System: This is your body's brake. It decelerates, helps you rest and recuperate, and returns your whole body to normal after the threat has lifted.

In a person who is healthy and in balance, these 2 systems coexist in harmony. That's because the need to survive is more important than spending all of the time in "rest and digest" mode (the parasympathetic nervous system) or in "fight or flight" mode (the sympathetic nervous system).

But trauma, chronic stress, and difficult experiences in childhood can seriously disrupt that balance. Some of us get trapped in our sympathetic system: always in overdrive, always on high alert, always a second away from doom, never able to relax. Others might have overactive parasympathetic systems, closing and detaching the moment conflict blows through the door.

My family never gave me a chance to regulate my nervous system. Between my father being an alcoholic, who could be violent, and a home life marked by loss and instability — including the murder of my uncle when I was 6 years old, whom I lived with, and the loss of my grandfather, whom I also lived with for a few years — my system was consistently awash with stress hormones. There was no safe window for my parasympathetic system to reclaim control and show my body a healthy "normal."

Polyvagal Theory: The Hierarchy of Relationship

In the past few years, an extraordinary model called Polyvagal Theory has changed the game in what we know about these responses, particularly how they occur in relationships. Created by Dr. Stephen Porges, this theory provides us with an ingenious, more complex palette in which to explore our states of nervous system(s) and understand how they affect our connections with others.

Think of it like a ladder with three rungs:

The Top Rung: Social Engagement (Ventral Vagal) This is where the good stuff in life happens, where healthy relationships are. When you're on that rung, you feel safe and connected and present. With a SMIZE (thank you, Tyra Banks), your face is light-hearted, you use prosody (emotional emphasis) in your voice, and then actually listen and care about what the person you're smizing at says in return. You can tap into empathy, curiosity, and playfulness. This is where love thrives.

The Middle Rung: Mobilization (Sympathetic) Here is where fight-or-flight occurs. When you end up on this rung, you are now in survival mode. Your heart is racing, your breath is quick, and your muscles are tight. You may be angry, anxious, or overwhelmed. Objectivity becomes subjugated to reflexes. In such a condition, connection is inconvenient or impossible.

The Bottom Rung: Immobilization (Dorsal Vagal) This is the response where freeze and sometimes fawn can be seen to occur. When you climb down to this ring, you stop action. You may feel numb, foggy, disconnected, or empty. Your energy levels drop, your voice may become monotonous, and you may experience a physical sensation of heaviness or immobility. This is the most basic survival response, and it shuts down connection entirely.

In healthy relationships, partners spend much of their time on the top rung, taking occasional trips down in times of stress or conflict, and then "repairing" the relationship to move back up. In troubled relationships, it is common that partners have routine ways of bumping each other down the ladder of opportunities and, once there, of becoming stuck on a lower rung, whether for hours, days, or years.

In my childhood, I was mostly confined to the bottom two rungs of this ladder. That top rung where I could feel safe and connected was a foreign country I rarely dared to visit. I was in sympathetic activation (fight or flight) or, more frequently, dorsal vagal shutdown (freeze) when my father was home. The never-ending cycling in and out of these states became my new normal, my home, and made it virtually impossible for me to form secure attachments or develop useful skills in relationships.

Knowing where you are at on this ladder can be a game changer for relationships. It helps you see when you are not in a place of healthy connection and gives you an explicit goal: climbing back into that top ring.

The Four Responses in Detail

Now that we have a general overview of these four survival responses, we can take a closer look at them individually and see how they reveal themselves in relationships.

The Fight Response

This fight response is about confronting threats face-to-face. What used to mean grappling with predators or rivals in the physical world in our pre-evolutionary past is, in modern relationships, what we see as:

- Arguing every point—even if it's over small matters
- Raising your voice, slamming doors, threatening to leave
- Defensiveness involves quickly forming an argument even before the discussion has started.
- Preemptive attacking before you can be hurt

- Controlling the behaviors of others

Individuals whose dominant response to a perceived threat is to fight might have grown up in situations where they had to be aggressive to get their needs met or where fighting was the only response their parents modeled in a conflict—they learned that the best offense was defense.

In relationships, the fight response can perpetuate cycles of heated conflict, with both partners feeling less and less safe and therefore, more and more inclined to remain in survival mode.

The Flight Response

The flight response is an impulse to flee danger. For our ancestors, this meant sprinting away from predators. In relationships, you will experience it as:

Physical leaving in arguments

Shutting down or disengaging emotionally

Avoiding intimacy when it gets hot

Extended hours at work or excuses not to be home

Venturing into substances, self-abuse, or self-sabotaging activities to "get away"

People who are heavily flight-emotion dominant typically were raised in an environment where flight was the only safe option or learned that if they had feelings and needs and expressed them, they were ignored or punished.

The flight response in a relationship fosters distance and disconnection, making partners feel left out or unimportant.

The Freeze Response

The freeze response is what happens when the options to fight or take flight seem to be unavailable. In nature, the phenomenon is called "playing dead," where animals freeze up to avoid detection or pull a last-ditch survival tactic. Here's how it appears in relationships:

Shutting down or freezing in your head during conflicts

Experiencing a sensation of physical heaviness or sluggishness

Dissociating or "spacing out"

Inability to express feelings or needs

On the outside, looking cool; inside, totally freaking out

Those with a dominant freeze response often had overwhelming childhood situations where they couldn't fight or flee, so they froze.

As a child, I experienced these feelings.

When my father unleashed his anger, I couldn't stand up to him — he was much too big, much too strong. I could not flee — where would I go? So, I froze. I was small, and quiet, and *nobody*. My body would shut down, lose touch with my mind, and I would wait for the storm to subside. This was a habit so deeply etched in my brain that many years later, in negotiations with friends, I would be thrown into that same frozen state by even mild conflict — eventually becoming unable to talk, think, or protect myself.

For partners, the freeze response can be especially puzzling because partners may experience it as apathy or disinterest rather than what it is—a complete state of fear.

The Fawn Response

The fawn reaction, outlined by therapist Pete Walker, is about placating threats with people-pleasing and compliance. Spoken words helped cement social bonds within groups, in evolutionary terms. In relationships it looks like:

Saying sorry too much and self-blaming.

You prioritize your partner's needs over your own.

You have a hard time setting or keeping boundaries.

Some men flip-flop opinions or switch preferences to become just like their significant others.

Some individuals fear expressing disagreement verbally or using curse words.

Individuals with a strong fawn response tend to have grown up in situations where their safety and acceptance were contingent on constantly performing for others (usually parents or caregivers).

After experiencing sexual abuse from my brother, I developed a prominent fawn response in addition to my freeze response. I grew hyper-attuned to others' wants and moods, scanning constantly for the needs of fantasy people in my life and trying to please them and evade any conflict. As an adult I fell into the same pattern, time and time again, giving too much and getting too little back in relationships. The fawn response had me convinced that love equaled self-sacrifice and that my feelings were not as important as making everyone else content.

In a relationship, having the fawn response fosters imbalance, resentment, and loss of oneself, as one half of a couple consistently sublimates their own wants and desires to the relationship to the point of harm.

Your Personal Blueprint

We don't all bank on a single response. We typically have one primary response to stress that we rely on, along with secondary responses that activate when the primary one is ineffective. Your specific blueprint was crafted through the course of your life, in particular during the early years of childhood.

Consider: if, when you were a child, you got punished for being frustrated (fighting), you probably learned to shut it down and rely on one of the others instead. If you couldn't fight or flee because someone physically imprisoned you (or was at least bigger and stronger than you were), you probably learned to develop a compelling freeze or fawn response.

"But how does this apply to me, and what if I didn't experience these same dynamics in my childhood?"

Great question, and I'm so glad you asked.

It should go without saying, not everyone will have a backstory of violence, betrayal, or abuse in their childhood. Some of you may not have experienced these traumas. Some of you may not have experienced any trauma until later on in life.

Traumas make up a long list, and some of them you may not even consider traumatic events. Here's a short list of recognized traumas:

Divorce or multiple divorces. Abandonment from a partner. Infidelity. Betrayal. Loss of a family member. Loss of a child. Physical handicap. Substance abuse. Neglect. Witnessing violence. Victim of a natural catastrophe. Victim of a crime. Loss of a job. Poverty.

Trauma is defined as: a deeply distressing or disturbing event that significantly impacts a person's emotional, psychological, and physical well-being.

Therefore, if a life event has affected your psychological, emotional, or physical well-being, you have experienced some degree of trauma. Therefore, your body—specifically your acute stress response (fight, flight, freeze, or fawn)—has at some point kicked in, <u>causing the wiring in your brain to change</u>.

With that in mind, your blueprint is not random. It's an elaborate adjustment to the particular threats you were subject to early on. Remember, your brain's chief function is to keep you alive—and it will remain committed to this function at all costs. The only trouble is, this blueprint, which helped you survive childhood, very well may be sabotaging your adult relationships.

The good news? Once you know your blueprint, you can begin to change it.

Training the Response: Transitioning from Military Life to Personal Relationships

By the time I turned 18, I was a lost boy… and yes, I said, "boy." I had little guidance, but a pressing desire to leave my situation, so I signed up for the U.S. Marine Corps during the first Gulf War. Boot camp was one of the most demanding things I've ever done, physically and mentally — yet, somehow, I was able to deal with the constant screaming of drill instructors better than most other recruits.

I should have been devastated, but it was a curious voice inside me that whispered, "Yes, I thought I would be this way," and instead I was oddly calm. The drill instructors who screamed in my face a few inches away didn't trigger my typical freeze reaction.

Why?

Because I knew this territory.

This was the dining table from my childhood.

This was my schoolyard playground.

This was any given afternoon in the backyard with my bullying older brother.

This was my "normal".

It was the "home" I grew up in.

Somewhere in my strange and twisted past, my traumatic childhood upbringing had prepared me for this specific aspect of military training. My nervous system had become accustomed to verbal abuse, akin to a UFC fighter's overexposure to the ring. I had been preparing for this my whole life—without even knowing it. I wouldn't understand this until much later in my adult life.

And much later, I had this awakening: It is possible to condition our responses with exposure and exercise. As surely as I learned in my childhood to "train" myself to handle the verbal aggression, we can train our nervous systems to respond differently to the triggers that challenge our relationships.

Survival Mode as Identity

For many of us — those raised in chronically difficult or traumatic circumstances — survival isn't just something that occurs periodically; it becomes our "normal," and our identity.

I spent decades of my life operating on a hair-trigger level of hypervigilance, constantly scanning around for threats, always ready to freeze or fawn. It wasn't something I did; it was who I was. It wasn't anything I could do any other way. It was how I had learned to survive.

This long-standing flare-up of our survival responses doesn't just impact our relationships — it defines our experience of life. It shapes our career path, our friendships, our extracurriculars, and even our sense of humor. It is a filter through which we see the world and where we stand in it.

I lived in survival mode so much of my life growing up that by the time my teens came around, it was the new normal, and I forgot, "This is how everyone goes about living," never considering it odd. My voracious reading of psychology books and the DSM was not just intellectual curiosity — it was my longing to know why I felt so different, so constantly on edge, so unable to relax into life in the way others seemed to do.

It is important to realize that you've entered a survival identity once your once-in-a-while responses for survival shift to survival for your "new identity" full-time. Because, although these responses are necessary for immediate threats, <u>being in a state of constant survival is immensely damaging to your body, brain, and relationships.</u>

The Blueprint in Your Body

A fundamental point to remember about the four responses, the fight-flight-freeze-fawn responses, is that these are not just psychological — they are as deeply physical as anything we can experience.

Activating your survival mechanism triggers a series of physiological changes in your body:

Stress hormones, such as adrenaline and cortisol, rush through your blood supply.

Your heart beats faster because your blood pressure rises.

Blood is redirected from your digestive system to your large muscles.

Your breath quickens and also becomes more shallow.

Your eyes allow more light to enter, which causes your pupils to dilate.

You become less sensitive to pain.

Your prefrontal cortex (the rational part of your brain) shuts down.

Ask any UFC fighter.

These physical changes are meant to prepare you to survive immediate physical threats. They're extremely effective for that use. But when they are triggered by relationship conflicts, work stress, or traffic jams, they can become problematic.

And chronic activation of this system has been associated with a range of health problems: heart disease, digestion problems, immune system suppression, and chronic pain, among others. You're just not meant to be in fight or flight around the clock. You weren't designed to live in that state 24/7.

Growing up in a house where danger could flare up at any second, my body rarely had the opportunity to fully calm down and heal. The chronic stress exacted a physical price that would follow me into adulthood — digestive issues, tension headaches, and chronic exhaustion. These were not just psychological symptoms — they were the bodily expression of a nervous system that was trapped in survival mode.

So, addressing these patterns is not just for your relationships; it's also for your health and longevity.

Conclusion: Knowing Your Blueprint

These fight-flight-freeze-fawn responses are not flaws in character or signs of weakness. They are complex survival mechanisms that have helped keep humans alive for millennia. Your issue isn't that you're having these reactions, but that they're getting engaged even when they're not helpful to you, including in the relationships that are most important to you.

Knowing this blueprint is the beginning of change. Accept these patterns in yourself, and you open up space between the trigger and the response—that space where choice lives.

In the next chapter, we'll take a closer look at the body's alarm system, including the hormones and nerve pathways that underpin these reactions. But for the time being, I want you to begin to notice:

What are the types of responses that you tend to go with under stress?

How do they appear in your relationships?

And, most important, can you start to watch everything with curiosity rather than judgment?

I want to remind you that these reactions are what helped keep your ancestors alive until you were born. They kept me alive during a childhood that could have destroyed me completely. They're not the enemy. They're ancient allies that could use an upgrade for modern life — especially when it comes to the nuanced, emotionally layered terrain of intimate relationships.

Your survival map got you to this point. And now it's time to rewrite it for the life and relationships you actually want.

CHAPTER THREE

THE BODY'S WARNING DEVICE

The first time I really understood what my body was doing through a stress response, I remember it, and there I was in my late twenties sitting in my shrink's office with an amazing man (formerly known as "shrink"), named Dr. Joseph Ruffin, attempting to understand why I had completely shut down during a fight with my wife the night before.

"I wanted to say something, anything, but it was like my brain suddenly had no signal," I tried to explain. "I felt that my mouth was dry, my heart was pulsing, and I just … froze."

Dr. Ruffin gave me a quick nod and pulled out a diagram of the human brain. "What you're describing is an amygdala hijack," he said.

"Another patient of mine told me that recently after she received hurtful news, she found her mouth went dry and her brain went blank, leaving her tongue-tied and, like you, unable to respond. What happened? Your body's alarm system took charge, dousing you with stress hormones and blocking your ability to speak."

For the first time, I understood what it was I'd been experiencing all my life—first as a kid with my father and then in relationships as an adult—as something other than a character flaw or my own weakness. It was biology. My body was working exactly as intended in response to a perceived threat. The problem was not my alarm system itself, but rather that my alarm was going off at inappropriate times without any clear reason.

My wife's response had hijacked my amygdala; she jacked my Amy.

You need to understand the body's alarm system, how it functions, why it is there, and how it can go wrong to transform your relationships. Well, it won't—at least not until you've learned what's really happening in your body in conflict and until you can do something about the automatic responses that were designed for physical survival, not for emotional safety.

The Chemical Mix That Promotes Stress

When your brain senses a threat, it sets off an alarm system that leads to a rush of hormones that prepare your body to either fight or run away. This mix of chemicals consists of:

Adrenaline (Epinephrine): The first on the scene. Your adrenal glands flood your body with adrenaline within a few seconds of a threat. This hormone gets your heart beating faster, makes your blood pressure rise, and stimulates energy supplies. It's what gives you that jolt of energy when you're scared or angry.

Norepinephrine: Adrenaline's evil twin? This hormone ramps up alertness, focuses attention, and can help you keep your mind on the perceived threat while ignoring everything else. That's why you can focus on your partner's tone or expression in an argument, even if you don't hear what they're saying.

Cortisol: The stress hormone that comes a little later to the party. Adrenaline and norepinephrine levels spike right away, but cortisol gradually increases and remains elevated. Cortisol is involved in controlling the body's processes that are active during stress, like blood pressure, blood sugar, and immune function. It's meant to help you respond to prolonged threats, but when it is chronically elevated, it can tear your body and brain apart.

Together, these hormones form what we feel to be the stress response — that unmistakable sensation of your body kicking into high alert.

My latest, personal anthem: Don't Jack my Amy.

My Alarm System: ON BLARE

I grew up in a home with an alcoholic, abusive father, so my alarm system was constantly being set off. It was a chemical cocktail that would rush through my small body on cue: every door slam, every raised voice, every heavy footstep walking up the stairs.

By the age of 14, I had already been through the painful experience of an absent mother, two stepmothers, sexual abuse, and innumerable eruptions of violence—whence my body had learned to remain in a constant state of alert.

And during times without a riot, my cortisol levels were likely even higher, as my nervous system remained braced for the next inevitable threat.

This is what scientists mean by a "sensitized" alarm system. My body's danger detector, like your smoke alarm going off when you're just trying to cook dinner, had become oversensitive, unable to tell the difference between true threat and the stress of normal life.

The sexual abuse of my brother was an ongoing exacerbation of this sensibilization. Although the event occurred only once, it left a significant festering wound in both my body and my soul.

Not only was home not safe, but my own body didn't feel safe, either. My identity, my boundaries, my self-esteem — all of it had been compromised. This made for a perfect storm for an alarm system that would stay on high alert long into adulthood.

The Hijacked Brain: What Suddenly Happens in the Brain with Addiction

To learn what goes on when conflicts arise in relationships, we need a brief tour of your brain's inner workings.

Various regions of your brain have evolved at different times during our evolutionary history. The most rudimentary portion, sometimes referred to as the "reptilian brain," regulates simple activities like breathing and heart rate. The limbic system, which the amygdala is a part of, helps manage emotions and memories. And the prefrontal cortex — the newest, most evolved part — processes complex thinking, planning, and social behavior.

These areas normally cooperate and work well together. Your amygdala's "Mayday! Mayday!" alert is what I refer to in our modern day as your personal Amber Alert. warning you to a potential danger, but your prefrontal cortex can assess whether it's a real threat and then select a suitable response.

But then your alarm goes off, and the beautiful night of harmony is shattered. Blood flow moves away from your prefrontal cortex and toward older parts of your brain, as well as to the large muscles. That is awesome if you need to slug it out or flee from a predator, but terrible if you are trying to have a subtle discussion about relationship problems.

This is what we refer to as a "hijacked brain." Your thinking brain — the part related to empathy, rational thought, and communication — goes out the window, and your survival brain takes over.

I experienced this hijacking many, many times as a child. When my father raged, I felt my mind would go blank, I would forget how to talk, and I would lose the ability to process information. I could only respond from that primal place of survival — often by freezing or fawning.

Years later—back to the Marine Corps Boot Camp chapter, I underwent another sort of hijacking. We were not allowed to sleep much in our first week, and stayed stressed on a 24-hour basis as well as verbally abused by the drill instructors, who were forcing us to battle our normal thought patterns and become Marines. Except this hijacking was voluntary, had a purpose, and was in service to something more important than survival.

Relationship Triggers: Why Words Can Sting Like Sharpened Blades

Now here's where this gets interesting for relationships: your alarm system—the Amber Alert—responds not only to physical threats. It reacts to these social threats as strongly, if not more so.

And it makes evolutionary sense. Being rejected by the tribe wasn't just "uncomfortable" for our ancestors — it could be a death sentence. Human beings crawled out of the muck via cooperation and connection. To be ostracized was to lose access to food, protection, and mates. Even though our brains treat social rejection as if it were a mortal threat, in many ways it was.

This is why some relationship dynamics can elicit such strong physiological reactions:

- Criticism can seem as though it's a physical blow.
- Silent treatment can be perceived as abandonment.
- One may experience a sense of expulsion from the tribe, complete with public humiliation.
- Betrayal can even seem like it's a threat to your very life.

Your rational mind may understand that your partner's criticism is not fatal, but your amygdala—*your Amy*—is not so discriminating. It senses potential harm to your social status or connection and hits the alarm button with the same urgency as it would for a physical threat.

For those of us with childhood abuse, these threats at a social level can feel even more triggering because they echo older, deeper wounds. When my ex-wife lectured me, I wasn't simply dealing with her words but with the bitterness of my father's tongue, the echo of never being enough, and the fear that love would always be tenuous and conditional.

The Body Keeps the Score: Somatic Symptoms as Signs of Activation

One of the best skills you can learn is to notice when the alarm goes off before you're taken over. Your body consistently alerts you, yet we've learned to ignore these warnings.

Here are some common physical signs that your stress response is intensifying:

Heart-related signals:

Increased heart rate

Sensations of heartbeats in the chest, throat, or ears

Chest tightness or pressure

Breathing changes:

Shallow, rapid breathing

Feeling like you're not getting enough air

Sighing frequently

Digestive signals:

Butterflies or knots in the stomach

Nausea

Dry mouth

Muscle responses:

Lockjaw, neck, or shoulder tension

Clenched fists

Anxious feeling "wound up" or on edge

Temperature changes:

Sudden feeling of heat or flushing

Cold hands or feet

Sweating

Sensory shifts:

Vision narrowing or tunneling

Muffled or loud sounds

Not in tune with the atmosphere around you

For me, the first warning sign is always in my stomach — a knot is slowly drawn so tight that it builds before I'm aware of having felt threatened at all. Next is a shift in my breathing to quickened, shallow breaths. My vision starts to tunnel, and I feel as though something is in my head, I can't think straight.

When I was a child, these feelings were so relentless it never occurred to me to think of them as unusual. They were just who I was. It wasn't until I joined the Marines and experienced periods of real safety that I knew what it was like to have a non-activated nervous system.

Three Speeds of Activation

Not all alarm responses are the same. Your system can kick in at varying levels of intensity according to the degree of threat you perceive:

Low-Level Activation: This is the equivalent of your car idling at a red light. You are awake, alert, perhaps a little bit anxious, but operating just fine. Your prefrontal cortex is still on; your mind works fine. This level of activation can actually aid performance — it's what keeps you attentive during the important presentation, or when you are trying to remain alert while driving in adverse weather.

Mid-Level Activation: You have some rev in your engine now. All that happens is your heart rate jumps, your breath speeds up, and thinking becomes even more narrow. You can still function, but you're also beginning to lose access to your most advanced cognitive abilities. In relationships, this is when communication starts to falter.

High-Level Activation: Your engine is at redline. Your body is in total emergency mode, awash in stress hormones. Your prefrontal cortex has essentially powered down, and you're in the hands of automatic survival responses. That's when you might end up yelling things you don't really mean, storming out of the room, or shutting down entirely.

It's how you notice yourself moving up the scale before you reach that redline zone where all productivity in communication is lost.

Past and Present Stimuli and Their Effects

What remains puzzling is how this Amber Alert alarm system links 'known feelings' with actual pockets of safety or danger. This is done, via a process known as "pattern matching," in which your brain quickly compares current sensory information with memories stored of a threat.

If your current experience has enough in common with past threats, your brain will sound the Amber Alert alarm — often before you even consciously register what it is that makes you so nervous.

That's why even a small trigger can provoke a significant reaction. The sound of your partner's voice could be like your father's voice before he turned violent. The frustration of being misunderstood could be similar to how you felt when your brother crossed your boundaries. The fear of abandonment when your partner requests space may resonate with the losses you experienced during your childhood.

For years, I couldn't understand why I would completely shut down in certain relationship dynamics. Why should so simple a disagreement render me speechless, mindless, and paralyzed? It wasn't until I understood the pattern matching that it started to make sense: my brain wasn't responding to the present situation but to the echoes of old trauma it heard in the present.

The Window of Tolerance: Your Relationship's "Safety Zone"

There's a term from trauma work, "window of tolerance," primarily associated with Dr. Dan Siegel, which refers to the zone in which you can function at your best. It's how a UFC fighter can exact an offensive or defensive strategy in the moment and seemingly make all of the right moves. Within this range, your feelings can be present without overwhelming you. You are able to think straight, express yourself, and be in touch with yourself and others.

When you're outside your window of tolerance, you're in either an upper or lower boundary of the two primary arousals: either hyperaroused (anxious, angry, panicked) or hypoaroused (numb, disconnected, shut down).

For those with trauma or chronic stress in their history, this window might be quite small. Subtle triggers, which others might not even find particularly stressful, can push you out of your window, activate survival responses, and impair your relationships.

My window of tolerance when I was growing up was razor thin. Even a whisper of conflict would shut me down to the point of detachment (hypoarousal) or, less frequently, send me screaming for the hills in a frantic bid to change my circumstances (hyperarousal). I had very little room to find a middle ground that allowed me to simply experience painful feelings.

Increasing your window of tolerance is one of the most important tasks when it comes to healing your relationships. It's never too difficult to embrace what is fuller, more loving, and more present—even during hard or conflicting times.

The Alarm in Practice: An Example from Real Life

Let me give you an example of how this can play out in relationships.

Decades ago, while living in New Jersey, I was seeing a girl named Sarah. One night she told me she needed some space and was considering spending the weekend on her own. I knew this made sense logically — everyone needs time alone. But within seconds the emergency response had kicked in across my body.

My heart raced, my stomach tightened, and waves of panic swept over me. I was either begging her not to leave (fawn) or completely shutting down, unable to articulate what I was feeling (freeze).

Sarah was confused, and for obvious reasons. She had confidence that she had just asked for a little personal time. From where I was sitting, or rather from where my amygdala (Amy) was sitting, she was threatening to abandon me, and my internal Amber Alert alarm was sounding the same warning it had sounded when my mother and two other stepmothers left earlier on during my childhood.

My reaction had almost everything to do with me and almost nothing to do with Sarah. Depending on our past baggage and how we interpret someone making a "scary" request, we respond with either a handful of love and compassion or a pound of protective fear and white-knuckled control.

Alarm Systems in Pairs: The Feedback Loop

Complications can ensue when two people with their Amber Alert systems meet. The stress reaction of one person can stimulate that of the other, somehow touching off a feedback loop that drives conflict out of control, beyond the control of either.

Picture this couple: One has an inclination toward the fight response when threatened, and the other slides into freeze. They start to argue, and their fight-response partner begins to argue back loudly and with animation. This triggers the amygdala's (Amber Alert) alarm systems of the freeze-response partner, who shuts down and goes silent.

That silence sets off the fight-response partner's abandonment fear, which leads them to pursue harder. This pressure only serves to drive the freeze-response woman deeper into shutdown. You both keep triggering each other's alarm systems, leading to a continuous cycle of escalation.

I've been in this dance a few times, typically on the receiving end as the freeze-responder. When one partner shuts off their alarm, it triggers anxiety in the other partner, and the more the anxious partner pursues, the deeper the first partner's freeze response becomes. Neither of us realized that we were trapped in a biological feedback loop powered by our alarm systems.

How to Turn Off the Blaring Warning Sound

The good news is that while your amygdala (Amber Alert) alarm system is strong, it's not impregnable. You can start to retrain your body's response to relationship stress through knowledge and practice.

Here are some initial steps:

Identify activation early: Know your own early-warning signs. The faster you can catch your body in the rev-up, the more room you have to shut it down.

Label what's happening: Being able to simply acknowledge in your mind (or out loud) "I am activating my alarm system" can engage your prefrontal cortex and lower the intensity of the response.

Breathe: Even: 30 seconds of purposeful breathing in and out—deep inhales and long exhales—can help start to adjust your state. This exercise stimulates the vagus nerve and counteracts the acute stress response.

When feeling stressed, the first thing to do is to remind yourself of your current location and that you are safe. Glance around the room and list objects you are currently seeing in order to pull yourself back into the present.

If necessary, take a time-out: If you know you are too activated for effective communication, it is perfectly fine to ask for a short break. Just set a definite time when you'll return to the conversation.

When I was in the Marines, I found that the best leaders were those who were able to stay calm when all hell was breaking loose. This is a skill they had to learn — they weren't born with it. And just the same, you can teach your alarm system to be more precise and less jumpy over time.

Conclusion: Your Alarm System Is Your Best Helper

Your body's alarm system is not your foe. It's an old, smart-as-hell survival skill that has kept your family line going for untold generations. The issue isn't that you have this system — I do! And I love it! The issue is that many of us, particularly those with trauma histories, need to recalibrate that system.

Learning about the hormones and neural pathways that underlie your stress response is not just esoterica; it can change how you relate to others. When you understand what is happening in your body during a conflict, you gain some control instead of being reactive.

In the next chapter, we're going to dive deeper into your brain's Amber Alert alarm system—the amygdala— and see how this little almond-shaped structure shapes your bonds and how you can work with it, not against it.

For now, I recommend that you become a student of your alarm system. Notice when it turns on, what turns it on, and how it shows up in your body. This is the first step to freedom from mechanical reactions that are (unbeknown) to no avail.

Repeat after me: the purpose isn't to never feel alarm; the purpose is to train your alarm so it's ringing at the right times, for the right reasons, and at the right volume.

If you learn to listen to your body's alarm system, it can help you form healthier, more connected relationships.

CHAPTER FOUR

THE AMYGDALA – YOUR RELATIONSHIP'S AMBER ALERT

In the last chapter, we covered the role of the amygdala and its function, but this is an incredibly important component of the acute stress response, and I want to dig a little deeper and give you some context behind the nickname "Amber Alert" and why I've chosen it as a metaphor. If some of this reads as redundant, just know that it's with intention; repetition is the mother of skill.

The Amber Alert of Your Brain

That jarring, high-pitched noise that sounds from your phone during an Amber Alert? The one that makes you jump, no matter what you're doing, that trumps whatever you're using, that demands your attention as soon as possible no matter the inconvenience?

We now know this as the amygdala. And there are two of them, located in the temporal lobes, one on each side of the brain.

These are the little almond-shaped structures that Dr. Ruffin told me about in one of our early therapy sessions. Again, the amygdala serves as the emergency alert system of your gray matter. It is in constant search of danger, making split-second judgments about what's safe and what's potentially threatening. And here's the kicker: It doesn't give two shits about your relationship goals or therapy insights, and it doesn't promise to "do better next time."

It sends out an alert when it senses danger. Noisy, inconvenient, and in your face. Period.

The amygdala lives in your limbic system, the emotional center of your brain. While other parts of your brain manage intricate thinking, planning, and reasoning, the amygdala is all about one thing and one thing only: survival. It mediates emotional reactions, notably fear and anger, and it does so with astonishing rapidity.

How fast?

The amygdala in your brain can produce a fear reaction about 20 milliseconds after that potential threat is detected. That is about 10 times faster than you can consciously think about what is taking place. By the time you realize your partner's voice got under your skin, an emergency alert has already been broadcast from your amygdala, sparking a chain reaction of physiological responses.

Your Amygdala: The Memory Bank of Relationships

Here's where things start to get really juicy in terms of relationships. Your amygdala doesn't only respond to blatant threats, like physical harm. It stores emotional memories in addition, especially those related to fear, threat, or pain.

And it does not differentiate between threats to our bodies and threats to our emotions.

To our amygdala, the pain of rejection, abandonment, or humiliation is all processed much the same way as physical pain. This is also why criticism from your partner can feel just as painful as being punched in the stomach. It's why the silent treatment can make you feel suffocated.

Your brain processes social pain and physical pain in many of the same areas.

But the amygdala doesn't just remember what hurt you — <u>it remembers the context surrounding it</u>:

The kind of voice that came before an argument.

The look he gave her right before he told her, no.

The times of day when arguments tended to occur.

The odor in the room when you got shamed.

It's why seemingly innocuous (trigger-ful) things can set off huge reactions in relationships. Your partner speaks in a certain tone, and instantly you're enraged. They sigh a certain way, and suddenly you're anxious. They're walking in front of you, and you are certain that they are ditching you.

You may rationally know your reactions are overblown, but your amygdala doesn't give a damn. It has picked up on a pattern that has led to pain in the past, and now it's freaking out in an attempt to protect you — like an Amber Alert that jumps in during your lunch break with urgent warnings of harm.

The Amygdala in the field: An example of Relationships

Let me provide a real-life example from my life.

There was my ex-wife and the way she said "fine" when she was not at all fine. The issue was her tone, which was clipped, slightly more nasal than her regular voice, and accompanied by a faint eye roll. Early in our relationship, this "fine" would be accompanied by days of tension, fights, or her shutting down emotionally.

For a while, simply that particular pronouncement of "fine" would send me into a tailspin. My heart would race, my palms would sweat, and I'd either suddenly start tearfully apologizing and promising change (fawn response), try to provide a defensive explanation (fight response), change the subject and physically remove myself from the conversation (flight response), or go momentarily silent because my brain short-circuited and I couldn't think or talk (freeze response).

Was my reaction logical? Hell no.

Was one word worth that much backtalk? Not rationally.

But, my amygdala was not interested in rationality. It had learned that this particular "fine" was a reliable signal that I was about to feel emotional pain, and it was activating its version of an emotional air-raid siren to shield me.

The problem is that these reactions usually made the situation worse rather than better. I hadn't learned to differentiate the errant thought from the terrorist threat in my head; to my jangly brain, a word wasn't just a word, it was a five-alarm emergency broadcast. My ex would get irritated at my "overreaction" to a single word, not realizing that my outsized reaction only worsened it, feeding a tiny spark of a simulation of breathless panic.

Your Attachment History, Embedded into Your Amygdala

Not only is your amygdala's sensitivity and response pattern influenced by your direct relationship at the time, but it's also reflecting your earliest experiences of love. They're deeply informed by your earliest attachment experiences — especially the ones you had with your primary caregivers as a kid.

If you were raised in a culture of consistent love, and you were responded to when you needed something, more than likely your amygdala was exposed to enough loving support that your relationship threat threshold is healthy. You learned that a fumble is not a fumble if it is repaired, that your needs are safe to express, and that people who love you return after a conflict.

But if you grew up in a chaotic, neglectful, or abusive environment, your amygdala made its own adjustments. It turned hyper-vigilant, throwing up warnings at the first sign of rejection or abandonment. Alternatively, it may have learned to completely tune out because there was no safe space for overwhelming feelings.

Think of it as the ability to adjust the sensitivity settings on your phone's emergency alerts. For some people, the whole thing is set to blare only the most extreme, imminent threats. Others are intended to sound the alarm at the first hint of potential trouble, even if that is miles off or unlikely to substantially affect them.

In my instance, having parents who would be emotionally unpredictable taught my amygdala to be in a very heightened state of alert all the time. A slight change in tone or facial expression could signify a pending blow-up or withdrawal of love. My brain learned very early that relationships weren't safe, and it brought that learning into my adult relationships.

That is why the same comment can roll off one person's back but put another into a trauma response. This isn't a matter of being "too sensitive" or "overreacting"—it's about how your unique brain was wired through experience to protect you.

The Four Fs and Your Amygdala

When your amygdala recognizes a threat and sounds its alarm, it activates one of the four survival responses we've been discussing: fight, flight, freeze, or fawn. But how does one person end up fighting, while another is the one who freezes? Much of it is based on what worked for you in the past.

If striking back kept you safe as a child, your amygdala learned that hostility keeps you safe. If fleeing or avoiding conflict kept you from pain, your brain was wired to break free at the first hint of danger. If freezing lowered the odds of making yourself a target, or if it enabled you to survive unavoidable pain, your amygdala recorded the new tactic. So if fawning — pleasing and placating others — made peace, keeping everything and everyone hanging on, well, that was your response to any kind of threat, your default to perceived danger.

Your amygdala doesn't give a flip if they're good for your adult relationships. It doesn't matter if it aligns with your values or the things you hope to achieve. There's one thing it does care about: keeping you alive. And to your caveman brain, the threat of rejection or abandonment can feel like a life-and-death threat, particularly if early experiences led you to believe that losing connection meant losing safety.

The UFC Fighter and the Amygdala

Remember that UFC fighter analogy from earlier? There's an interesting connection here.

Elite fighters have trained their amygdalas to remain regulated even under the most extreme stresses. When fists are coming at their face — something that would send most of us into full-body panic — their amygdala remains fairly chilled out. That's not because they don't have an operational alert system. It's because they have repeatedly conditioned themselves to face these threats in safer, controlled circumstances, training their brains to believe that they possess the necessary skills to overcome them.

It's akin to first responders learning to function calmly in the face of catastrophes that would render most people inert. They have better control over their alert system, so they can think straight even when the alarms are going off.

That is precisely what we need to do in our relationships. We have to teach our amygdala to stay regulated when we meet emotional threats. Not by repressing our reactions or denying that we're feeling something, but by steadily introducing ourselves to relational triggers in safe, supportive situations where we can practice new responses.

A fighter is not great because he is a dodger or a runner. They become great by confronting them over and over again, learning from each experience, until they build new neural pathways that help them stay in the present and be strategic rather than reactive.

Neuroplasticity: Your Amygdala Is Not Set in Stone

Here's the good news: Your amygdala isn't fixed. Because of neuroplasticity — the brain's ability to reorganize itself by forming new neural connections — you really can rewire your emergency alert system over time.

This doesn't occur overnight. The same way a fighter doesn't win the title after one day in the gym, you won't change the emotional part of your brain in one shot. And your emotional intelligence is a balancing act with your intellectual intelligence — which means you need to work at it. However, with practice and the proper techniques, you can slowly train your amygdala to be more selective about what it deems to be a real threat.

The first step is awareness: when your internal Amber Alert is sounded. The best indication of this is how your body feels. All that racing heart and tight chest, churning stomach, and that surge of energy or the opposite—that is all your emergency alert system engaging.

As you become aware of this activation, you can begin to create a gap between the signal and your response. That doesn't mean stunting your response. This is not about searching for solutions so much as stretching the space to opt for how you will respond versus being pulled along by automatic patterns.

Over time, with practice, you can teach your amygdala that certain "triggers" in a relationship — a certain tone of voice, a certain kind of criticism, a partner needing space —aren't actually life-threatening. They can be uncomfortable, even really unpleasant, but they do not need to justify the full emergency broadcast that your brain is giving them right now.

Your Amygdala's Relationship Memory

The most potent feature of the amygdala is how it records relationship memories. They're not conscious — narrative memories, such as "On June 15, my partner criticized me at dinner. They're implicit emotional memories that are automatically activated in similar contexts.

Your amygdala not only remembers how painful that criticism was; it also remembers the entire sensory experience of that hurt. The lighting in the room.

The music, which is playing as background music. The smell of the food. The time of day. The clothes your partner had on.

This is also why relationship triggers can feel totally random and incredibly confusing. Your partner may be totally mystified about why, seemingly out of nowhere, you shut down or lash out, not understanding that something about the present moment recalls a wound from your past.

You know how a particular song or smell might instantly take you back to a specific moment that comes with all the emotions attached? Your amygdala lays down these super-strong associative memories around relationship experiences, especially painful ones.

If only I'd realized this back then. It can be so liberating! It lets you know that your reactions are not, in fact, crazy or irrational —they're just the product of your brain doing the very thing it evolved to do: trying to keep you alive based on past experience.

Daily Practices to Work with Your Amygdala

So how do you start to work with this incredible emergency alert system in your brain? Here are some practical approaches:

- Name it to tame it. Just naming what's happening (say to yourself, "My amygdala is sending out an alert right now") can reduce its charge. Research has found that the process of putting feelings into words activates the prefrontal cortex in the brain, which is associated with control of emotions.
- Track your triggers: Begin to take note of your specific circumstances, words, tones, or behaviors that give rise to your internal Amber Alert. Keep a journal if it helps. The more conscious you are of your triggers, the less instinctively you'll react to them.
- Pay attention to your unique physical cues: When you are triggered and your amygdala gets fired up, you will always have physical signals, but these are unique to you. Some people feel it in their chest, and some in the stomach or the throat. Some get hot, others cold. Knowing your activation signals is an early warning system.
- Practice regulation tools: Simple practices such as deep breathing or a physical or sensory grounding practice can help to quiet your amygdala when it gets over-fired. We'll talk more about these in future chapters.
- Create new experiences: Intentionally create new, positive experiences in situations similar to your triggers. If criticism around a dinner table is a trigger, you can work on giving and receiving gentle and kind feedback about food at the dinner table in a safe space.

The Amygdala in Your Relationship: Both Sides Count

It is important to remember that you and your partner both have amygdalas that are always scanning for danger. Relationship conflicts often go out of control because each person's emergency alert systems are triggered by the other.

Have you ever heard the sound of an Amber Alert going off on your cellphone, only to experience it doing the same thing on someone else's cellphone nearby—all within the space of a few seconds?

Or, maybe it's happened while you were in a department store, and suddenly several people are fumbling through their back pockets or purses trying to shut off the alarms going off on their cellphones? This illustrates how our individual amygdalas can react in similar ways to certain stimuli.

IT CAN GET QUITE NOISY REAL FAST!

You say something with a certain intonation, which trips your partner's amygdala. You flinch defensively, firing your amygdala. Seconds later, you both feel as if you're in survival mode and are unable to reach the parts of your brain that hold empathy, complexity, and connection.

It's two emergency broadcast systems setting each other off in an endless cycle of escalating feedback. The wailing grows louder and louder, to the point that neither of you can think or communicate properly.

That's why learning about the amygdala isn't only about managing your responses or other people's responses; it's also about recognizing when your partner's amygdala has been triggered and knowing how to help both of you find your way back to safety.

Conclusion: Recalibrate Your Alert System

It bears repeating: Your amygdala is not the enemy. It's an essential part of your brain that has been working hard to keep you safe since the day you were born. It's not that you have an emergency alert system; it's that this Cro-Magnon survival mechanism never updated its firmware, its threat-assessment algorithms to differentiate between a saber-toothed tiger and a sarcastic remark from your partner. There are no auto-updates that are turned on; you have to do the work here.

But with insight, patience, and practice, you can recalibrate this alert system. You can teach it to tell true emergencies from false alarms. It is something you can train to stay on guard but not necessarily broadcast at maximum volume for each and every perceived threat. And you can, in the process, turn your relationships from places of survival into spaces where growth and connection are possible.

In the following chapter, we'll look at how these survival mechanisms can become a way of life — how the sporadic firing of your emergency alarm system can develop into a chronic state of readiness that informs your identity and habits for relating to others.

But for now, I want you to keep this in mind: your amygdala's alarms are not faulty or broken. They were created by a genius system doing what it was optimally set up to do. We must tune the alarms to sound only in emergencies, not at every fleeting shadow.

Respect your body's Amber Alert warning, a.k.a., the amygdala.

Get to know it.

Master it.

Don't jack my Amy.

For me it's not just a silly warning to others; it's also a mindset. I don't want to walk around in life jacking anyone else's Amy, either.

CHAPTER FIVE
───────────────

SURVIVAL MODE AS A LIFESTYLE

I felt things start to form a new normal in my life when I was twenty-eight. I had recently landed a middle-management job promotion with a company named America Online (AOL)—the premier Internet Service Provider (ISP) in those days. I was working at one of their call centers in Oklahoma City.

The promotion in itself was a long shot for me : I had no college degree, but all of my peers did. I'd never held a management position before, but in me there was always an innate leader, strong in the fight — to fight (take the impossible long shots)—and it was that way of thinking that started showing itself to me.

In my first six months as a manager, I accomplished what everyone said was impossible: I led and coached a team of 28 retention agents — those whose job was to save anyone who called in to cancel their monthly internet subscription — and I turned "us" from one of the worst-performing teams across five massive call centers nationwide into the number one, highest-performing team in the company.

They reached 100% "X of X," exceeding every performance benchmark—something that had not been accomplished in the history of an America Online call center.

From the outside I was doing great. My colleagues respected me. My team adored me. My superiors were impressed. I was the embodiment of professional success.

But during that time – unbeknownst to my peers – I was also being treated by Dr. Joseph Ruffin, who had diagnosed me with bipolar disorder (something I would later conquer) and was providing psychotherapy and medication management for my condition. Early in our three-and-a-half years of work together, he wired me up to an EKG to check my heart rate. He brought me the results a week later, with concern written all over his face.

"Something fascinating happened when you were revealing that memory of your father's abuse," he said. "Discussing trauma puts most people's heart rate up. Yours dropped significantly."

I did not realize the significance at the time, but Dr. Ruffin said that this was a classic sign of a freeze response — my body had learned to conserve itself, almost play dead, in the face of traumatic memories — I did not even have to think of that moment; my body just automatically went there. Indeed, a simple conversation about those experiences has, many years later, elicited the same physiological shutdown that once protected me as a child.

I was hit with an unfortunate reality: throughout my childhood, I had been so traumatized that I had actually wired my brain to act with "calmness" in the face of extreme duress.

This juxtaposition—how well I seem to be doing on the outside compared to the time bomb of response ticking away on the inside—precisely captures what it's like to live with survival mode as your default setting. Outwardly, I was battling and prevailing. On the interior, parts of me were still frozen in trauma, still running on the survival program installed in childhood.

When Something Some of Us Thought Was Temporary Becomes Something Permanent

Evolution designed the stress response we've described in earlier chapters — the release of adrenaline, norepinephrine, and cortisol; the changes in blood flow; and the state of heightened vigilance — to be transient. Our bodies activate this system in response to immediate threats and deactivate it when the danger is over so they can rest and recover.

But what happens in the lives of some of us out there where the danger never actually goes away? What does it mean when preschool children are raised in a world where potential threats are constant and unpredictable?

The reality is, the temporary becomes permanent. The exception starts to look like the rule. The panic button has become the default setting.

By the time I was eleven, living with my father, his third wife, my older brother, and my stepsister, my body had surely forgotten what it felt like to be truly at ease. My father's unpredictable rages and the terror they caused, the abandonment I felt when stepmothers walked out on me, the violation of boundaries in the abuse from my brother—all of them had taught my nervous system that the world was a fundamentally unsafe place.

My body reacted in kind, staying in a low-level state of stress even during the relatively peaceful times. Why? Because I knew from experience that calm was always simply the prelude to the storm, that safety was an illusion, and that the next explosion was always around the corner.

This is what it looks like when survival mode becomes a way of living:

Your body ceases to fully reset back to baseline between stressors.

Your sympathetic nervous system is still dialed halfway up, ready to jump to full emergency mode when the emotional triggers have all shown up.

There is never a full return to normalcy of your stress hormones, and your brain remains hypervigilant.

Chronic Survival Mode Begins in Childhood

For most people who live life in that chronic survival mode as adults, the template was forged in childhood. Our nervous systems are mostly plastic — most easily shaped by experience — when we are young. The established patterns then serve as the template for how our bodies and brains react to stress throughout our lives.

As I look back at my childhood, I can see how the perfect storm of conditions gave birth to a lifetime of survival mode:

My parents' separation, which occurred when I was seven, shook my sense of order and security.

My father's alcoholism and drug use, which caused him to act unpredictably and scared us a lot.

The physical and emotional abuse directed at my mother, my brother, me, and even our dog, Mopey—taught me that nobody was safe from my father's anger.

When I was 6, my uncle was shot dead, which introduced the idea of sudden violent death into my young imagination.

The cycle of my father's marriages and divorces, building attachments, but then severing them, over and over again.

The night my stepmother was lying under the stairwell after she was beaten and then left for good the next day. I felt as crushed as she did, which proved to my subconscious that love is fleeting and that safety could never be achieved.

The sexual abuse by my brother at age 10, trespassing the most fundamental boundaries of my body and identity.

Any one of those events would have been sufficient to sensitize a child's nervous system. As a team, they provided a perfect manual for how to live a life in a state of constant survival mode.

The Intense Physical Burden of Chronic Survival

The constant survival mode is also incredibly taxing, physically. Our bodies just aren't meant to stay on red alert all the time.

Think of how it might sound if your car engine ran at high RPMs, 24 hours a day, for years. Systems do eventually collapse. The same is true for our bodies when stress hormones are consistently elevated over time:

Suppression of the immune system: Chronically increased levels of cortisol suppress the ability of your immune system to defend you against illness.

Digestive problems: Under stress, blood is shunted away from the digestive organ and can result in such issues as irritable bowel syndrome, acid reflux, and poor nutrient absorption.

Cardiovascular stress: Chronic high blood pressure and elevated pulse pressure can stress your heart and blood vessels.

Muscle tension and pain: Chronically tense muscles can create chronic aches and pains such as backaches and headaches, etc.

Disrupted sleep: The hypervigilant brain doesn't exactly take time off in favor of deep, restorative sleep.

Hormone imbalances: Chronic stress throws off the body's hormone balance, wreaking havoc on everything from metabolism to reproductive health.

Accelerated aging: Studies show that chronic stress literally makes our cells age faster by shortening the length of telomeres, the caps on our chromosomes that help protect our cells from aging.

What Dr. Ruffin saw in my EKG there was a physical imprint of how my body had responded to chronic trauma. Instead of a response of fight or flight under stress, my lower-than-average heart rate meant my body adapted into the conserve mode: slow my heart, reduce my metabolic needs, and prepare my body to withstand rather than flee the inescapable. I had become so conditioned to this freeze response that it would kick in like clockwork, even when I felt safe inside a therapist's office, secured as an adult from any danger.

The Impact on the Mind: When Survival Becomes Who You Are

The mental cost of chronic survival is likely more significant than the physical cost. When your nervous system has been molded by trauma, by chronically elevated levels of stress, it's not just a part of the body that's affected — it changes the way you perceive yourself and the world.

Here are some of the mental patterns that result when you're in survival mode for a long period of time:

Negative expectancy: Expecting the worst to happen in any situation.

Hypervigilance: Scanning for threats all the time, never able to relax or simply be.

Black-and-white thinking: You see situations, yourself, and others as either all good or all bad, safe or dangerous, with little in between.

Trouble trusting: Believing that other people are going to hurt, leave, or betray you at some point.

Shame and self-blame: Taking to heart the idea that you are inherently bad or undeserving.

Control fears: Trying to control everything and everyone in your immediate surroundings because that "makes me feel safe".

Challenges with boundaries: Either having rigid, impenetrable boundaries or almost no boundaries.

Emptiness: A sense of feeling disconnected from your true self and your true desires and needs.

These are not character flaws or signs of weakness. They are adaptive responses to a childhood environment in which these beliefs and behaviors may have been required for emotional or physical survival.

The psychological impact had complex effects for me.

On the one hand, I became a good leader of people—to motivate and to inspire — skills that I leveraged later at America Online. Conversely, I struggled with low self-worth and often felt different from everyone else.

My America Online success wasn't despite my trauma history — in certain ways, it was because of it.

That same hypervigilance, which prevented me from relaxing, made me incredibly attuned to the needs and motivations of my team members. The same mechanism of proving myself, rooted in childhood feelings of worthlessness, drove me to accomplish things no one would believe possible. The capacity to operate under such stress that I had developed as a child served me well in the high-powered corporate world.

But there was a catch to these adaptations. As Dr. Ruffin's EKG showed, pieces of me remained stuck in trauma, still reacting to the world as if I were that powerless 3-year-old kid. None of that professional success could salve those wounds — it could only cover up the scars briefly.

The Next Relationship: Survival Mode—a Repeating Cycle

As adults, we bring our survival-oriented identity into our intimate relationships, and the result is everything from painful to confusing for both ourselves and our lovers.

The attachment system, which is closely tied in with our survival systems, is the key system affected in a close relationship. The vulnerability of genuine intimacy can feel literally life-threatening to a nervous system trained to be on high alert all the time.

This happens in ways that are remarkably predictable:

Testing and Distrust: You constantly (but often unconsciously) test your partner to see if they'll hurt or abandon you in the way you've been hurt or abandoned in the past or, in some cases, as a defense against what you fear might or is already happening. This is a form of what I call, "diasterful-projecting".

Emotional reactivity: Minor points of disagreement evoke exaggerated emotional responses, as each new confrontation gets mixed with the emotional intensity of past traumas.

Trouble with emotional intimacy: Either distancing oneself to the extreme or becoming very anxious and clingy, always seeking reassurance.

Recreating familiar dynamics: Unconsciously picking partners who resemble systems we learned as children but that might have been dysfunctional or hurtful.

Self-sabotage: Wrecking relationships as they begin to feel too good, too safe, too close — because safety feels unfamiliar and therefore dangerous.

I have experienced all of these patterns and, in fact, sometimes transitioned back and forth between them within the same marriage. Even while I was riding high professionally at America Online, my personal life was frequently messy and difficult. The person who could lead a team to a level of unprecedented success couldn't keep an intimate relationship together. The same person who was able to inspire other people in his professional circles was unable to connect with his children on even a most basic level at home.

It raises a cruel irony that the thing we most want — true connection — is actually what our terror-based identity sees as the grossest danger.

The Blessing of Adaptation: Strengths Become Weaknesses

My time at American Online has also been an example of a fascinating paradox of survival adaptations: the same traits that help us to survive trauma can be huge strengths in certain environments — but debilitating weaknesses in others.

That same fighting spirit is what set me apart and served me so well in my professional career—the ability to overcome adversity, to never give up, and to guide others when times were tough. Without the education and experience of my peers, I accomplished what no one else had. My team was a record-breaking team for the company. I was respected and valued.

And yet this same fighting spirit was a guest that often let me down in intimate relationships, where vulnerability and surrender can be more crucial than strength and control. The hypervigilance that made me an attentive manager made me an exhausting partner. The engine that propelled my career success depleted my ability to rest and play.

Meanwhile, as Dr. Ruffin's EKG showed, parts of me were still frozen in trauma. I could fight well professionally but would seize up if I were triggered emotionally due to past childhood battles. My heart rate would actually slow down — a biological marker indicating that my body was kicking into conservation mode, preparing to endure (not escape from or face down) the presumed threat.

This split in escaping responses—fight in some cases, freeze in others — is typical of people with complex trauma histories. We've evolved multiple survival mechanisms, and some of them can appear to be in conflict with one another. To colleagues, I probably seemed confident and assertive. Close friends may have perceived me as aloof and emotionally distant—this continued well into my 40s, by the way. Each of these perceptions represented a facet of the survival identity I developed, which depended on various aspects of my traumatic history.

Identifying Survival Mode in Yourself

The most insidious thing about chronic survival mode is that it feels entirely, infuriatingly normal to those who exist in it. When you've spent your entire life with your nervous system cranked to 11, there isn't much of a "relaxed" to feel in the first place.

That was certainly the case for me. Until Dr. Ruffin showed me that EKG, I was not aware of how much my body was reacting, in a deep, physical way, to emotional triggers. I believed that everyone faced life with the same level of vigilance and paranoia as I did. I thought I was just being myself, and no offense, but that's how I reacted.

The first step to change is learning to know when you're in survival mode. Here are some warning signs to look for:

Shallow, rapid breathing

Constant muscle contraction, particularly of the jaw, neck, and shoulders

Effect on stomach: Digestive problems (that get worse with stress)

Rapid heartbeat or palpitations (or, as in my case, a slowing heart rate)

Sleep disturbances

Fatigue you can't shake with rest

Emotional indicators:

- Feeling jittery or on edge all the time or suddenly.
- Cutting off one's own emotions or feeling nothing.
- Irritability and a short fuse
- Excessive anxiety around the event
- An inability to feel pleasure or happiness
- Shame waves, or severe self-criticizing

Cognitive indicators:

- Thoughts that race or mental "chatter."
- Difficulty concentrating
- Pessimistic future predictions
- Black-and-white thinking
- Catastrophizing (imagining the worst-case scenario)
- Hyperawareness (watching for danger all the time)

Behavioral indicators:

- Escape to avoid the uneasiness-eliciting situation.
- Discipline or obsession with perfectionism
- Use of substances as a way to cope with or escape feelings.
- Workaholism and busyness
- Inability to be present or mindful
- People-pleasing or lack of conflict
- Runs from a conflict

If you relate to more of them, you're likely in survival mode, not safety and choice.

The Positive Feedback Loop of Survival Mode

One of the most insidious things about chronic survival mode is that it becomes self-reinforcing. If your nervous system is chronically on high alert, you are more disposed to interpret neutral circumstances as threats and consequently turn on more survival responses that reaffirm the pattern.

For example, if you are already in a state of hypervigilance, you might perceive your partner's neutral facial expression as an angry or disapproving one. This belief activates your survival mechanism in 1 of 4 ways: you attack, you withdraw, you shut down, and you over-accommodate. Your partner, upset by your reaction to their neutral face, will confirm your initial read of the threat in their eyes.

"See?" your survival brain says. "I told you they were angry! Good thing we were prepared!"

This forms a nasty feedback loop, in which your survival responses appear to be confirmed by your life situations, while life situations are themselves being generated by the very responses you're wanting to change.

I was stuck in that cycle for years. My hypervigilance would cause me to misperceive others' intentions, which would then get acted out in ways that led to the rejection or conflict that I dreaded, which would then foster a cycle where I would believe more and more that people couldn't be trusted and that the world wasn't safe.

Even while I found success at America Online, this process was working its magic under the covers. Although I'd been able to make use of my hypervigilance in the workplace — foreseeing potential problems and staying one step ahead of the curve — when it came to my personal relationships and feeling safe within my body, it only created more terror.

TRANSFORMATION FROM SURVIVAL IDENTITY TO TRUE SELF

Perhaps the most damaging effect of chronic survival mode is that it disconnects us from who we really are. When you've trained yourself to always be on the lookout for danger, when you already have a predisposition toward seeing danger everywhere in the world, and when you've been taught since birth to always be prepared to fight, there's not any energy left for discovery or joy or creativity or true connection.

Your survival identity — the constellation of adaptive behaviors, beliefs, and patterns that helped you cope with trauma — is not your true self. It's a protective shell fashioned around your true self, designed to keep you and your emotions safe in a cruel world.

The issue is that many of us get so identified with this defense mechanism that we actually think it is ourselves. We believe that our hypervigilance, control issues, people-pleasing tendencies, and emotional numbness define who we are. We can't imagine who we would be without these patterns, because we've never had the safety to learn.

Certainly, I found this to be the case. Even when I was being hugely successful at America Online at age 28, I was still mostly in my survival identity. My leadership skills, although authentic, were being channeled through the filter of trauma adaptations — needing to prove my worth, the hypervigilance that let me notice what other people needed, and the fighting spirit that had kept me alive as a child.

The therapy work with Dr. Ruffin was my initial baby step in learning to separate who I was in survival mode from who I really was deep down. The EKG results were a physical manifestation of just how embedded my survival responses were — so automatic, they functioned without my ever having to consent or take notice, altering the very physiology of my body in response to thoughts alone.

Peeling away the survival identity to reach one's true self is a journey, one that demands safety, time, and assistance—people who can see you more rationally than you're able to see yourself.

The First Move Out of a Life in Chronic Survival Mode

It's not a quick or simple transition to stop living in chronic survival mode. Your nervous system has taken years or decades to learn those patterns, and it will take time and steady work to create new ones. But it is possible. I know this is possible because I have experienced that transformation myself, and I can observe it occurring in other people.

Here are some early steps on this journey:

Build external safety: Before your nervous system can begin to calm down, you must receive a real, physical sense of safety from your environment. That might mean leaving an abusive relationship, striving for financial stability, finding a safe place to live, or drawing boundaries with toxic people in your life.

Cultivate awareness in your body: Learn to track the physical sensations of stress and safety in your body. Healthier habits like mindfulness meditation, yoga, or somatic experiencing can also help you cultivate this awareness.

Develop a window of tolerance: Gently expose yourself to mild distress to gradually increase your capacity to remain regulated and expand your range to stay grounded and present even in the face of stress.

Foster co-regulation: Organize time with people whose nervous systems are well-regulated. Just as anxiety is contagious, so is calm. Your nervous system will start to mirror that of people in your surroundings.

Stimulate the parasympathetic nervous system: Anything you can do to turn on your "rest and digest" system can counteract chronic sympathetic activation. Long, deep breaths; humming or singing; cold exposure; and certain types of movement may have strong effects.

Find support: Receiving help from a trauma-informed therapist, a somatic practitioner, or some other healing professional can be incredibly valuable on this path.

Use self-compassion: Last but not least, be as gentle and patient with yourself as possible going through this process. You adapted survival responses for good reasons. They shielded you from danger as long as you needed to be shielded from danger. Honor them as you even seek to reform them.

The path out of chronic survival mode started, for me, with that work with Dr. Ruffin — the realization that my body was still relating to the world as though I were in physical danger, even as my life had proven, repeatedly, that I was safe and successful. This journey included years of therapy, somatic practices, and relationships that both triggered and healed my ancient wounds, along with the ongoing slow evolution of truly understanding who I am beneath the calluses of self that we build to cope.

Conclusion: Beyond Survival

When stuck in chronic survival mode, imagine the world projected under a funhouse mirror—more threatening, more frightening, and more overwhelming than it really is. This was formed and polished by your first experiences — the ones of suffering, trauma, pain, loss, or chronic stress.

The good news is that you can replace this lens. Although it won't happen in a day or without effort, the situation improves gradually with support. Your nervous system can learn that the world isn't such a menacing place as when you were small and defenseless. Your body can remember how to receive rest, play, and feel safe in connection with other people.

At America Online, I learned that you can be successful on the outside and living on the inside of survival. The struggle I experienced during my childhood, which was necessary for survival, transformed into my strength in the corporate world. But real healing takes more than professional success — it's about reconnecting with who you really are underneath the survival adaptations.

Dr. Ruffin's EKG revealed an essential truth: our bodies keep the score.

They remember what hurt us, and still, they respond to it long after the danger is gone. But this same bodily wisdom holds the secrets of healing too. By listening to our bodies, learning to notice when we're in survival mode', and slowly building new patterns of safety and connection, we can start to live from choice instead of reaction.

This isn't to say you should deny or forget about the real dangers you have encountered. It does not involve pretending that the world is a safe place or that people will never cause you harm. This is developing the ability to judge situations now and not to see them all as if through naked wombs. It has options in how to respond as opposed to being governed by automatic survival reactions.

In the next chapter, we'll look at how you can figure out what your usual stress responses are and how they're manifesting in the way you show up in your relationships. But for now, I urge you to just observe:

How much of your life is life-threatening?

How would it be if you felt fundamentally safe in your body and in the world?

The stretch is from survival to safety, from reactivity to response, and from protection to connection. This is quite possibly the deepest work we can do as humans. It begins with the small (but huge) realization that the coping mechanisms that once protected you may now be the very things that keep you from the life, relationships, and self you want.

CHAPTER SIX

WHERE DO YOU LIVE?

Alright, listen up.

If you've gotten this far into the book, it's not because you're doing me a favor by reading it. Something deep inside of you is dying for answers. Part of you knows that the way you've been living — the way you've been loving —isn't working. And it is time to do something about it.

We have come a long way in the first five chapters.

We've been on a tour of the ancient survival blueprint that's baked into your brain.

We've also looked at your body's (amygdala) Amber Alert alarm system flooding you with hormones that hijack your rational thought processes.

We've explored how your amygdala sends out Amber Alerts whenever there's any chance of relationship trouble. And we've watched how all that can become not just a response you fall into every once in a while, but an approach to living your life — how you are in the world.

But without action, knowledge is just mental masturbation. It might feel good in the moment, but it doesn't produce any new psychological possibilities.

Now, we are going to be honest and straightforward. We're going to determine exactly where you are residing — which of the four survival responses is now your default home address. Because you can't chart a course to where you'd like to go until you know where you are.

Remember that UFC fight I mentioned earlier, between Conor McGregor and Nate Diaz? McGregor was the overwhelming favorite, the best pound-for-pound fighter in the division. But when the going got tough — when Diaz began to find success with his punches and McGregor tired — we saw his default mode kick in. McGregor went for a takedown on Diaz, a classic fight-or-flight reaction that masquerades as a fighting move. He was fleeing the onslaught of punches, and it resulted in his defeat when Diaz took him down and put him in a chokehold.

Even the world's best fighters revert to their survival programming when taken past a certain point. Except they study them. They review the tape. They acknowledge their weaknesses in order to take action to improve them.

That's what we're doing now. We're watching the tape of your life.

When I was in the Marines, our drill instructors would tear us down to build us up. They weren't being mean for their own sake — they were trying to get us ready for circumstances where our lives might hinge on our reaction. They knew that in battle, you don't rise to the occasion — you fall to the level of your training.

It is the same for people who are in relationships. When you face strife, when trust is tested, when vulnerability is necessary — you don't magically turn into your best self. You revert to your most hardwired habits. You drop to the level of how your nervous system is trained.

So, think of me as your relationship drill sergeant for the next few pages. I'm not here to coddle you. You've invested some money in me by purchasing this book. My task is to help you see yourself clearly, perhaps for the first time. For your life — your ability to love, connect, and truly experience joy — depends on it.

The Four Survival Territories

Visualize the four types of survival responses (fight, flight, freeze, and fawn) as different types of land or acreage suitable for living. Each has its own terrain, its own climate, and its own native customs and traditions. Every one of them served a function in your development, the terror of your childhood environment.

But just because you lived in a territory doesn't mean that's where you're supposed to live for eternity. Let's explore each one:

The Fight Territory

This is the land of confrontation, of showdowns, of taking perceived challenges by their gnarly horns. In its healthy state, the fight response helps you establish boundaries, represent yourself, and protect what you have. In trauma's form, it becomes chronic defensiveness, aggression, and control.

Signs you're living in Fight Territory:

You get angry or irritated easily.

You are frequently in fights or power struggles.

You need to be right or to win.

You're on guard for possible slights or disrespect.

With you, agreeing to disagree is a struggle; you find it difficult to concede when you're wrong.

You have a tendency to blame others when something does not go your way.

You are using criticism or disdain as defensive weapons.

If you don't control your life, you don't feel safe.

For years I sublimated my fight response into professional success. At America Online, I led a troubled team to achieve record-breaking results. I battled for them, nudged them, and would not tolerate mediocrity. My survival response became a true strength in that environment.

Yet in my most intimate relationships, the same fighting energy was controlling, defensive, and alienating. The same characteristic that allowed me to lead effectively rendered me a challenging partner.

If Fight Territory is your home community, there's a good chance you were raised in an environment where you must be strong to survive, or showing weakness might get you beaten, or you observed aggression as the go-to option for dealing with opposition. Your nervous system learned to be the best defense; you have to be the best offense.

The Flight Territory

Here is the land of evasion, of withering away, of fleeing imagined danger before it has a chance to turn you into a victim. Emotionally healthy, the fight response helps you get away from genuinely dangerous situations and allows you the opportunity to process your emotions when feelings are challenging. This is the trauma version of the fight response; it involves chronic avoidance, unavailability for one's own emotions, and disconnection from feelings.

You know you're living in Flight Territory when:

You hide when things get tough.

You are either always running away or physically present but mentally absent.

You "check out" with work, screens, substances, or other behavior.

You suck at emotional closeness.

Instead of feeling things, you intellectualize them.

When the conversation gets too close, you change the topic.

You feel more comfortable with space, whether it be physical or emotional.

You're constantly trying to figure out a way out of relationships.

Flight was never my go-to mode of response, but I have certainly been in this territory. I had thrown myself into my work after my divorce, into exercise, into whatever would keep me from feeling the pain of what had happened. I pushed forward to avoid confronting my feelings. I kept busy so I didn't have to face the emptiness.

If you come from Flight Territory, that's likely where you grew up, noticing that escape really was the best option, that your feelings were not validated or were punished, or that you were raised to believe that relying on others is dangerous. Your nervous system figured out that the way to be safe is from a distance.

The Freeze Territory

This is the land of the immobilized, the land of shutdown, the land of making myself invisible in an environment of perceived threat. The freeze response, however, in its healthy expression, is about buying yourself time to determine if you are in danger or, in some cases, where neither fight nor flights are an option, to conserve your energy. In its trauma-shaped version, it's chronic disconnection from your body, emotional numbness, incapacity to take action even when you need to.

Why you could be living in Freeze Territory:

- You shut down in the face of conflict or stress
- You experience times when you are feeling numb, or simply feeling empty inside.
- You have a hard time making up your mind; you hesitate when taking an action
- You tend to shut down or "space out" when feelings are overwhelming
- You feel trapped. You feel trapped in situations you don't want to be in.

- You may seem calm on the outside but are panicking inside

- You struggle to find out what you need or to let others know.

- You are less fearful when you are invisible, when no one sees you.

This was my old stomping ground here for a good portion of my younger years. And so, when my father would rage, when my brother trespassed over my boundaries, when my world kept moving around underneath me as stepmothers flew off in and flew off out, I would freeze. I go silent, I am still, I am invisible. As Dr. Ruffin's EKG would later confirm, my heart rate would, in fact, plummet, a physiological hallmark of the freeze response.

One or more if this was your experience growing up, there may be a home for you in Freeze Territory: You could not fight back or get away from an attacker; you learned it was no use, resistance was futile; you were confronted with an event so powerful, horrible or overwhelming it was simply too big for you to respond to actively. Your nervous system learned: Safety is in the disappearance, even if it's just inside yourself.

The Fawn Territory

This is the land of people-pleasing, accommodating, of attempting to purchase safety by addressing others' needs to the detriment of your own. In its healthy iteration, the fawn response helps you to attune to others and stay connected in social networks. In its trauma form, it is chronic self abandonment, codependency and lack of identity.

Indicators that you might be living in Fawn Territory:

- You say "I'm sorry" too much, maybe for things that aren't your fault

- You're very clued-in to other people's moods and needs
- You're changing what you believe to resonate with what others are thinking
- You're taking too much responsibility for others' feelings
- You are needy and insatiable with your need for approval
- To be non-adversarial, you put yourself last
- It is safe when others are pleased with you

I developed a strong fawn response in addition to freezing in response to the sexual abuse by my brother. I was superattuned to everyone else's wanting and moods, scoping every situation for how to please versus how to say no. This was something that followed me into adulthood, winding me up in relationships where I constantly was giving and not receiving.

If Fawn Territory was the place you called home, you may have spent your childhood being forced to take care of other people's feelings and moods in order to feel safe, or you may have learned that you didn't matter compared to others, or that the only thing of value you could bring to a relationship was an ability to do things for others, and simply being yourself wasn't enough, or that your worth was in how useful you were to others, rather than a person in your own right. Your nervous system learned that safety is in making yourself useful and agreeable.

Hybrid Spaces and Shifting Homes

But most of us don't exclusively inhabit one of those territories. We're all gathering here at our principal dwelling, but we also have vacation houses or timeshares in other jurisdictions that we use in limited circumstances.

You may, after all, inhabit Fight Territory in your professional life, but retreat to Freeze Territory in your intimate life. It is possible that when friends encroach too close, you'll default to Flight Territory. Your survival geography is particular to you, a product of your own experience and the specific dangers you've confronted.

And your address is not static, it can change. Major life events, entering new relationships, going to therapy or just getting older can have the power to change which terrain feels like home. I've lived in the territory states at various times in my life, though Freeze and Fawn were my homes for many years.

The objective isn't to move to some perfect realm, which doesn't exist. Every answer has its context, its wisdom, and its utility. The aim is to have freedom of movement amongst territories — to choose your response, rather than being driven there by the nervous system's out-of-date GPS (Global Positioning System).

Taking Inventory: Where Are You Living?

Is your ideal career your actual career? Not the honesty that's a punch to the gut or a stick in the eye, but the honesty that sees clearly and allows us to decide wisely.

Here are a few examples. For each one, what response feels closest to home, feels like your "normal" mode of pattering?

If someone criticizes you, do you:

- Fight back - On the offensive or counter-attacking, *(Fight)*
- Discontinue the topic, or remove yourself from the conversation *(Flight)*

- Blanking-out unable to answer, or think *(Freeze)*
- Say "I'm sorry" too much and try to make the person like you *(Fawn)*

When your partner desires more closeness than you'd like, are you more likely to:

- Get frustrated and pick arguements with them *(Fight)*
- Keep yourself busy with work or other things *(Flight)*
- Feel swamped and devoid of emotions *(Freeze)*
- Fawn over them, override your own squeamish feelings to give solace

Some things you do when you're feeling vulnerable or scared?

- Fly into a rage or struggle to assert control of the situation *(Fight)*
- Give yourself a way to distract or excuse yourself *(Flight)*
- Shutting down, emotionally or physically *(Freeze)*
- Concentrate on solving for someone else *(Fawn)*

When someone you love is offended by you, do you:

Defend yourself or counter-attack *(Fight)*

Steer clear of them, or tone down the significance of the matter *(Flight)*

Sit in silence not sure how to engage *(Freeze)*

You are trying to get back into their good graces *(Fawn)*

If you're like most people — and especially if you're an introvert — when you're thrust into a group situation that feels awkward, I'm guessing you do one of the following things:

- *DOMINATE* the conversation, or *CRITICIZE* the group *(Fight)*
- Find an excuse to exit early *(Flight)*
- Get silent and hope you don't get caught *(Freeze)*
- Work on being useful or at the very least entertaining. *(Fawn)*

As you think about these examples, you will start to see a recurring theme. You might recognize that you lean more consistently into one or two of these responses than others. These are your default domains — the territories where your nervous system swiftly steers you when it senses danger.

Your Loyalty to Territory Vs. Loyalty to Partner

One of the most interesting things about these survival territories is how they effect our attractions and the dynamics that come up in our relationships.

We are often subconsciously attracted to people who activate our familiar survival responses—not because we like to suffer, but because these patterns feel like a "home" to our nervous system, even when it wasn't a healthy one.

You may be drawn to lovers who fight, who resist, who dance the dance of conflict that feels so familiar if you were raised in Fight Territory. Or, maybe you attract submissive partners who enable your controlling tendencies.

Flight Territory is your home, you may be attracted to partners who are emotionally unavailable, or have some avoidant features, leading to relationships where no one gets too close. Or, you can end up with anxious, seeking partners who activate that need you have to maintain distance.

Individuals living in Freeze Territory often attract dominant partners who make choices and act, taking the actions for the fighting to be frozen unchallenged. Or they end up among other freeze-types, forming relationships based on inertia and unspoken needs.

And if you also happen to live in Fawn Territory, the people you are attracted to may be those who you can care for, who are unassuming of what they want and need over and above what you want and need, or who reward you with infrequent validation of your caretaking efforts.

I have lived this cycle over and over again. It had all led up to me leaving that marriage with only a backpack and $900 — years and years of fawning, of trying to save someone who didn't want to be saved, but also of abandoning myself in the process. I was playing out the dynamic of my youth, seeking to win love by proving how much I could give up and give away to others, much like how I had once tried to secure safety with my unpredictable father.

Understanding where your territory is helps you see those patterns very starkly, maybe for the first time. It helps you know when you are choosing partners for the purpose of re-creating the known rather than the possibility of the new.

The Price for Not Moving

Let one thing be very, very clear: there is a price for staying in your default. A cost to your well-being, your happiness, your ability to have real connection with people.

Prolonged fight response, for its part, manifests itself as follows:

- Relationships based on power rather than partnership
- Health hazards of continually being angry and being tense

- Aloneness as people step away from so much of your closing up
- A life where you're respected, but seldom intimately known

The flight or fight response, when it becomes chronic, will cause:

- Relationships that never grow deep or close
- Feeling empty and disconnected from yourself and those around you
- Opportunities for growth and connection lost
- An existence of movement without meaning

When the freeze response becomes chronic, we get:

- Connections that leave your needs unsaid and unmet
- Such a deep feeling of helplessness and feeling stuck
- Shut-down and depressed state of body
- A life lived in observation and not in fullness or fullfilment

Fawn mentality, when chronic, results in:

- Relationships in which you are put on this earth to meet others' needs
- Bitterness hidden underneath a happy face
- Identity loss and disconnection from your own wants
- A life that appears good in the eyes of others, but that feels hollow in your own.

I've paid the price in all these forms at different stages of my life. These automatic survival reactions have cost me relationships, health, opportunities and years of my life. I don't want that for you.

The good news is: You do not have to keep living where you've been living. As I mentioned previously, your nervous system is incredibly plastic. Through consciousness, training and support, you can gain the freedom to choose your response, breaking free from trigger-based, kneejerk responses.

This does not mean throwing out the wisdom of your survival responses. All of them were created with good intentions, and all of them have value:

- The fight response gives you the ability to establish boundaries and speak up for what is important.
- The flight response allows you to determine when a little space can prove to be a very good thing.
- The freeze response allows you access to stillness; to the collected wisdom of not acting.

What the fawn response grants you is empathy and attunement to the needs of others; what you learn from that stage of your life is how to put aside your own needs for the desires of those you love.

The goal is not to get rid of these responses, but to integrate them — to have them accessible by choice, but not by force.

Conclusion: The Decision Point

So here you are at a decision point. You've been shown the map of the four lands. You've done an inventory of the place where you've been living. You know the costs of staying are high.

Now what?

You could close this book right now – and it's likely that many already have. The content has likely triggered many people to do so. It's reality, and it is what it is. This isn't easy reading.

And maybe you've been triggered as well, and to you I will say, thank you for your brave conscious decision to stay in the "fight," with yourself.

Still, you might say, "Hmm, interesting information," and be on your way to your default habits. Many people do. It feels good there, in a familiar kind of pain way.

Or, you could make today the day that you take the first steps along the path to a new address—to a life where your actions come from a place of choice, rather than from compulsion, from current awareness rather than past conditioning.

This journey isn't easy. If it were, everyone would have already completed the journey.

Make no mistake about it: I've researched and written this book out of an immense and sometimes overwhelming amount of pain. It has been quite painful to look into the mirror for much of my life, and even more during the time I've been writing this book.

It takes courage to look at the truth of your patterns. Testing out new ways of being takes vulnerability. It takes discipline to retrain neural pathways that have been strengthening themselves for years.

But as someone who has many times chosen the latter, I can tell you from personal experience (mine and all the other people I have seen follow this path): It's worth it. The freedom, intimacy, and peace, which is possible on the other side of this work is greater than most people ever get to taste in their response systems.

So, I want you to promise something to yourself:

Decide to look at yourself plainly, without distortion, judgment, or shame. Decide to be curious about your patterns, not critical of them. You have a choice what to do with them now. You can opt to allow them to coast on autopilot, running the same painful programs in your relationships. Or you can elect to wake up, and break that automatic cycle and do something different.

The choice is yours. And it begins right here, right now, with a simple question that only you can answer:

Where are you, and where would you like to go?

PART II THE IMPACT OF CONNECTION

CHAPTER SEVEN

RELATIONSHIPS IN SURVIVAL MODE

I recall having been seated across from my therapist, my psychiatrist, Dr. Ruffin, in the first year of our work. I was sharing with him another tale of a relationship gone down in flames.

"I don't understand," I said, rubbing my hands through my hair irritably. "I'm successful at work. I know how to lead teams, solve hard problems, deal with pressure. But as soon as I start taking the relationship seriously, it all goes to hell. I feel like I'm someone else."

Doctor Ruffin leaned another forward. "You don't metamorphose into someone else," he said. "You are who you had to be to survive your formative years. In this case, however, unlike on the job, those survival skills are not working for you. In personal relationships, they stab you in the back."

That conversation was a game-changer for me. It was what taught me that the same reflexes that kept me safe as a little boy — and got me to where I was in my professional life — were exactly the reflexes that were dooming my chances at connecting.

This is the paradox of survival mode and relationships: The very coping mechanisms that saved us once upon a time are now the bars of the emotional prison in which we imprison ourselves.

Where Survival Mode and Intimacy Collide

In this book, we've looked at the four survival responses (fight, flight, freeze, and fawn) and how they appear in your life. We've seen how these responses wire into your nervous system through early experiences. We've looked at them as being part of your default way of living in the world.

But no place will such reactions cause more havoc than in close relationships.

Why? It's that being in close relationships sets off your attachment system, the primal, hardwired urge to connect with others that's been there since you were a baby. And your attachment system is also hardwired to your survival responses.

Consider the process: As an infant, your very survival literally relied on staying connected to your parents or caregivers. To be abandoned, or left alone, or in some way rejected was not just emotionally painful, they realized — it was a threat to their life. Your immature body and developing brain were unable to differentiate between threats to your relationships and threats to your physical survival, because such threats were one and the same.

Fast forward to adulthood.

You don't think an argument with your partner is life-threatening with your rational mind. Although, I must be transparent as I'm thinking about it – for me it did feel life-threatening at times. There have been times throughout my 6 marriages when a threat of a break-up or a divorce on the part of my wife felt like a threat to my very existence, and that by the way, was a key indicator of my co-depency, which took me a lifetime to discover. But I digress; that's for a future book.

Your nervous system, though, especially your amygdala, that Amber Alert of a relationship we discussed before, doesn't parse these distinctions very finely. It senses a potential threat to connection, and with a brain that evolved to scan for danger, it sounds the alarm, tapping the survival response that got you through it all when you were a kid.

And suddenly you are no longer an adult talking to someone you love. You're a child coping with trauma, and you're doing it with the survival mechanisms that you constructed to protect yourself in the first place.

The Close Battle of Relationships: What Actually Occurs

Allow me to provide you a sense of what this looks like in day-to-day life. I have lived these situations, and I have seen many others live them as well.

Think of a couple: we'll call them Mike and Sarah.

Mike was raised by an emotionally unpredictable mother who would fly off the handle one moment and smother him with love the next. His survival strategy was essentially hypervigilance (keeping an eye out for the slightest signs of anger), and people-pleasing (trying to ensure that she was happy no matter the cost). In short, he has developed a powerful fawn response.

Sarah's parents were emotionally unavailable to her, ignoring how she felt, and what she needed. Early on, she learned that being vulnerable meant being rejected or ignored. She survived on a default pattern of self-sufficiency and non-involvement—the ancient "flight response"—a way of coping with a world in which you know your needs will never be met.

Now they are in a relationship, but they are bringing those same survival patterns along. Here's an example of how a typical exchange plays out:

Sarah's day at the office was terrible, and she comes home exhausted, withdrawn. She's not in the mood to talk, just wants some space to unwind.

Mike, who has been hyperattuned to the emotional temperature in his household for years, suddenly feels Sarah's recusal. His amygdala goes off like an Amber Alert: "Danger! She's pulling away!"

His shiny, needy inner-child kicks in.

"What's wrong? Are you mad at me? Can I get you anything? Did I do something?" he inquires, following her from room to room.

Sarah, who is already depleted, is now under pressure to contain Mike's anxiety. Her flight instinct takes over and she is quickly becoming annoyed. "I'm fine," she says flatly. "I just need to be alone for a while." She runs back to the bedroom and slams the door.

To Mike, this retreat is abandonment. His anxiety spikes further. He taps politely on the door, suggests he could make her some tea, pleads to know how he made a mistake, makes one last, fruitless attempt to switch the magic on again.

For Sarah, this quest is an assault. Her need for distance is greater. Mike isn't listening to Sarah's request. She would get colder, more distant.

And round and round they go, each survival response into the other's, defending themselves from one another in a way that perpetuates itself, making the other person feel progressively less safe, and less connected.

It's not that either of them is wrong or bad. And that's because they are both acting out of old survival programs that served them when they were children, but are a complete disaster in adult relationships.

The Four Horsemen of Marital Armageddon

If survival responses are running the show in your relationships, they tend to play out in predictable ways of relating. In, *The Four Horsemen of the Apocalypse*, relationship researcher, Dr. John Gottman one of the world's foremost experts on loneliness—has discovered that there are four particularly destructive styles of conflict that indicate that a relationship is in trouble. These four horsemen, all direct manifestations of a survival response, include:

Criticism (argument from aggression): Attacking your partner's personality or character instead of his or her actions with, "you always" or "you never" statements. "You're so selfish. You never consider what I need."

Defensiveness (form of fight or flight response): Not listening or accepting your partner's point of view, counter-attacking or distracting. "Well, what about when you did it last week?"

Contempt (an over-the-top fight response): Being disgusted, hostile or disrespectful toward your partner. Eye-rolling, sarcasm, aggressive humor, name-calling.

Stonewalling (freeze or flight): Shutting down emotionally, refusing to speak to your partner or leaving and refusing to talk about it.

I've ridden these four horsemen at different times in my marriages.

Whenever my wife would give me a piece of her mind, I'd either defend myself (fight) or stonewall her (freeze), depending on how much I felt threatened. Neither did anything to help us work out any resolution; all they did was make a situation worse or drag it out further.

These patterns aren't random. They're what you get when your survival brain seizes your ability to connect.

When Survival Instincts Clash: The Dance of Distress

What's so interesting — and sad — about the responses to survival in relationships is the way they compound each other. Some combinations produce predictable "dances" that couples get locked in, each partner's reaction serving as a cue that triggers the other's response and makes it worse.

Here are some popular pairings:

The Pursue-Withdraw Dance

I suspect this is one of the most common patterns I see in stagnating relationships. The dominant partner tends to come from a fight or fawn response who likes resolution, discussion and connection. The other partner then shuts down, freezes up, withdraws, needing space, or is overwhelmed.

The longer the pursuer pursues, the more the withdrawer withdraws. The more the withdrawer pulls away, the more the pursuer pursues. Round and round they go, each feeling more and more misunderstood and alone.

I experienced this dance during my own marriages. I'd shut down when there was a conflict or shut people out, and I couldn't get through. It would set off my wife's anxiety and she would push harder — more questions, demands for answers, following me from room to room. I'd shut down even further, which in turn would make her more anxious and pursue harder.

Neither of us knew we were engaged in a dance for survival. I wasn't electing to shut down; my freeze response simply took over. It wasn't that she was electing to pursue; her fight/fawn response was on reflex. We were both victims of nervous systems wired by our childhoods.

The Attack-Attack Dance

If both partners loop to fight (as opposed to fight-or-flight), disagreements inevitably escalate into pitched battles in which the priority is not understanding but winning. Each one perceives the other's aggression as a threat and is forced to escalate.

This dance usually involves: Raising voices, interrupting, name-calling, subtle references to past mistakes and transgressions. Neither feels heard or understood, and both leave feeling injured, resentful and more confident than ever that the other is the issue.

I know what that feels like, because I've also been in situations like that, where the two of us would both go right to our fight responses. These were intense relationships, physically and emotionally — lots of sex and lots of fighting, lots of long breaks, sleeping in separate bedrooms, weeks of silent treatments, dramatic arguments and equally dramatic reconciliations. It was exhausting, and in the end legally written off as, *irreconcilable*. Totally…toxic.

The Freeze-Freeze Dance

When both partners default to freeze, conflict doesn't even look like conflict. There is no "fighting for your love" — the end doesn't come by building walls or breaking plates. It shows up as a disconnect, disengagement, and unfulfilling emptiness even with them in the same room.

Such couples tend to say that they "never fight," which they see as a positive. But no open conflict isn't the same as a healthy relationship. Indeed, it quite often means both of the people are too closed down to even get to the issues between them.

It's a dance that looks like both silence, emotional flatness and the dance of which you live parallel lives and not shared ones. Issues are not resolved because they are not addressed in the first place.

The Fawn-Fawn Dance

When couples function mostly from a fawn response, the relationship may appear perfectly fine but never real. Both go out of their way to please the other and to avoid conflict, to such an extent that neither communicates their actual desires or emotions.

Such couples are often the ones who say that they "never fight," or that they "agree on everything," but lurking beneath the surface are resentment, unmet needs and a feeling of being a stranger to one another. The relationship works just fine in practical terms– it just doesn't feel right emotionally.

I too, spent years in relationships with these dynamics, with two people too afraid of displeasing the other to try to get what we want. We'd smile, and nod, and say everything's fine while dying inside." These relationships were not explosive like the fight-response ones — they were just as unfulfilling, and ultimately not viable.

The Cost of Love Under Fire

In relationships that function primarily from survival mode, there is a high cost paid by both individuals:

- Emotional exhaustion: Living in a fight, flight, freeze, or fawn state constantly saps your energy and resilience.
- Lack of intimacy: Real intimacy involves vulnerability, which you can not really possess when you are in survival mode.
- Health effects: Long-term stress in your relationship can manifest in your body in the form of increased stress hormones, inflammation, and a suppressed immune system.
- Trauma reinforced: Your survival responses knit deeper pathways as each new trigger hardens and becomes more automatic for you.
- Collateral damage: kids, friends, family members — they all be affected by your relationship nightmares.
- Potential squandered: Maybe even more tragic, however, is what doesn't get to happen — the joy, the growth, the healing that can happen when relationships create safety instead of engendering survival.

I have paid all of those prices in my relationships. The chronic activation of survival responses had me emotionally exhausted, physically unwell and increasingly convinced that real connection was not possible for me. Each broken relationship fortified my darkest convictions: that I was simply unlovable at my core, or that love was real only as long as a Phish song and not even for 20 minutes before the damnable suffering began.

Breaking the Cycle

So how can you begin to change these patterns? How do you transition from relationships based on survival reactions to ones that promote safety, connection, and expansion?

Step One - Awareness. You can't alter patterns you can't perceive. Here's what you can start to be mindful of when it comes to your survival responses in your relationships:

- What situations predictably activate your fight, flight, freeze or fawn response?
- What sort of feelings of sensations go with these responses?
- What gets triggered in you, that causes these thoughts and beliefs to emerge?
- What are your survival mode activities?

Just the act of watching these patterns without judgement starts to create space between trigger and response — space opening the possibility of choice.

Step Two - Ownership. This doesn't mean blaming yourself for responses that were hard-wired into you, at least not by you. It means accepting that though you didn't write your own code, you are responsible for what you do with it now.

How you would use it: "I recognize that I feel threatened right now and would like to close off. This is my freeze response kicking in. If we look at how I was raised, it works out, but is it what will help me right now?"

Step Three: Communication. Obviously, the third step is communication. Once you have some insight into your patterns, sharing that with your partner can be transformative. This isn't about your history as an excuse for being a jerk (or worse). It has to do with creating a context and inviting understanding.

Communication sounds like: "When you told me that you needed space it made me feel a rush of panic. I think it set off my old fears of abandonment, ones that had originated in my childhood. When you left, my first impulse was either to hold onto you, or to shove you away before you abandoned me. I'm working on how to recognize, process and intervene in this pattern in a different way."

These measures will not be a quick fix. They are the start of a process — a process that takes time, vulnerability, patience, practice and, in many cases, professional help. But, they are a key pivot from involuntary response to voluntary response.

A Different Kind of Strength

In the Marine Corps, I discovered that real strength is not the absence of fear. It's not that, it's about feeling the fear and doing the work anyway. It works the same in relationships.

Sure, the ultimate power of relationship isn't in never getting triggered into survival responses. It's about knowing when you are triggered and walking a different way, anyway. It's about, let's say, overcoming the instinct to protect one's self and remain vulnerable. It's about not disengaging when you want to run, speaking up when you want to shut down, listening when you want to pounce, and holding boundaries when you want to please.

This strength isn't something that is natural. It's earned through repetition, through falling and arising, through deciding to take the harder path of growth instead of the easier path of protection.

Conclusion: From Battlefield to Staging Ground

As I sit here tapping these backlit keys, I reflect on my own track record in relationships, I survey a battleground strewn with the fallen of my unchecked survival reactions. Marriages that failed, engagements that shattered, friendships that were unable to hold the weight of my unhealed trauma.

But I also recognize a classroom — every relationship revealing something about me, every experience leading me to greater self-awareness, every painful pattern exposing where I was in need of healing. Believe me, it's still not 100% easy when the subject of relationships or marriage comes up, and I'm the guy saying, "I've been married…6 times."

In between marriages and divorces – even up until the end of the fourth – I would try and avoid being too deep into the conversations (flight at work). I feared the "my turn,"—that inevitable feeling of the oncoming question: "how about you, Phillip? Married, divorced?"

But the uneasiness I now feel is not due to my record. It's the bias that exists for the divorced/remarried, and the multiple instances of this that often play into the fact of the matter: I may be judged and ostracized, or not fully accepted when someone in the group is turned off by my honest answer. Knowing this judgement could take place is a disappointing reality to entertain as the conversation is being had. I've had to learn to be ready to accept it. At the same time, the liberation that has come because of my transparent approach is always the silent reward to my soul.

Your relationships can be a battlefield or a training ground. The battlefield is about survival, about getting out with minimal damage. In a training environment, the intention is to evolve, to learn new tactics, to become stronger and smarter with every new struggle.

The choice is yours.

You can still continue to run your relationships to the tune of your survival responses and continue to create those painful old patterns time and time again. Or, you can take your relationships to be laboratories in which you experiment with healing, places where you see the triggers that set you off, interrupt automatic reactions to them — and explore new possibilities of connection.

This focus on the four instinctive survival responses will be the focus of the next four chapters, where we take an in-depth look at how each survival response expresses itself in relationships, and what special challenges and potentials these activations offer. We'll begin with the fight response — or when protection turns to aggression — and how it can both help and hinder your ability to create authentic relationships with others.

But for now, let's take a moment to simply observe: Where is survival mode showing up in your relationships? What's the dance you are locked in with your partner? And what if you could step out of battle and into the training ground?

CHAPTER EIGHT

THE FIGHT RESPONSE:

WHEN PROTECTION BECOMES AGRESSION

I had just come back from Marine Corps bootcamp, I was on leave for 10 days before I had to report back to Camp Pendleton to start Marine Combat Training (MCT). I was on fire, I was so confident and I felt like nothing could harm me, I was fearless and unafraid of anything—or so I thought.

I was just so over-ego'd, looking back. And yet, I was stronger, in the best shape of my life, and I was now experienced in hand-to-hand combat. For the past 16 weeks, I'd been wired for war, taught to cultivate a killer instinct.

My older brother, who had been mean and abusive to me for as long as I had lived, was waiting to take my measure.

And at 6'2" and 230 pounds, he still thought he could wrestle me into place as he always had. While staying at his apartment one afternoon, with his wife, it happened. He had overheard me on the phone with an ex-girlfriend and he didn't like the idea that I was falling back into an old relationship. That afternoon, he attempted to relive the big bully brother image I'd known, and he aggressively approached me. What followed for us both was unexpected.

On instinct, I stepped forward — unafraid — and punched him in the face. He looked stunned, but kept coming toward me to fight. I grabbed his arm and in one continuous movement, tossed him over his coffee table, spun around his back as he was trying to get back onto his feet and put him in a chokehold. Within seconds he started to whimper, and his wife was begging me to let him go.

I eventually did.

He stormed off to the bathroom and I spent a few moments after listening to him sob on the phone with our father about how I had "attacked him." The irony was epic — how many times had he pummeled me during our youth and had never faced repercussions for it? And how many of those times did I allow it go unreported to our father?

As I stood there — in my brother's living room, heart racing, adrenaline blazing through me, I realized something clearly for the first time in my life: I had an UNHEALTHY FIGHT in me. Years of being frozen with fear when I was around him, years of fawning and also in flight, trying to avoid his wrath — all of it added up to a pressure cooker of rage that the Marines had simply enabled me to express.

I'm not proud of what I did on that day. Violence should never be glamorized. But that confrontation was an origin story for a seismic paradigm shift in how I thought of myself, and of how I was confronted by threat. For the first time in my life, I had access to my fight response in a relationship where before I'd only previously experienced flight, freeze and fawn.

It wasn't the Marines who had handed me the fight response, it was always there, buried somewhere under all the layers of fear and helplessness. What the Marine Corps given me was permission to use it, training in how not to be eaten alive by it, and enough safety for me to touch it even in situations that had overwhelmed me before.

That moment with my brother was the beginning of a tangled journey with my fight response — one that brought me empowerment and disillusionment, one that made room for the healthy boundaries that saved me and the aggression that cost me so much throughout my childhood.

The Double-Edged Sword

Fight may be the least understood of all the survival responses. We believe it's inherently bad, like it's aggression or hostility or even violence. But the fight response, like all survival mechanisms is there for a reason. It's not inherently harmful, it only harms you when you're using it incorrectly or when it becomes your only tool of getting through stress.

At its heart, fighting is about self-preservation and regulation. It's the part of you that says "no" to violation, that defends your needs, that guards what is precious. Without some healthy access to fight energy, you become a sitting duck for exploitation and abuse.

You have trouble setting limits or speaking up for yourself.

You are a doormat on which everyone wipes their feet.

But when the instinct to fight is the only, (or) dominant way you know how to respond to the stress of being in relation, things get tricky in a different way. You get defensive, controlling, critical or aggressive. You push people away. You make a fight where a fight does not exist. You hurt those you love most.

The point is <u>not</u> to get rid of your fight — it's to include it. It's to harness its energy rather than be drug around by it, to fight for people you care about rather than fighting with the people you love.

"Never End the Fight": The Combatting Heroism

There is one scene in the movie "Lone Survivor" that haunts me.

Taylor Kitsch plays Navy SEAL, Lieutenant Michael Murphy: Lt. Murphy finds himself on a mountainside in the mountain ranges of the Kunar province in Afghanistan with a four-man SEAL team and an outnumbered chapter of approximately 80 Taliban soldiers.

They are outgunned, outnumbered, and with no way out.

Lt. Murphy understands the only possible way they can be saved is to climb high enough to find a signal on their satellite phone and summon air support.

Lt. Murphy tells his teammate, Marcus Luttrell (Mark Wahlberg), "Never end the fight."

Then he does something unthinkable: He puts himself in the enemy's direct fire, scaling the rocky slope as rounds zip all around him. He gets to the top, calls for help and as he's finishing the climb, gets shot several times. There he dies, on his knees and gazing at the mountains ahead.

He did not fight for himself or to protect others. Not in anger, not in vengeance, but in love, and in duty.

This is the fight response at its best — the capacity to face insurmountable odds, not in ego, not in anger, but in service to something greater than yourself. It's the warrior energy that defends, not destroys, that serves, not enslaves.

My own battle with my older brother, and what Lt. Murphy gave, couldn't be a starker contrast.

In both cases, it was the fight response that was triggered, but in my experience with my older brother, it sprang from years of pent-up rage and newly found power. Lt. Murphy's was disciplined courage and selfless love.

My fight caused damage; Lt. Murphy's saved lives.

This contrast makes sense, and demonstrates a fundamental truth: The fight response is a spectrum. At one extreme is reactive aggression based on unprocessed trauma and fear. At the opposite is conscious courage motivated by love and calling. Most of us live somewhere between the two, moving up and down the spectrum, depending on the circumstances and our own level of consciousness.

The point is not to forever avoid a fight. Occasionally, we must be like Lt. Murphy — we have to engage in combat — for our relationships, for our values, for those we love. The idea is to fight deliberately, to decide when and how we engage, rather than acting on reflex.

The Biology of Battle

Before we get into further how the fight response can manifest itself in relationships, let me first explain what's happening in your body when this response kicks in.

When your brain senses a threat, it activates the sympathetic nervous system, the "gas pedal" of your autonomic nervous system. This triggers a chain of physical responses that are meant to ready you for action:

- Your pulse and blood pressure rise

- Blood is directed to your large muscles

- Your breathing is faster and more shallow

- Your eyes dilate to allow in more visual information

- Stress hormones such as adrenaline and cortisol are released into your system

- Your digestive system slows or grinds to a halt

- You notice your sense of pain is reduced

These changes aren't random. They are literally readying your body to fight — to protect yourself from some perceived threat. The problem is that your body does not know how to differentiate between a saber-toothed tiger and a sarcastic remark from your partner. Both have the potential to elicit the same physiological response.

In those years that I led that team at America Online to peak performance, I was tuning my fight to that constructive end. The spunk, focus and determination that accompany such a response and make it an asset in the moment. But at the same time, the physiology that helped me rise up the work ranks could wreak havoc on my intimate relationships, where a softer touch was required.

The Childhood Roots of Fight

As with all the survival responses, your relationship with the fight response developed in response to your early experiences—specifically how the adults around modeled, responded to, and navigated both anger as well as the need for and setting of limits.

Some of us were raised in households where fight was the default. We observed parents who screamed, blamed and became physically aggressive when under stress. We learned that safety had power and control was currency. We were taught that vulnerability was dangerous and to best protect ourselves, the best defense was the good offense.

Some of us were raised in homes where the fight response was discouraged. If there was any anger or boundary asserted, we were punished, cut off from loving, or abandoned. We learned our needs didn't matter, that keeping the peace mattered more than telling the truth, and that "good" meant compliant.

And again, some of you who didn't necessarily have these dynamics in childhood, may have very well learned them through other traumas: a divorce, a loss of a child, a pink slip from an employer, a physical handicap, a car accident, or any other life-event that caused a trauma in your life, which ultimately may have rewired your subconscious with a new set of biochemical responses.

And some note mixed reactions to their fight energy. Sometimes it was permissible, even encouraged; other times it was severely punished.

This conflict leads to confusion surrounding when it is and isn't ok to fight.

I had a very difficult relationship to fight given my experience as a child. My father exhibited an extreme, frequently frightening form of the fight response — an explosive anger that could be unpredictable and unexpected at any time.

And yet, I couldn't feel my own anger or set boundaries. I could not stand up for myself without more violence or more punishment.

So, I had this really split relationship with my fight response. Part of me was terrified of it — I associated it with my father's rage and the mess it left in its wake. I was, in a way, fascinated by it — because it afforded him power while my freeze and fawn responses had made me feel powerless.

That division carried into adulthood with me. I was able to access fight energy productively in some situations, such as in my work. In relationships, though, or other intimate relationships, I did one of two things: I either bottled it up entirely and felt quietly resentful until I finally blew (like a smaller version of my father) or, I expressed it in a way that almost exactly replicated my father's toxic behavior.

It's key for healing to understand those childhood foundations of your relationship with fight. It makes you realize that the patterns you are in now are not just random patterns or ingrained in you — they're mostly learned patterns for specific situations. And what's learned can be unlearned and replaced with healthier options.

Arguing in Relationships: The Red Flags

What does the fight response tend to look like in relationships? Here is a breakdown of some common symptoms:

- Criticism: The statement you made reflected on the nature of your partner rather than the behavior. "You're really lazy" for "I get really annoyed when the dishes stack up."

- Defensiveness: Reacting to feedback or requests by retaliating or explaining. "Yeah, but what about when you did the same thing last week?"
- Control: Trying to control your partner's action, decisions or feelings in order to reduce your own anxiety. "You can go out with your friends but every hour you need to text me."
- Contempt: Making your partner feel repulsive, inferior, or unworthy and above you. Eye-rolling, making fun, name-calling.
- Black-and-white thinking: Thinking in all-or-nothing terms about situations, people, or conflicts. "You are either all in for me, or I don't like to use the word, but you are a loser."
- Escalation: Intensifying a conflict beyond its level of merit. Transforming a conversation about house-cleaning duties into a referendum on the relationship as a whole.
- Throwing something back: Repeating a past mistake or conflict to bring it back into an argument. "This is like when you did that three years ago with the..."
- Interrupting: When you cut off your partner mid-sentence so that they're unable to complete their thoughts or express their feelings.

- Physical intimidation: Using your own body to create fear or obedience, with or without violence. Looming over your partner, standing in doorways, punching walls.

Sadly, I have done all these things at some point in my relationships. In my earlier marriages, criticism was often my default reaction when I felt a threat or was not being listened to. I'd zero in on my wife's imperfections instead of articulating my own needs. It was simpler to attack than to be open.

In another relationship, I was controlling — always looking at my wife's phone, asking her about male friends, setting rules about when and how she could go out. I didn't understand at the time that my need to control wasn't about her trustworthiness; it was about <u>my</u> unhealed abandonment issues from childhood.

Another Relationship Example - A very clear example from my own life, that demonstrates: what happens when fight takes over an interaction in relationship.

Several years into my relationship with Sarah (not her real name), we were out to dinner at a restaurant when she casually mentioned seeing an ex-boyfriend earlier that day. There was no purpose to the casual remark, just her recounting part of her day to me.

But that's not how my (Amy) amygdala heard it.

It quickly issued an Amber Alert: "Danger! She's thinking about her ex! You're going to be replaced!" Seconds later, my body had gone into full fight mode — heart racing, muscles tensing, breath coming all shallow.

The words that came out of my mouth after that bore almost no relation to the actual situation and everything to the fact that my fight response had switched on: "Oh, so that's what you were checking your phone? Planning your next meetup?"

Sarah looked stunned. "What are you talking about? I, uh, I just saw him in the coffee shop. It was a two-minute conversation."

But I was too deep into fight mode to listen to her. "It's like you're unhappy with me, you can say it. You don't have to keep secrets and pretend."

"I'm not keeping secrets! I just told you, literally, about running into him!"

It was all downhill from there. I got more and more accusatory; she got more and more defensive. What should have been a nice dinner turned into a strained, tearful evening, and we went to bed angry and disconnected.

I can see so much more clearly what happened as I look back. Talking about an ex-boyfriend alone made my childhood fears of being abandoned—of people abandoning me—come to the surface.

My fight kicked in as a protective mechanism against feeling the pain of being left again.

But rather than keep me safe, it broke the connection between us that I most feared would happen. My fight response that I thought was keeping me safe was actually endangering my relationship.

When Partners Have Mismatched Fight Styles

The situation gets more complicated if one partner has a different relationship with the fight response. And this very difference ... often results in that painful pattern, that vicious cycle tendency that leaves both people feeling that the other just doesn't get them, and they are one of a kind, all alone.

Take for example: you grew up in a fight-centric household; for you, direct confrontation might be considered normal and good. It might feel natural to raise your voice, to express your anger, to argue passionately.

But if your partner was raised in a household where fight was forbidden or dangerous, these exact behaviors might feel terrifying or abusive to them. Their nervous system could shut down altogether at what you call a "normal" expression.

If, on the other hand, you learned to deny your fight response, you might react to more direct expressions of anger from your partner with feelings of overwhelm or emotional shut down. You may recoil or people-please, or both in response, and your partner may feel ignored or condescended to.

And these differences are not character flaws or matters of romantic compatibility. They are delivered from the bodies of nervous systems that were formed by different environments and learned different ways to cope with threat.

Recognizing these differences is the first step in their reconciliation. It enables you to see your partner's response doesn't mean they don't care, that it's not a personal assault — it is as if their even/odd strategy or soothing paired with efforts to flee is their nervous system doing exactly what it learned to do to survive.

The Costs of Chronic Fight

The Price You (and your partner) pay when the fight response becomes your go-to strategy for dealing with relationship stress, you and your partner both pay a heavy toll:

- Physical health: Chronically expressed anger and hostility are associated with heart disease, hypertension, compromised immune function and reduced life span.
- Mental health: Existing in a state of constant fight can lead to anxiety, depression and burnout.
- Relationship quality: Spouses of chronically defensive or critical individuals report lower satisfaction in their relationships and higher levels of contemplating divorce or separation.

- Emotional intimacy: Real intimacy involves vulnerability, and that is impossible when you are in fight defense mode.

- Resolving conflicts: Paradoxically the fight response ofter prohibits resolution of the underlying cause of the conflict.

- Role modeling: Children who observe habitual fight reactions in their parents are more likely to adopt similar patterns in their future relationships.

These are the costs I have paid in my relationships. I was always on the offensive, my fight switch turned on, and it literally wore me out and made an emotional recluse of me, more and more convinced that real connection with other humans wasn't even possible for me. And with each relationship failure, my deepest fears of being essentially unloveable, and that love was a lie confirmed.

Regaining the Health of the Fight Energy

Don't get me wrong: it's not that you should erase your fight response. As I learned that day with my brother after graduating from Marine boot camp, some angry combat energy is crucial for establishing boundaries, fighting for what you need and protecting what matters.

The trick is to learn how to use this energy consciously instead of being highjacked by it. Here is a powerful tactic that has helped me and a lot of other people transform their relationship with the fight response:

- Create a Pause: As soon as you realize that your fight response is getting triggered, the best thing that you can do is to put space between

- the trigger and your reaction. This pause is when choice becomes available.

Some good ways to pause would be:

- Inhale and exhale, 3 times, lengthening your exhale, all the way out.
- Move back Physical backing off or spacing away.
- Say: 'I need a moment' and take a short time-out
- Silently count to ten
- Hand on your heart or belly

The pause won't fix the problem, but it will stop you from making it worse by automatically fighting back. It allows your prefrontal cortex — your thinking brain — time to come back online.

Get Curious About the Trigger

There's a perceived threat behind every flight response. It can help to become curious about what is triggering you exactly, so that you can respond more effectively.

Ask yourself:

· What am I afraid of in this moment, truly?

· What does this remind me of in my past?

· What do I want that I'm not getting?

· What do I seek to preserve?

So, when I drafted my fight response to Sarah casually mentioning her ex-boyfriend, I discovered something: I wasn't actually afraid she was cheating. I was afraid of being left, of being too much or not enough, of being replaced — all dreads rooted in early experiences of loss rejection, and abandonment.

This awareness doesn't automatically alter the response, but helps you see that your reaction is frequently more about your history than your current life.

Express Needs, Not Criticisms

The fight one crops up as blame, likely due to feeling safer attacking someone than having my guard down. But criticism almost never actually gets your needs met. It just causes defensiveness and distance.

Get comfortable articulating your underlying needs with him/her directly:

- Not: "You're not listening to what I'm saying. You're always on your phone."
- Try: "I'm feeling disconnected from you. I need some dedicated time sharing a bubble without distractions."

Instead of: "You're the worst. You never even called to say you were going to be late…"

- Attempt: "I was concerned when I didn't hear from you. I need to know when plans get modified to know your safe."

This movement from criticism to expression of need isn't simple. It involves vulnerability, and that is a scary thing when you have a fight response turned on. But it's the only way to cease the cycle of emotional violence and establish true connection.

Reshape Your Fight Energy into Something More Positive

The energy of the fight response is not bad unto itself. It can be driven in directions that can be helpful to you and in your relationships:

· Use it to establish clear, firm limits

· Aim it at the problem and not at people

· Turn it into passionate support of the things you stand for

· Crush it out with some good physical activity

· Use it for protection when you absolutely must

At American Online, I learned that I could direct my fight energy towards leadership—leveraging its intensity and determination to defend my team and break through barriers. This was the fight energy in service of, instead of in resistance to creation.

Repair Relationship Ruptures

Try to have control over yourself as unfortunately there would be moments in which your fight response will take over. When the tissue becomes damaged, repair is necessary.

Effective repair includes:

- Owning what's yours with no excuses
- Showing true regret for the impact of what you did
- Making meaningful amends
- Agreements to make changes in the future
- Don't anticipate instant forgiveness

I stewed for hours after that godawful dinner with Sarah until I finally calmed-the-F-down and could see how my fight response had got the jump on me. I specifically apologized for my accusations and explained the fears that had activated me. I didn't justify anything I had done, but I did explain what led me to behave the way I had, and in the same process, allowed me to finally understand what had happened.

Fighting For, Not Against

The goal isn't to eradicate anger altogether: You don't want to discard your fight response. It's to change how you operate on this energy — have it invested in your relationships rather than expended against your partners.

It looks like "fighting for your relationship" in the following ways:

· Addressing patterns that cause frustration or distance

· Resisting the intrusion of external threats to your relationship

· Focusing on your needs, and your partner's needs

· Not quitting when it gets hard

· Protecting the fences that maintain the strength of your relationship

Some of the ways I'm most proud of how I've showed up in relationships involve using fight energy in these constructive ways — standing up for my partner against others' criticism, pushing through my fear of vulnerability to stay in and shift difficult conversations, fighting against some of my more automatic responses in order to create something healthier.

Conclusion: The Heart of the Warrior

In many spiritual traditions, this model of the warrior is less about unthinking aggression than disciplined strength in service of what matters. The warrior doesn't fight because they hate or fear, but because they love and are committed to something that is bigger than they are.

This is what your fight response in your integrated state is capable of: It's the force of protection rather than destruction, of uniting rather than dividing, of growth rather than immobility.

"*Never end the fight,*" says Lt. Murphy, but in this circumstance that is a tough pill to swallow. Sometimes the most important battle isn't the one outside of you, but inside — the battle to stay awake when everything in you wants to go unconscious, to remain open and be transparent when everything in you wants to close up and attack or defend, to choose love when everything in you wants to choose fear.

I still have work to do with my fight response. I still get hijacked. There are times when the old patterns hijack me, where I find myself struggling against, rather than for. But those moments are ever less frequent and intense. I'm learning to harness rather than be harnessed by this energy.

Your journey with fight energy is going to be yours. It will be molded by your history, your particular triggers and your own nervous system. But all of us have the same basic choice to make:

Will you let your fight response be on autopilot, reproducing the same old painful patterns of before? Or will you put in the work to recollect that fragment of self, to assimilate it, to turn it into a resource for healing, for connection?

The battle is not always easy. It takes bravery, practice and support from others in many cases. But it results in relationships that are strong and tender, boundaried and vulnerable, protective and connected.

In the next chapter, we'll explore the flight response—how the instinct to flee from danger can become a pattern of fleeing from intimacy, and how to move this energy from flight to fight.

CHAPTER NINE

FLIGHT: RUNNING FROM INTIMACY

I was in my garage, sitting in a cloud of cigar smoke, when I finally acknowledged what I was doing. It was 2 in the morning and I'd already been out there for hours, after another fight with my wife — my sixth wife, if you're still counting.

It wasn't the first time I found myself in the garage during an argument. It had been my sanctuary, my cave – or you could call it, *my inner prison.*

As tensions mounted, when I'd hear her voice go into that place, she couldn't help but make it sound the way it must've sounded all those years coming out of my father's mouth, the tightness in my chest would return, that longing to just not be in that room anymore. So, I would go — to to the garage, or my bedroom, or sometimes just "away," with no endpoint in mind.

Flight.

It was how I was answering in that marriage, like I had in so many in my life. But as I sat in the garage that night surrounded by the evidence of my escape — the cigar butts, the drained empty plastic water bottles, the hours spent deflecting rather than attending — I asked myself a question that broke through my justifications:

What was it about this relationship that made me shut myself in from the start?

It was a retreat. A running away from myself, from my unhealed wounds, from the work that I knew I had to do and yet didn't. I'd married woman number six, still laden down with gobs of the previous five, still operating from that part of my wounded child who had been held in varying forms of the acute stress response.

People in toxic and abusive relationships regularly ask: **"…why do I keep attracting the same type of (man or woman) …?"**

Maybe a better question to ask is: **"Why do I invite them in, and give them the keys to my house?"**

Maybe an even better question to ask is: **"Why am I still living in the same house?"**

I don't blame my ex-wife or any of my exes for our failed relationships. I blame myself.

The one thing that each of those relationships had in common was **me**—my unhealed trauma, my unconscious patterns, my inability to stick around when relationships became challenging. I was the one who needed healing, who needed to figure my stuff out before stepping into doomed-from-the-start relationships.

This particular marriage – my sixth – had pressed every button of unresolved hurt from my childhood. Up until the rockiness emerged, I thought I was doing well, or at least doing better. But rather than confronting the cycles, I'd done exactly what I'd always done — I'd fled. Not physically at least…not initially. I would run emotionally, withdrawing, clamming up, pulling back into my internal bunker, where she couldn't get me. I was running to save my life.

Until the day I actually did walk, as I wrote about in the first chapter of this book, none of it made sense. That last flight was merely the last in a thousand little flights that had been taking place all throughour our time together.

It's funny… that word, *together*.

TO-GET-HER.

I never figured it out with any of my exes: how <u>to get her</u> – and I'm not saying, "get" as in, acquire, obtain, control, but "get" her: Understand her. Know her. Love her for who she was.

Back to the flight response… It exists to save your life in dangerous situations. But when it's the way you lead with when dealing with relationship stress, it doesn't save anything. It just delays the inevitable while obliterating the prospect for real connection.

The Anatomy of Escape

It is one of our most fundamental survival reflexes: the flight response. When we feel threatened, our bodies gear up for flight — to avoid physical hazard and fight another day.

The heart will race, the blood will flow into the big muscles of the legs, breathing will become faster, stress hormones will pour into the system — all designed to help us run faster and farther.

It's this capacity for response that has kept our species alive for millennia. Whether our ancestors could outrun predators across the savanna could make the difference between life and death.

In the relationships we have these days, there are few or no flesh-eating predators to flee. Instead, there are bad feelings, hard conversations, vulnerability, intimacy, struggle — experiences that may register as threats to our nervous systems, but aren't truly dangerous to our lives.

But our bodies don't always distinguish this way. To your amygdala, that relationship Amber Alert system we mentioned, the emotional threat of potential rejection or abandonment can be just as hazardous as an actual threat. It evokes the same physical response: Get away. Run. Escape.

Flight takes various forms in relationships:

- Physical distance: Physically escaping the room, the house, or the relationship during conflict or emotional activation.
- Emotional withdrawal: You simply check out - you stay in the room, but you're gone - you numb-out, dissociate, go away.
- Avoid conflict: Deflect attention with humor or by changing the subject, or refuse to discuss difficult or challenging issues.
- Busyness: Packing one's schedule with work, hobbies or other activities that don't leave much time — or energy — for deep connection.
- Distraction: Feeling bad? Plug in, zone out; snort what you can.

- Chain-dating: Quickly replacing a partner with another, never allowing yourself to go deep enough to touch your attachment wounds.
- Workaholism: Substituting career as a socially acceptable means of avoiding the intimacy of relationship.

I've employed each and every one of these escape tactics at some point in life.

The Childhood Roots of Flight

Just like all survival responses are rooted in our earliest experiences, our habit to flee is a product of the past: the way our caregivers responded to us as we sought action and connection also left a mark on our subconscious.

When the people who cared for you refused to acknowledge or listen to what you needed: you as a child learned: "there's no use in asking or hoping for support." It was better to take care of things yourself, to stand on your own two feet, to not be dependent on anyone.

When emotions were terrifying to your caregivers: when a caregiver responded to your big feelings with anxiety, anger and/or shutdown, the younger version of you learned: "emotions are dangerous and should be avoided or repressed."

Connection isn't safe: When children who grow up in unpredictable relational conditions feel unsafe many, if not most, of the time, they come to avoid emotions and connections because these things come to represent threat and danger.

Conflict and the desire to escape it, or at least dominate another person, is the most common reason why people abandon, become violent with, or withhold love from their partners: When children who hear or see children experience traumatic events, post-conflict, be it a parent that leaves, becomes violent, or withholds love, they are often learning that they should do anything they can to avoid conflict.

All these things together shaped my own fight-or-flight response. I was raised by an alcoholic, abusive father and the parade of stepmothers who entered and left my life, so I learned long ago that connection wasn't safe or reliable.

The people who were supposed to love you, you discovered, could hurt you, could control you, could abandon you. Safer to maintain a distance, to not get too close, to always have an escape route in place.

My brother's sexual abuse drove that point home even further. My body, my limits, my very being had been violated by someone who should have had my back. Where would I be able to go and feel safe after that?

The answer, for my young psyche, could be found nowhere physical — only inward, away from the pain, into an emotional cocoon of detachment.

When I got married the first time, never mind the sixth, these patterns were in place. I was trying to figure out how to be present in the middle of conflict. I didn't know how to hold my emotions without being swallowed up by them. I didn't know how to trust that we could still be connected even through disagreement and disappointment. Even more unhealthy in my first marriage, I didn't know how to communicate like a normal, functional adult; I only knew I wasn't getting what I wanted. I only knew from past experience with my father that the way to get what you want was to fight: yell, intimidate, push, hit.

And, other times – in subsequent marriages and relationships, I just ran — the running sometimes literal, always emotional. Not that I didn't care, but that I cared too much and I didn't have any tools to deal with the vulnerability created by that caring.

Flight and Relationships in Action

I can give you an example from a previous marriage of flighty behavior in relationships.

My wife and I were making plans to get away for a weekend to visit her family. My visits there were always stressful — her family was loud, opinionated and had a communication style that felt combative to my nervous system. But I knew the visits meant a lot to her, so I'd reluctantly agree to go, bracing myself for discomfort.

The night before this one, as the specific trip in question approached, my wife informed me her brother would be at the house too, and he was someone who triggered me quite a bit, particularly with his really aggressive teasing that uncomfortably resembled that of my own, older brother.

I felt my flight response engage the moment I saw him. My heart rate began to soar, my chest constricted, and my mind frantically looked for an exit strategy.

But without giving it a second thought, I found myself blurting out, "You know what, I'm sorry, but I just remembered I have a major work deadline on Monday!" I ought to stay home and work on that, shouldn't I?" You go ahead without me."

My wife's face fell. "You're doing it again," she said. "Any time something doesn't go your way, you give yourself an out."

She was right, of course.

But in that moment, all I could sense was the force of my wanting to avoid — to avoid her disappointment, and her family, and the awkwardness of not having control over a situation that I did not know how to control. The deadline for the work was out there, but it wasn't exactly pressing. That was just an excuse to flee.

Then it was an argument about how I don't care about her family, and me defending that I, "need to be responsible about work." Neither of us was acknowledging what was going on — my nervous system was in full flight mode, reacting to perceived threats that had more to do with my history than my current surroundings.

I stormed off to the garage to cool down (and, yes, flee), and she went to bed angry. She visited her family the next day without me, and we both remained (individually) stuck, feeling isolated and misunderstood.

This was repeated on numerous occasions over the course of that marriage. Any situation that caused me their discomfort would set me to flight, and I'd have a reason — it was always rationale-sounding, it was always justifiable — for making my escape. Repeated flights over time that chiseled down on that trust and connection in our marriage until finally I took the ultimate flight and left the marriage altogether.

Review: The Paradox of Flight: When Running Makes What You're Running From

One of the harshest ironies of the flight response in dating is that it typically achieves the exact effect you're trying to prevent.

If the threat of rejection has brought you to this place, whether that rejection is emotional, sexual or something else, your emotional or physical absence will likely ensure that your partner will eventually stop trying to create a deeper connection with you — sound familiar?

If you've become a runner due to your fear of being controlled, your avoidant pattern will tend to elicit a pursuer pattern from your partner, which causes them to chase after you in order to win your love and affection, or commitment—thus, creating that sense of being controlled that you've been running from.

If you're running because you're so worried that conflict will make the relationship shatter, your failure to have the conversations you need to have causes more harm by creating resentment and distance than addressing the stuff honestly and openly does.

That was certainly the case in my marriage.

My flight was ultimately based in a fear of being controlled or criticized — something I learned to avoid during experiences with my father as a child. But my cycle of emotional retreat and physical absenteeism pushed my wife to work even harder to capture my attention and involvement. She'd chase more, criticize more, demand more again — all of which elicited even more intense feelings of flight within me.

Back and forth it went, both of us tapping into the worst fears and most ingrained patterns of the other. My flight stoked her fight/pursuit, which stoked further flight from me, which stoked further fight from her. Neither of us knew that we were in a biological feedback loop, created by each of our nervous systems interacting in patterns born out of our youngest wounds.

The Costs of Chronic Flight

The stakes, for both you and your partner, couldn't be higher when flight becomes your go-to solution for relationship stress, both you and your partner lose out.

- Emotional intimacy: True intimacy isn't possible without being present and being vulnerable. Flight terries both, building relationships that can work in a practical sense, but never truly in an emotional one.
- Trust: Routine emotional or physical absence wrecks trust. Your partner is learning you can't be trusted to stay in the game when the going gets tough.
- Problem solving: That which isn't solved doesn't exist. They go under ground, where they fester and fester until they are too big to be denied.
- Personal growth: Growth is to be found on the edge of your comfort. When you're habitually running away from discomfort, you're losing opportunities to cultivate emotional depth and relationship skill.
- Connection: Perhaps most painful of all, chronic flight fosters a deep sense of isolation — for your partner, who can't get through to you, as well as for yourself, huddled up inside your protective cocoon.

All of these costs I have borne in my relationships. It was as if my flight response had left me disconnected to a depth that held me physically present despite a lack of emotional participation in the partnership. With each relationship, another place to visit but not dwell in, another situation with which to cope, instead of engage. You end up living a life of paying for your inability to reconcile who you are, and you do so, in installments.

By my sixth marriage, in some ways I'd come full circle and was willing to do whatever it took to keep it together, but this where my childhood trauma reared its ugly head, big time. There were dynamics that had surfaced – which hadn't surfaced in previous marriages – that brought me back to square one, as in, my 6-year-old-inner-child-square one. The marriage wasn't like previous marriages and relationships, the ones where "flight" was just how I rolled—always with one foot out the door, always with an escape hatch plotted, a grim-if-necessary exit, on standby, always ready to skedaddle when things got too, well, real, too intense, too dangerous to my tenuous self-sufficiency. The sixth ended because I began a healthy fight response for myself. More on this in a later chapter.

The Flight Spectrum: Healthy Boundaries to Chronic Avoidance

Flight, like fight, comes in a spectrum. Healthy boundary-setting and space-taking (taking a step back when you need to, giving yourself time and space to process, recognizing when distance serves your good) is one end. At the other end is chronic avoidance — the incapacity to remain present with discomfort, to work through conflict, to continue to engage when relationships become difficult.

It's just the choice/force thing that's different. A successful flight is made up of conscious choices about when space is in service of the relationship. Unhealthy fleeing is instinctive, fear-based rather than wisdom based, and usually occurs at a time when presence is most essential.

Through my marriages my flights were not conscious decisions. They were reflexes, reactions automatic to me in my perilous state of mind. I wasn't in my book-writer head thinking "I need some space to process this so I can come back and engage in a more productive way." I was just being hijacked by a survival mechanism that was far, far past its sell-bydate.

Understanding this spectrum reminds us that the end goal isn't to never take space or set boundaries. Sometimes distance is the best relief. The point is to make those choices consciously, rather than being led by unconscious survival responses that simply create more problems than they solve.

Focusing on Presence: Turning Flight into Engagement

Even if those are the costs of chronic flight, the answer is not to snuff out your capacity to walk away when you really need to. Like any survival response, flight is helpful. The trick is learning to direct this kind of energy, rather than being engulfed by it.

Here are several approaches that have worked for me and countless other people in changing that relationship with flight:

Identify Flight Triggers

Begin to observe the times and places, or the certain interactions or feelings that trigger your desire to run away. The most common flight triggers are:

- Open criticism or speculation
- Outpouring of emotions of all degrees by people
- Demands relating to emotional exposure
- Conflict or disagreement
- Feeling Dominated or Railroaded
- Feeling as if you have disapproval or disappointment

The biggest flight triggers for me were any time I felt controlled or criticized. When my wife expressed disappointment in me or made direct requests that felt like demands, my flight response would trigger immediately. The first step to responding in a new way is to identify those triggers.

Becoming Aware of the Physical Senses of Flight

There are always signs your body sends you that your flight response is kicking in. Learning to detect these early warning signs allows you the opportunity to make a different decision.

Common physical signs of the flight response are:

- Feeling restless or fidgety
- Superficial breathing, or not breathing at all
- Pressure in your chest or throat
- A powerful need to escape or get away
- Glancing, for an escape
- You suddenly feel tired or checked out
- A feeling of being detached or unreal

For me, in my most recent relationships, the first tell was always a tightening in my chest and a sudden fascination with anything other than the conversation at hand. I would start to look at my phone, I would glance at the door or I would be mentally planning something unrelated. The earlier I can catch these signals, the better my ability to stay present.

Name What's Happening

Just recognizing to yourself (and sometimes verbally to your partner) that your flight response is kicking in can help interrupt the cycle.

Giving the process a name helps engage your prefrontal cortex — the thinking part of your brain — which can modulate the more primitive survival response. It also casts light on the situation for your partner, and makes them realize your withdrawal isn't personal, it is bio-logical.

Stay in Your Body

The flight response does something much worse; it pulls you out of your own body — into your head, into the future, into juvenile fantasies of escape. One potent antidote is to intentionally refocus attention on physical sensations in the here and now.

Some of the effective grounding practices are:

- Sensing your feet in contact with the floor
- Seeing your breath, without trying to make your breath do anything
- Closing your eyes and resting a hand on your heart or belly
- Touching what you are wearing or something nearby
- List five things you can see right now in the room in which you are sitting.

These very simple habits can help root you in the present while your fight response is attempting to pull you out.

Employ the "Pause and Stay" Practice

The next time you feel the desire to run (whether physically or emotionally), try this simple practice:

- Recognize the desire without judgment
- Take three deep breaths
- Commit to hanging in for just two more minutes

Two minutes later, see if you can actually take the space or continue engaging.

Typically, the first wave of the flight response will have passed after two minutes, so that you could stay present. If you need space after the pause, grab it with a little more consciousness rather than reactivity.

Express Your Wish for Space

Sometimes you actually do need space to process emotions or regulate your nervous system. The trick is to consciously and communicatively take the space.

Communications that work about space look like:

- "I'm all frazzled and need a few minutes to think. How about if we step away from this for 15 minutes and then return to it?"
- "I care about what you're talking about and want to show up for you. I am starting to wind down now. I need to take a quick break to respond and then we're going to have a discussion."

This strategy respects both your temporary need for space and your partner's need for closeness and closure.

Practice Gradual Exposure

In the same way that someone might spend time slowly acclimating to higher and higher heights (here it might be a fear of heights), I would like you to spend time building your capacity to be with and stay with emotional discomfort.

Begin by tolerating your discomfort with mild flight tendencies — in lower-intensity conversations where the urge to run is gentle — and try to stick with the experience of non-flight. As you get better, you can grow towards these increasingly-triggering interactions.

This is not a matter of "sucking it up" in the face of infection. It's about increasing your window of tolerance — like the UFC fighter who trains for years, sparring so that they can be comfortable in the uncomfortable — the span of emotional intensity you can experience before becoming hypervigilant, checked out or off the rails.

Returning Home to Yourself: The Deeper Healing

Beyond these practical strategies, however, is deeper healing: healing the complexity of childhood wounds and expectations that underlie the impulse to fly.

For me, that's included a lot of therapy, somatic practices, and an openness to revisiting and reprocessing early experiences of being abused, controlled, criticized and manipulated. It has meant learning that I can experience difficult feelings without being torn apart by them, that I can battle without losing, that I can be close without losing myself.

Most fundamentally, it has been recognizing that I've been running — not just from other people but myself, from my own feelings, needs and wounds. The greatest journey has been learning to come home to myself, to cultivate the internal safety that doesn't rely on conditions being the way I'd like them to be.

Because the thing is, no matter how far you run or fast you go, you are always there. Healing arises not from discovering the perfect escape but from building the capability to stay — with yourself, with your feelings, with the messy, beautiful truth of human connection."

Conclusion: Running Away to Running Toward

My relationship with the flight response goes on. There are still moments when the desire to flee — physically or emotionally — but they no longer feel unbearable. I'm better now at recognizing what's happening, and I can make a conscious decision instead of being swept along by automatic habit.

I'm learning how to convert the flight energy of running away from discomfort into the flight energy of running toward growth, scurrying away from what scares me into intentionally scurrying toward whatever matters, most.

This transformation isn't about having to never (not) take space or set boundaries. It's more about doing so purposefully, and in service of deeper connection, and less as a means of avoiding it.

Everyone's process with the flight response is their own and personal. That will be colored by your unique story, your specific triggers, your body's nervous system. But the choice we all face is the same: Will you let your flight tendencies drive you mechanically away from your most important relationships? Or will you do the hard work to take back this energy and turn it into a capacity for healthy autonomy and authentic engagement?

The way of presence isn't easy. It takes courage, practice and, often, help from others. But it results in relationships that are both authentic and intimate, both with healthy boundaries and genuine vulnerability, both free and deeply connected.

In the next chapter, we'll look at the freeze response—what happens in your body when you're hardwired to go into immobility in the presence of danger—and we'll learn to break out of the freeze pattern, or emotional shutdown, that might stem from this deeply ingrained survival mechanism, so that you can thaw the frozen places in yourself that still need to feel and connect.

CHAPTER TEN

THE FREEZE RESPONSE:

THE SILENT KILLER OF CONNECTION

There is a moment of scary clarity in the first fight between Conor McGregor and Nate Diaz. If you watched it, you know what I'm talking about. If you haven't, allow me to set the scene, with a little more detail this time around. I am intentionally bringing you back to this story.

McGregor, the cocky, confident fighter who had become the badass of the UFC, is fighting Diaz as a fill-in opponent.

First round, McGregor is looking good, landing punches, dictating the pace. He's there, in his element: the incarnation of the fight response at its fastest, brightest, most capable. Diaz is holding his own, managing some good boxing strikes, along with some leg kicks of his own. Three and a half minutes into Round 1, and you hear the commentator make mention of blood dripping from the right eye of Diaz…and then mentions something critical and noteworthy:

Diaz had accumulated a lot scar tissue around both eyes over the years from having so many open gashes caused by strikes.

Scar tissue for a fighter is interesting.

Interesting in that, a scar represents healing on the surface. It says, "there was once damage here," but it's healed. However, physically speaking when it comes to scar tissue, the skin may not have its whole and complete structure to it that it once originally had, though it may appear to be whole on the surface.

I wonder how many of us are walking around today with scar tissue – scar tissue on our soul, on our hearts. Perhaps we are more easily wounded today – if hit in the same spot again. Just something to think about.

Round 1 comes to an end with McGregor ahead on the scorecards.

A minute and a half into Round 2, and McGregor has caused more bleeding to Diaz's face, but just a minute later and Diaz cracked McGregor hard in the face, forcing him to step back, and suddenly something shifts.

McGregor shrugs and holds his hands in the air, in a gesture that seems to say, "All right...you tagged me good — let's go!"

But if you study the expression on his face in that moment, what you see is not fight or even flight.

- It's freeze.
- His eyes get a distant look.
- He grows more and more unsteady on his feet.
- There's a stammer in his answers that wasn't there before.

Diaz tags him with a couple of good punches. McGregor tries to defend, landing a few combinations of his own – but McGregor's almost done.

Joe Rogan yells out, "Conor is in serious trouble!"

It's a subtle thing, but unmistakable to anyone who can track the signals: McGregor's mind is frozen, caught in that no-man's-land, where the brain has no plan, no idea what the body is supposed to do next.

He's tackled to the ground seconds later and then gets submitted by a rear-naked choke to conclude the fight.

In his post-fight interview with Joe Rogan, McGregor says something insightful: "I didn't use my energy efficiently; he was much more efficient with his energy." But was what he was actually communicating, "I didn't know what to do… and I was frozen"?

I've contemplated that moment frequently for one reason: I've lived it — not in the octagon, but in my relationships.

That moment where something smacks you in the mind, where all the things that have always worked, suddenly don't work anymore, where you can't properly fight or run because you're staggering around blind, lost, and alone.

You're just... stuck.

Stuck in time as life moves on around you and over you.

The Freeze Response

It's probably the least glamorous of survival reactions, the least well understood, but in many ways, the most dangerous — particularly in relationships. It's the "freeze" aspect of the flight-or-fight-or-freeze response — the one not so obvious, not so portraited in movies, not so talked-about, and not so easy to escape, because while fight sounds loud and flight looks like distance, freeze can look like calm acceptance from the outside and be a hell of a prison from the inside.

And, like McGregor, in that fight, many of us are frozen not by one punch but by all the punches — the wear and tear on us from being emotionally pummeled each day, the fatigue from being in a constant state of defense, the futility from putting up a fight and having nothing change.

We get stuck in groundhog days of patterns that keep replaying themselves in relationships — the same arguments, the same sensations of disappointment, the same cycles of disconnection, all happening over and over while we pretend to stand by, knowing we have to make a change, but for the life of us we can't make that change in any way forward toward anything.

It's the relational freeze, the silent killer of intimacy that leaves us stuck, physically present but emotionally AWOL, knowing we need a new way, but unable to do anything about it, hungry for change, but paralyzed by the very trauma that change would address.

More Than Fight or Flight: The Ventral-Vagal System and Survival Freeze

Fight or flight are the two most well-known stress responses.

They are dramatic, visible and easily recognizable. But freezing does not exploit this channel. It's what happens when neither fighting nor fleeing feels feasible — when the threat is too much to bear for an aggressive response yet escape options seem cut off.

The Freeze response has several distinct purposes in nature:

- Pretend to be dead: Most predators prefer to attack live prey than something that looks dead.
- Becoming invisible: Predators don't have as much to focus on when you're not moving.
- Saving energy: When flight is not a viable option, the best solution is to simply freeze and save energy until escape is possible.
- Pain relief: The freeze response naturally produces endorphins that dull physical and emotional pain.

The same mechanisms that lead animals to survive physical threats can also be activated in humans facing threats to relationship—criticism of a partner, risk of rejection, feelings of conflict that seem unsolvable, or emotional environments that serve as a reminder of trauma from childhood.

The freeze response in relationships may show up as:

- Emotional numbness: Clearing out emotions in order not to be overcome by them.
- Dissociation: "Checking out" when you're actually present (other common feelings: like you're not in your body; that you, your partner or the situation is not real).
- Analysis paralysis: The tendency to think through and then overthink through every possibility, ultimately to the point that you take no action at all.
- Compliance without engagement: Saying yes to whatever your partner wants but not being emotionally there.
- Procrastination on relationship-related decisions: Always deferring necessary conversations or decisions in or about your relationship.
- Feeling "stuck": Being aware that something needs to change but not knowing how to change.

- Learned helplessness: You believe nothing you do will make things better, so why bother?

Each of these forms of freeze has appeared at some stage in my relationships.

Toward the end of my previous marriage, as hyper-verbal emotional abuse from my alcoholic wife would escalate beyond my tolerance, I'd find myself staring blankly ahead—physically there but emotionally shut down and unable to either effectively solve the problem or to just get up and walk away.

I would sit across from her at dinner and nod at the appropriate intervals while … feeling nothing, a flawless theater of engagement masking total private shutdown. I would lay awake at night ruminating upon all the things I could do to try and make things better for the two of us, yet I would never actually do any of them; most of them I had already attempted once…or a few dozen times. Still, I would agree with myself "today is the day".

I'd draw a line in the sand or recommend therapy, then lose the will to force the issue when the moment came.

This was not the same as my flight response, though from the outside it could have appeared similar. Flight was active avoidance — me being the one to leave — head to the garage for hours, smoke cigars, read, and be alone. Freeze was when I couldn't move in any direction but desperately wanted something to change.

The Biology of Immobility

What's going on in your body when you're freezing? When your brain concludes that the threat is unavoidable, it activates a different part of the nervous system from fight or flight.

Whereas fight and flight turn on the sympathetic nervous system (the gas pedal), this extreme freeze turns on the dorsal vagal branch of the parasympathetic nervous system (an emergency brake). This then triggers a series of physiological changes:

- HR and BP decrease
- Breathing becomes shallow
- Muscles become rigid or limp
- Digestion slows dramatically
- Body temperature decreases
- There's a narrowing of consciousness, even sometimes a sense of dissociation

Endorphins are also released, leading to a decreased perception of pain.

These changes aren't random. They're getting your body ready to be still — to endure life by shutting down, by making yourself small, by expending as little energy as possible until the danger goes away.

Because the thing is, relationship stressors don't generally just "pass." Also, unlike a predator that might get bored and move on, relationship dynamics don't simply move on, but rather get stronger when they are not corrected. And so, the freeze response, meant for short-term survival, becomes a long-term way of being that slowly strangles connection.

When things were at their worst in my marriage, I would have these physiological responses every day. My pulse would actually feel like it dropped when we fought — I would get cold and my wife would be working up a sweat from the force of her emotions. Remember in an earlier chapter, when I told you the story about that day at Dr. Ruffin's office – when he told me that my heart rate dropped when reflecting on moments of abuse with my father?

My breath was so shallow that I'd find myself lightheaded now and again.

There were times my muscles would lock themselves into a tense position that had me dealing with never-ending pain in my neck and back.

Perhaps the most disconcerting was when I'd kind of disappear into a moment of dissociation and feel like I was watching the exchange from outside of my own body, or when minutes of time would pass without me having any real recall of what had been said. My awareness was contracting to shield me from what felt like too much emotional pain.

The Childhood Roots of Freeze

The freeze response, like all of our survival responses, is rooted in our earliest experiences—namely, how our caregivers responded to our needs and emotions.

Freeze children are conditioned to freeze first as their primary response when they are indirectly taught that:

Fighting back or running away don't work for them: When children learn that fighting back leads to more punishment or that the show of resistance is futile, and that running away is either impossible or will result in being found and punished even worse, they freeze.

Their feelings are threatening: If sharing feelings would cause rejection, punishment or abandonment, kids learn to deny feelings by freezing them.

Learned helplessness (a core element of the freeze response): They are unable to improve their situation, and when this pattern is repeated over and over throughout childhood, children then internalize that they are incapable of changing their circumstances (self-efficacy).

Invisibility equals safety: When visibility results in abuse or criticism, children are taught that being invisible — making themselves physically small, emotionally contained, not verbal — is the safest place to live.

Mine was a type of freezing response, and in all of these ways.

I grew up with alcoholic, abusive parents and early on learned the futility of fighting back and the utter lack of a safe place to run. The only choice I had was to freeze — to shrink, to try to disappear so that my emotions wouldn't spark his anger, to go along with the orders and disappear inside myself so deeply that nobody could ever get to me.

The sexual abuse by my brother only solidified this dynamic.

My body, in those times, physically stopped—couldn't fight someone bigger and stronger, couldn't flee, and so my nervous system did what it is supposed to in cases like that: it immobilized me and fired endorphins to shut down the pain.

These early encounters wired the neuropathways that would light up when I felt similarly threatened in my adult relationships. By the time I got into my marriages, the freeze response wasn't a conscious decision–it was a reflex, a reaction to certain emotional triggers that my body interpreted as life-threatening based on past experiences.

Freeze in Action: An Example of a Relationship

Here's an example from my last marriage, showing how that freeze dynamic plays out in relationships.

My wife and I were at a dinner party with some friends, an evening that should have been fun but often felt startlingly stressful for me (if not for her) thanks to the caprices of her (at the time) increasingly erratic behavior after drinking wine for hours on end.

Partway into the evening, she'd started to insult me in front of our friends — belittling cutting comments about my career decisions, my parenting style, even my looks.

With each of her increasingly piquant comments, I could feel the old chill start up. My body temperature dropped. An expressionless look crossed my face. By then my mind was blank and I could not think of one answer to defend myself, nor to change the subject. I sat there, nodding every so often, forcing a smile here and there, though inside I was totally shamed down.

Our friends looked as if they wanted to say something, but they didn't. We moved on to other topics, but I sat there, frozen near the fireplace, for the rest of the evening. At the appropriate times, I made casual talk, but I wasn't actually there. I'd fled to that internal bunker where nothing could get to me.

On the way home, my wife scolded me for being "boring" and "aloof" and "disengaged" at the party.

"You sat there like a rotting corpse," she said. "You made me look foolish in front of our friends."

I wanted to tell her what had happened — how, when she criticized me publicly, my freeze response was triggered, how I quite literally could not respond in any physical way. But I knew the words would fall on deaf ears. Even though she complimented me from time to time as being "brilliant" in my understanding of psychology and neuroscience, those attributes in me didn't count when it came to her, or to "us". I sat quietly, listening to her onslaught. I was still; I was emotionally paralyzed.

So, in an attempt to move on from her commentary, I nodded and apologized and vowed that I would "do better," clearly seeing that unless we worked through our imbalance, the same scenario would come to play over and over.

This cycle — trigger, freeze, criticism for freezing, deeper freeze — happened hundreds of times in our relationship. I had learned helplessness and each time, two or three or four or more times, I branded "nothing will work," or "this will not work" and it was just "make it through this," but, "do not have any reaction or feeling about this assault."

The Groundhog Day Effect: Stuck in Time

The problem with the freeze response in relationships is that it reinforces destructive patterns -which I refer to as the "Groundhog Day Effect" after the movie in which Bill Murray continually relives the same day over and over.

When you are chronically frozen, you stop including new learning in your repertoire and are unable to make behavioral changes as a result. Instead, you end up arguing about the same things, dealing with the same issues, suffering the same disappointments over and over.

And nothing changes because, well, your freeze response is preventing you from doing the things that would actually help make a change.

I had the same fight with my spouse about her drinking literally dozens of times throughout our marriage. The script never varied:

- I'd worry about her drinking
- I'd tiptoe around her heightened, conflict-seeking-behavior
- She would get defensive about anything and attack at will

My boundary in those instances was my own level of tolerance, but it was beyond my ability to keep my cocoon safe in certain interactions.

She'd escalate until I apologized for mentioning it.

"You'd just do it again the next day or the next week, and nothing would be different" – I thought.

Each time I'd settle in with renewed resolution: this time I'd be steadfast; this time I wouldn't get derailed; this time I'd press for meaningful change. But, every time that freeze would kick in at the first sign of danger, there I would be: immobilized and unable to protect myself.

This is what it looks like when freeze is a relationship prison. You can sense the walls - you understand that you are incarcerated, but you cannot locate the strength or the path to freedom. You are not locked down by force, but by your own nervous system's reaction to threat perceived.

The Costs of Chronic Freeze

Because when the freeze response is your go-to strategy for dealing with relational stress, you and your partner both pay a high price:

- Loss of self: Freezing chronically severs you from your own needs, desires and boundaries until you do not even recognize who you are any longer.
- Emotional deadening: The numbness that initially serves as a defense against pain also prevents you from feeling joy.
- Physical health: The physiological side effects of chronic freeze — muscle tension, shortness of breath, digestive issues — are legitimate physical problems over time.

- Frozen relationship: Growth needs change and Freeze is prevention against change, stuck in the same, rut for a relationship.
- Reservoir of resentment: Frozen emotions don't just evaporate and disappear — they go underground, and on some level continue to accumulate, creating a reservoir of resentment that poisons connection.
- Time lost: Most painfully, freeze steals time — months, or years, lost in states of paralysis that could have been spent growing or experiencing joy or discovering healthier relationships.

All of these costs I have paid, a million times over, in my relationships. Toward the end of my last marriage, I had almost ceased to exist at all. My friends attested to this after I left, and after the marriage was over.

The vivid, fiery, expressive man I had been had morphed into a shell of compliance and numbed emotion. I had physical symptoms of chronic pain, extreme digestive issues, debilitating fatigue — that I now realize were my body's expression of my largely constant freeze response.

Time is always a sacrificial lamb: six years frozen in the depths of a relationship that was slowly killing me, six years that I will never get back, six years I could have been healing, growing, and creating a life that was me.

The Freeze Reflex Spectrum: From Healthy Pause to Disease Response Collapse

Like fight and flight, freeze is also a continuum. One end is the healthy pause — the ability to step back internally, make room for consideration before responding, cool your emotions before reacting. At the other end is chronic shutdown — the inability to feel your authentic feelings and needs, to take effective action, to stay emotionally present amid emotional stress.

The distinction there is between choice and constraint. A wise pause is a concerted effort to take time to think before acting. Danger freeze is mindless; fear reacts for us, even after it has already been clear that reflection would be helpful.

The freezing during my marriage was not a conscious choice to pause and reflect. It was a survival shutdown caused by my nervous system's perceived threat. I didn't think, "I need to step back and take a moment to process my feelings before I say something.'

I was just getting hijacked by a survival mechanism that was no longer useful.

That phrase I mentioned in chapter 3 and 4, about the amygdala – I'm serioiusly considering having it printed on a t-shirt:

"Don't Jack my Amy." – meaning, "Don't hijack my amygdala".

Let me know if you want one.

Seriously now, appreciating this spectrum helps us see that the aim is not to never break or grieve. Sometimes you just want some internal space. The aim is to make decisions like this consciously, and not as a replay of subconscious survival dynamics which create more problems than they solve.

Trauma and Freeze: The Wound That Doesn't Show up

Among all the survival responses, *freeze* is most emblematic of trauma; specifically, of what psychologists refer to as "inescapable attack." When a threat seems insurmountable and there's no chance of winning or fighting the innate response is freeze, a desperate act of self-preservation.

It is why freeze is so prevalent in survivors of childhood abuse, domestic violence, and sexual assault — victims who, whether physically or psychologically, could not fight back or flee.

The tragedy is that the very response that helps people survive trauma can also interfere with their healing from it. Freeze maintains traumatizing experiences wrapped up, undigested, frozen in time. The sounds, smells, and feelings, the fear, anger, and helplessness stay with you and continue to act as though the trauma were still happening, it shows up as symptoms and not as memories, which can be stored and integrated with, and healed.

My own freeze response was both a trauma response and a conceptual barrier to my own healing from that trauma. The numbness that insulated me from unbearable pain also made it impossible for me to process the pain. The disconnection that enabled me to survive intolerable moments also isolated me from the very feelings I needed to experience in order to heal.

Melting this chronic freeze involves getting to the root trauma—bringing enough safety into our nervous system that we can actually start to thaw out the freeze in our experiences, not all at once, but not so slowly that the makeshift dam bursts.

Unthawing the Freeze: Getting Your Feelings and Actions Back

Despite the price of perennial freeze, by no means should this be to lose one's ability to take a reflective pause, when called for. Freeze, like all survival responses, is important. It's learning to operate with this energy rather than being hijacked by it.

Here are some tactics that have worked well for me and for the many people I know who've been able to shift their relationship to the freeze response:

Recognize Your Freeze State

Begin to pay attention to the familiar sensations, thoughts and actions that let you know you are in freeze. Common signs include:

- Feeling numb or empty
- Trouble thinking clearly or making decisions
- Sudden onset of heaviness or fatigue
- You don't feel "in" your body
- You are unable to get in touch with your emotions
- Feeling trapped or helpless

For me it always started with a drop in body temperature and my face turning into a mask, as if what I was feeling inside had already taken over the surface with its blankness. If I figure these signals out in time, I'm in a much better position to avoid total shutdown.

Regain Safety in Your Body

The freeze response kicks in when your nervous system senses insurmountable danger. The antidote is to help you body understand that you are safe in the present moment — you have options and resources that weren't present during whatever traumas you may have experienced in your past.

The following are several successful strategies to help restore a sense of safety:

Orienting to the environment around you: Look around and name what you see, to remind your nervous system that you are right here in the present, not back there in the past.

Physical movement: Small shifts or small movements such as moving your finger or toes, even small movements can start to unlock the immobility of freeze.

Rhythmic activities: In some cases, tapping or swinging or humming may also help to regulate a dysregulated nervous system.

Do a temperature change: Splash your face with cold water or hold an ice cube, or take a warm shower to get feeling back into your body

Grounding Techniques: Zone in on physical sensations that root you in the present moment — the feeling of your feet on the ground, your breath going in and out, the fabric touching your skin.

I even found that while I was married to my now ex: splashing cold water on my face sometimes helped me break out of an impending freeze response during an argument. The sensation was enough to jolt me out of the autopilot shutdown mode and offer me some minutes of clearer thought.

Practice Pendulation

Pendulation was designed by the trauma expert Peter Levine; it's a process of gently moving your attention between sensations (feeling distress, and feeling a sense of resource or comfort). This helps guard against emotional overload, as well as gradually increasing your ability to remain present with challenging emotions.

The practice looks like this:
- Take note of where you are tensing or going numb or uncomfortable in the body

- Mind, can you move unpleasant thoughts elsewhere, maybe to a part of your body that feels fine and neutral or even good?
- Wobble and change, flitting between, sticking with one only a matter of seconds, to start.

You extend the amount of time you can bear to meet your discomfort.

It was this simple practice that helped me start thawing frozen parts of my experience — feeling emotions that had long been numbed, but without becoming overwhelmed by them.

Reclaim Your Voice

Freeze often appears as an inability to speak your truth – to communicate needs, establish boundaries, or express true feelings. Finding your voice is a literal and figurative way to warm up the freeze response.

Begin in low-risk situations:

- Write in a journal what ever thoughts come to mind and write any free-flowing feelings you may have.
- Practice with saying simple truths out loud when you are alone: "I feel sad," "I need help," "I'm angry."
- Practice speaking out the hard conversations with a trusted friend or expert therapist
- Start with smaller boundaries within safe relationships before trying more difficult ones

As you become more confident, build up to being more expressive in more difficult relationships. Just remember, this is not about picture-perfect communication so much as it is about overcoming the silence that a freeze dictates.

Build a Support Network

I do not believe that healing from chronic freeze is something we can do with ourselves alone. The inertia of freeze itself makes it difficult to engage in those actions necessary for change. Support people who can see your patterns and gently encourage movement is worth its weight in gold.

This support might come from:

- An experienced therapist who understands trauma and its freeze response
- Friends who know your patterns and can mirror them with compassion
- Groups designed to help survivors of similar situations
- Body-based therapists who can aid you in re-establishing a connection to physical sensations

My own healing became exponential when I finally met a therapist who saw freeze not as an issue of poor character but as a response to survive, who could help me understand and see how I was still protecting myself from dangers no longer around.

Conclusion: From Frozen to Flowing

I am still working through my own freeze experience. There are some days I still find that familiar numbness creeping up, when words desert me and it seems impossible for me to actually do something. But here's what's changed: I am now generally able to know what's going on and do something to thaw myself out before the shutdown gets too drastic.

I am learning to shift freeze energy from helpless immobility to the healthy capacity for thoughtful pause — from stuck to being still by choice, from emotional numbness to emotional regulation, from paralysis to presence.

This change doesn't mean not getting a freeze response. Our nervous systems will of course always respond to perceived threats by relying on past experience. It's learning how to cultivate awareness and skills to move through those freeze states more quickly, and to have our frozen parts be thawed out, with compassion rather than judgment.

Your experience with the freeze reaction is your own. It will be molded by your particular history, your own particular triggers, your very own nervous system. But the basic choice is the same one for all of us: Will you allow your freeze response to keep you entrapped in patterns that no longer serve you? Or, will you roll up your sleeves and get to the business of reclaiming your ability to genuinely feel and authentically act?

It's not an easy path of the thaw. It takes courage, time and often support from others. But it results in relationships capable of being equal in emotional candor and thoughtful choice, vulnerable and clear-acting, deeply feeling and free-acting.

I will add one more, extremely important side note to close chapter.

The first 6 months into my separation and divorce from my wife, I slept *a lot*. I found myself so tired and fatiqued throughout the days, and this was alarming to me. My whole life up until this point I'd lived off of 5-6 hours of sleep per night, consistently.

Suddenly, I was sleeping 8-10 hours per day, and found myself napping sometimes in the afternoon.

One day it finally hit home – and this is something for you to consider if you're dealing with the same issue: this very well could be your body's need for rest after living under the Acute Stress Response for so many years.

Remember what I shared in previous chapters: your body was not designed to live in the Acute Stress Response. At max, 15-20, maybe 25 minutes would be considered normal under the ASR.

This need for rest is your body's way of telling you: "I've had enough. Let me rest – or we die."

Okay – perhaps a little dramatic with that last line. Point is, give your body and mind a break and allow it to rest.

Allow it to heal.

You've heard it said, "Many things will naturally reset if you just shut them down for a while and power them back up – including you."

The next chapter gets more into the fawn response — how the drive to appease, to avoid conflict can lead to a pattern of losing yourself in relationships, and how to reclaim your true self while still remaining connected.

CHAPTER ELEVEN

THE FAWN: PEOPLE-PLEASING

AT THE EXPENSE OF SELF

"It was my fault, and you don't have to feel bad for spanking me."

And I can still hear my 10-year-old child-self saying it to my father, the man who had just beat me with an electric cord, the man whose furies had left me shaking and bruised. And yet there I was, trying to comfort him, to make him feel better about what he had done to me, trying to make him feel innocent.

I had forsaken myself to give him empathy.

This pattern—this frantic effort to get a response, to mollify those who had hurt me—didn't seem aberrant to me then. It was simply survival. In a household in which fighting back meant escalating punishment and running away was never an option, I learned that the best way to survive was to be whatever my father needed in that instant.

I had forgotten to anticipate his moods.

I had forgotten to own his feelings.

I had forgotten to be useful, compliant, invisible when necessary, soothing when needed.

I was doing a masterful job at the fawn response years before I learned about the term.

The fawn response is something that has only been recently introduced to our understanding of trauma responses.

Fight, flight, and freeze are well-known psychological concepts, but the concept of "fawning" was coined by therapist Peter Walker during the early 2000s to describe what he observed in some of his patients who had been through complex trauma—specifically family abuse throughout childhood.

Walker observed that if fight, flight, and freeze responses have not been able to ensure safety, many people who have experienced trauma develop a fourth trauma response: to become helpful, compliant, and reactive to their abuser, in order to minimize any additional harm.

Like the fawn that cowers before the predator, they had learned to give up their own needs, their own boundaries, even their own identity in their attempt to keep the people they depended on happy.

This answer — this knee-jerk people-pleasing at my own expense — became how I defaulted to operating in the world. And it trailed me well into my adulthood, affecting my relationships, my career decisions and my own sense of self for decades to come.

The Unseen Survival Plan

Of the four Fs, fawn is also probably the most instilled response from a societal standpoint, and the least vilified as problematic. As a culture, we've learned to applaud and reward self-sacrifice, often in roles and relationships. We applaud the partner who is always there for their loved one, the employee who will never say "no" to more work, the friend who is available no matter what the personal toll.

But what may appear to be a generous, selfless thing to do from the outside can be a trauma response in disguise, a way of trying to feel safe by making yourself indispensable to others, by never upsetting them, by becoming so useful to them that they would never abandon or hurt you.

In relationships, the fawn response can show up as:

- Difficulty saying no: Saying "yes" to things you don't want to do out of fear of disappointing others or making them angry.
- Chronic apologizing: Feeling responsible for things that are not your fault, including other people's emotions and responses.
- Loss of identity: Becoming a chameleon who morphs opinions, interests and values — at least temporarily — to coincide with those of whosever company or influence you are currently under.
- Avoiding conflict: Taking whatever measures necessary to avoid arguments, including sacrificing your own needs and wants.
- Codependent loyalty: Staying in toxic relationships for much too long because your self-worth is based on being of value to another.
- Trouble determining what you crave: Feeling genuinely stumped when you're asked what you want because you're so used to paying attention to other people's wants.

I used to be each of these people. I was whatever the person in front of me needed me to be — the supportive husband, the agreeable employee, the friend who never wanted or needed anything. I spent so much time managing other people's emotions that I started to lose touch with my own. I became an empty shell, containing only reflections of the people I was surrounded by.

This pattern played out most acutely in my marriages, crescendoing in my last. And with each new relationship, I would lose more and more of myself — my interests, my boundaries, my voice — as I fought to keep the peace, to be the perfect partner, to avoid the abandonment I feared above all.

By the sixth marriage, I was a master of self-abandonment. If my wife challenged me, I would right away apologize, even for wrongs I hadn't committed. And when she'd get mad, I'd be the one, smoothing things over, absorbing the feelings she couldn't manage, carrying them as my own to repair.

Whenever she would make demands that did not respect my boundaries, I'd talk myself into the idea that my boundaries were the problem — that I was being selfish to even have needs.

I had deserted myself for her, the same as I had deserted my child self for my father. It was a cycle that had repeated. Again, my childhood wiring at work.

Fawning and the Origins of Childhood

Like all survival responses, this fawning has its origins in our earliest experiences—in how our caregivers responded to our needs, emotions, and attempts at autonomy.

Children will pull out their fawn response primarily if they find out that:

Their needs come second: When children see that caregivers always prioritize their own needs or emotions over theirs, children learn that the only chance they have to get some of their own needs met is to attend to the needs of the caregiver first.

Their emotions are too heavy: If a child has authentic feelings and receives negative social conditioning, such as rejection, punishment or abandonment, they learn to shut down the feelings and figure out how to manage the emotional state of the caretaker instead.

Their love is conditional: If love and approval are offered to the child only when the child does or says or behaves in certain ways, the child learns the message: my value comes not from who I am, but how useful I can be to others.

Their boundaries aren't honored: When a child's "no" or personal boundaries are not acknowledged or are punished, they learn boundaries are unsafe and that safety comes from meeting others' demands without question.

My response, the fawn response, was forged out of all these elements.

I learned early on, while being raised in such an abusive, alcoholic family that my needs and feelings were irrelevant or at best, provocative. To cry, be afraid or angry would have only made him more volatile. Boundaries were an impossibility. The only safety I found was in meeting his demands terrifyingly well at that moment, in making myself useful enough that dealing with the chaos he would make by hurting me would be genuinely inconvenient.

I learned to read the most infinitesimal of cues — the slight narrowing around his eyes that indicated brewing anger, the cadence of his particular sigh that warned me he was ready to blow, the timbre that meant danger lay just ahead. I developed hypervigilance, watching the world for danger, constantly on the lookout for how I could prevent threats, defuse them with my helpfulness, my compliance, my will to take blame.

"I wasn't supposed to make you angry." Those words became my chant, my shield, my fervent plea to turn myself from target to compatriot in my father's battle with himself.

This dynamic was further reinforced by my brother's sexual abuse.

When a more powerful person violates your most basic boundaries, there's no one there to protect you, and the fawn response often feels like the only possible means of survival. I couldn't fight him off. I couldn't leave the house where we had lived.

I learned how to dissociate, to go numb, to make myself say what I was supposed to say so that the abuse would be less violent and painful and soul-destroying.

These early experiences formed neural pathways that would fire on cue when I felt threatened in adult relationships. When I got married, the fawning neuro-response was no longer a conscious choice — it had become second nature to react that way to even a whiff of disapproval, anger, or possible rejection.

Does Fawning Look Like: A Real-Life Example

Here's a specific example from my last marriage that is an example of the people pleaser/fawn response in action.

My wife and I were preparing for a family vacation. For months, she'd been telling me how much she wanted to go to the beach — "just anywhere near the water." I'm not beach people; I can't stand the excessive heat, the sand, and the whole process is stressful, not relaxing.

What I really wanted was to go to the mountains, walk in the cool forest air to unplug from technology and plug back in to nature… and of course, smoke cigars.

But when the moment of decision of course it came, I said none of this. Instead, I accepted with great enthusiasm two weeks at a beach resort and even proceeded to research the "best" beaches and give my wife a choice. We planned the trip, and almost every trip we planned thereafter? You guessed it – had a beach, sand, and…water.

When a friend asked me why I would opt for a beach vacation when I did not even like beaches, I can still recall saying, "It makes her happy, and that's all that counts."

This probably seems loving and sacrificial on the surface. But what was really going on was much more convoluted, and much less fulfilling: I was scared expressing my wishes would lead to an argument, or for her to be disappointed in me, or even to reconsider her decision to be with someone whose needs didn't perfectly match hers. Was she wrong? No. Was I wrong, yes. I had an issue with vocalizing my preferences.

I had had as miserable a vacation as could have been anticipated for me—two weeks of hot burning sunshine and sand where sand was absolutely never meant to be, things I didn't enjoy but, "at least everyone else did."

I never complained. I did such a good job acting excited that my wife had no inkling I was hating every minute of it. It was indeed the perfect beach vacation companion, all the while marking off the days in my head that we get to go back home… even if home meant…Home.

It wasn't just vacations — not this pattern, this utter surrender of anything I might need or want for myself. It played out in small daily decisions (what to eat, what to watch) and in large life choices (where to live, how to spend our money). I deferred to her automatically in either instance: if I was asked my opinion, I would carefully calculate what answer would make her happiest.

This resulted in a connection that was built upon a fiction — my wife was in love with a *me* that didn't exist, a perfected persona that was cultivated to keep the peace and establish attachment at all costs. And I was becoming more and more disconnected from my true self, increasingly unclear about what I truly wanted or needed, except that the most pressing thing was to not have the relationship end.

Now, I cannot restate this enough: though it may seem like I am blaming my ex – I alone am the one to blame. I allowed it. Maybe she wasn't nice. Maybe she did have an addiction. Maybe she too, wasn't completely whole, but this I know for 100% certain: I was the sick one.

The Pandemic Paradox of Fawning: When Pleasing Pushes Us Away

The cruel irony of the fawn response in relationships is that it frequently creates exactly the outcomes you're trying to prevent.

If you're a suck-up type personality because of the fear of abandonment, then your continued unoriginality will keep the whole relationship at a non-real depth, where true intimacy and sharing is not possible, the next form of abandonment even though your partner is physically around.

If you are a *suck-up* in order to avoid conflict, it will come in other forms whether it's passive/aggressive behavior, repressed needs/emotions, or even dis-ease from the otherwise unhealthy energy that is created by your energy instead of that of honest disagreement.

If you're fawning because you think your worth depends on your usefulness to other people, you'll magnetize people who uphold this idea by treating you in terms of what you can do for them as opposed to acknowledging you as an entire person—thus confirming your darkest thoughts about how little you have to offer at a fundamental level.

And certainly, that was true in my marriages. My endless efforts to avoid conflict by never acknowledging what I truly felt or needed didn't produce harmony — they produced relationships with very little, true intimacy.

My wives didn't know me because I never let myself be known. The connection that I desired so badly was thwarted due to the very strategies I was using to make it happen.

And then, even when I did everything I could to be the ideal partner, we fought. And when they did explode, they were all the more damaging because they were not about whatever specific thing was happening at the time – they were about instead the stockpile of resentment, the unmet needs, the unexpressed emotions that had been simmering below the surface of my stage-managed happiness.

By the time we broke up, or a marriage ended, we knew nothing of each other — or with me, because I'd never really shown her my real self, and her, because I'd never given her room to know that "self".

The fawn response, which is based on a survival strategy to create safety through connection, had in fact created deep isolation between the two of us.

The Costs of Chronic Fawning

When the fawn reaction becomes your go-to strategy for dealing with relationship discomfort, you and your partner both pay a high price:

- Self-loss: The most hurtful price of all, and probably the one we are least aware of, as the self is washed away over time and true needs, desires, and values are indefinitely denied for more in favor of others.
- Resentment: Between the ears, it looks something like this: The conscious mind buys into the story of selfless giving, but one's unconscious is balancing an invisible calculation sheet of sacrifices made. This is simmering, unidentified, underground resentment that ultimately throws a monkey wrench into relationships.
- Attraction to exploitative relationships: The fawn response tends to attract others who take advantage of your giving without giving back in return.
- Physical symptoms: The pressure of keeping yourself bottled up can often result in physical conditions: chronic pain, digestive complaints, autoimmune disease, chronic fatigue.
- Depression and anxiety: Living in a state of disconnection from your most authentic self, always externally monitoring to know what others needed of you, it's a perfect setup for mental health challenges.

- Spiritual bankruptcy: At its deepest level, chronic fawning results in feelings of deep emptiness — a life lived in service of others' desires rather than one's own values and meaning.

Again – not to sound repetitive: I have endured all these costs in my relationships. With marriage No. 6 came mysterious physical ailments, profound depression and disconnection from my authentic self, and I could not determine why I was so sick and sad, because I could not really accept that I had a problem. I was something of a shell of a person: adept at anticipating and fulfilling the needs of others, while profoundly out of touch with my own.

The spiritual void was perhaps the most painful. Even with all the exertion to get it right, to <u>belong</u> by self-abandonment, I was desperately lonely. In the words of the poet David Whyte, "The price of our vitality is the sum of all our fears." I had given up my vitality — my true, rooted self — on the altar of my fears and it wasn't safety and belonging I got, but a gruesome sense of isolation and pointlessness.

That Fawn Response Spectrum: From Noble Giving to Self-Betrayal

Like any survival response, fawn occurs on a sliding scale. On one end is healthy giving — the capacity to pay attention to the needs of others, make compromises where appropriate, and take delight in being there for those you love.

At the other end lies chronic self-abandonment — the inability to both identify and honor your own needs, to set boundaries, to exist as a self within relationship.

The big difference is choosing to do something vs. having to do something. Healthy giving means making a conscious choice about when and how to put the needs of others first. Unhealthy fawning is knee-jerk and fear-based, and often occurs just when you most need to prioritize your own needs to be physically and emotionally healthy.

Being married, I didn't give from a place of choice and love and abundance. It was a compulsive tactic fueled by fear — fear of rejection, fear of conflict, fear of being perceived as selfish or unlovable. I was not exercising agency—that is, I was not making an active decision to give my partners' desires precedence in certain instances and my own in others. I was defaulting to just what they wanted IN ALL THINGS, regardless of damage to my own physical, emotional, or spiritual well-being.

By understanding this spectrum, we can start to see that the goal isn't to never acknowledge the needs of others or to never make sacrifices for the things and people we love. Sometimes the most honest expression of your values can be putting the needs of a loved one ahead of your own. The idea is to <u>make these choices deliberately</u>, rather than being led along by automatic survival-related responses that cause even more trouble than they resolve.

Codependency and Fawning Are Two Sides of the Same Coin

The fawn response is closely tied to what psychologists call codependency — a learned behavior sometimes prompted by abuse or neglect in childhood, although, essentially, it means depending on another person's approval to feel a sense of identity, purpose and worth.

Codependency can really be considered as the relationship pattern that occurs with one or both of the partners acting mostly from the fawn ingrained response. The basics are all there: hyper-attending to others' needs while neglecting your own, struggling to create boundaries between yourself and others, your sense of worth based on how needed you feel, and losing yourself within relationships.

My own codependent journey started in childhood, as I was programmed from a young age to become hyperaware of my father's emotional status as a means of survival. This pattern continued for me into adulthood, and I became what therapists like to call a "human doing" rather than a human being—only ever feeling worthy, or like I had an identity, when I measured what I did versus who I was.

This codependent component of my internal wiring was also – and is also one of the core mechanisms that drives unsuspecting males and females from all race and creed to be drawn back into toxic, abusive, dysfunctional relationships time and time again. But that's a different book, maybe my next one.

In my marriages, this translated into needing to be responsible for my partners' feelings, the neverending need to "save" them from their problems, even when they didn't ask me to and equating my self-worth with the degree to which they needed me. When one relationship would end, I would promptly search for another, terrified of confronting myself flat without the defining context of being someone's boyfriend, someone's caregiver, someone's husband, someone's step-father, someone's emotional crutch. Keep in mind, this is someone with 6 marriages under his belt, and someone who's had a total of 12 step-children along the way. A LOT of experience in where I'm attempting to teach from.

The connection between the fawn response and codependency shines a helpful light on why "just set better boundaries" doesn't usually work for chronic people-pleasers. The problem isn't that we don't know how to set boundaries — it's that the whole nervous system is organized around an assumption that boundaries are dangerous, that safety comes from merging with others rather than being a separate self with personal needs and limitations.

Take Back Your TRUE SELF: Turning Fawn into Healthy Connection

Now, despite the costs of chronic fawning, the answer is not to remove your capacity to care. Like all survival responses, fawn has a role. It's all about learning to give from true choice, not from fear-based obligation.

Here are a few methods that have helped me to change our relationship with fawn:

Recognize Your Fawn Triggers

Begin observing which particular situations, which interactions or which emotions turns on your desire to people-please. Common fawn triggers include:

- Conflict or threat of conflict
- When they need him/her, or when they come to him/her for help
- Not sure what people want from you
- Picking up on another's distress

My largest fawn cues have been anything that smacks of disapproval or anger from authority figures or partners. When someone I cared about appeared upset — a certain tone of voice, an expression, a sigh of exasperation — my fawning response would automatically kick in. And those particular triggers were the first step to responding differently.

Practice the Pause

When you can feel your fawn response kicking in, practice putting a little space between trigger and action. It is in this pause that choice enters.

Some ways to add a pause:

- Take a deep breath
- "Let me think about that and get back to you".
- Excuse yourself to go to the bathroom or get a glass of water
- Count to 10 Before Speaking
- Pose a clarifying question as your way to buy time

The pause doesn't solve the problem, but it keeps you from robotically betraying yourself with reflexive people-pleasing. It provides some time, also, for your prefrontal cortex — your thinking brain — to snap back online.

Tap Into What You Really Want

You could have lost your connection to yours, through years or decades of train riding, living in major part, the lives of other passengers. The fundamental thing to change the fawn response will be to reconnect with who you really are.

Some practices that can help:

- Journaling a few times per week about your feelings, needs, and wants
- Seeing a therapist who specializes in codependency or people-pleasing
- Wondering "What do I want?" in small, low-risk ways every day
- Recognizing bodily sensations as possible indicators of unmet needs
- Making time in your calendar to just be with, undistracted

For me, this started with some very basic questions that I found myself unable to answer:

- What foods do I actually like?
- What kind of music do I like?
- What do I want to do with my free time?

The fact that I found those simple questions about preferences so blank, exposed just how disconnected I had become from my real self.

Start with Small Boundaries

The idea of setting boundaries in the wake of a lifetime of people-pleasing is scary. Start with small, low-risk limits so that you can build your confidence, and help your nervous system that having limits doesn't result in abandonment or harm.

Some small examples:

- Asking for what you want at a restaurant instead of going along with others
- Deciding not to attend an optional social gathering you have no interest in participating in
- Saying what you like the sound of for a movie or activity
- Allowing yourself time to breathe without apologizing, explaining or feeling guilty

Every time you set a teeny tiny boundary and live through it, you forge tiny new neural pathways which eventually take over the belief that your safety requires self-abandonment.

Practice Authentic Giving

Once you start connecting with your true self, you will learn when to distinguish between fawn-giving (giving from fear and obligation) and authentic giving (giving from love and choice).

Authentic giving:

- Is motivating, not really exhausting
- Comes with no obligations of reciprocation
- Is defined, rather than infinite
- Respects your desires as well as others'
- May even contain a real "no" when suitable
- Comes from a place of plenty rather than of scarcity

Learning to authentically give has been one of the most curative parts of recovering from chronic fawning. I've found that when I give from a place of choice, rather than from fear, the giving itself is joyful rather than draining. And ironically, that more contained, real giving, creates a more connected experience than the old pattern of self-depleting sacrifice ever did.

Develop Self-Compassion

Finding your way from chronic people-pleasing to authentic connection is not a linear path. There will be relapses — moments when you slip back into old ways, when fear gets the better of your best intentions, when you realize you've abandoned your needs, your cravings and desires — and submitted instead to the comfort of the familiar hand-licking behaviors you find yourself turning to, that allow you to shut down.

In these moments, self-compassion is your most important tool. Beating yourself up for people-pleasing only offers another chance to leave yourself. Rather, try to greet these moments with the same kindness that you extend so easily to others.

Some exercises in self-compassion:

- Putting your hand on your heart when you notice you're beating yourself up

- Conversing with yourself the way that you would to a cherished friend going through a rough time
- Recognizing the real fears and needs that exist below the surface of people-pleasing behaviors
- Remember that changing long habit patterns takes time and patience
- Appending a handful of victories rather than consistent losses

For me, the process of learning self-compassion has been the most difficult and the most rewarding when it comes to recovering from chronic fawning. After a lifetime of defining my worth in terms of what I could do for others, I've had to reorient my whole sense of myself in relation to my place in the world and how I take care of myself.

Concluding: Self-Forfeiture vs. Self-Recovery

My struggle with the fawn response goes on. There are still times, although far fewer these days when I get that familiar desire to forfeit myself, my needs and my body, and morph into whomever someone in my presence wishes me to be in order to get love by disappearing. What is different now, generally, is that I can see what's going on and can make a different choice – I recognize I have a choice – and choose to stay with myself even as I'm with someone else.

I'm learning how to use fawn energy to that end — how to move it from reflexive self-abandonment to conscious connection, from accidentally merging with others out of fear to engaging with them as a whole, separate self capable of both giving and receiving, both compromise and boundary-setting, both care for others and care for self.

This doesn't mean you have to care less or become selfish. It's about becoming real — about bringing your whole, authentic self to your relationships rather than some idealized version you believe will please your partner. Ironically, such authenticity actually opens the door for more profound and meaningful connection than people-pleasing ever will.

Your fawn response journey will be as individual as you. It's a product of your unique history, your particular triggers, your individual nervous system. But the underlying decision is the same for all of us: Will you continue to abandon yourself in an attempt to receive connection by force? Or will you do this work to reconnect with your true self, recognizing that real connection is only born from real presence?

The road to authenticity is not an easy one. It takes courage and practice, and, often, the assistance of friends. But it results in relationships defined by mutual respect rather than codependence, by reciprocity rather than abuse, by loving you, not what you can do.

In the following chapter, we will dive deeper into how these four survival responses (fight, flight, freeze, and fawn) interact with each other to create intricate patterns in relationships that can either keep us stuck in cycles of disconnection or that, if we understand them and transform them, will allow us to have closer, more authentic relationships than we ever dreamed we could have.

CHAPTER TWELVE

THE DANCE FOR SURVIVAL:

WHEN THE RESPONDING PATTERNS CLASH

I was sitting in the office of yet another marriage counselor with my wife, (2nd one, if you're keeping up) when I saw something that would change my life forever: I was with someone who experienced things differently than I did.

My wife and I had both been recounting our most recent fight. it was something smaller — like dinner plans or a long overdue kind act that hadn't played out the way we'd hoped — that had ballooned into a life-and-death standoff in which neither of us felt seen or heard. As we sat beside each and told what happened, the counselor listened thoughtfully before offering a piece of advice that has followed me to this day:

"What I am observing is that classic pursue-withdraw pattern. 'When you' — she gestured at my wife — "feel disconnected, you go to him with criticism and demands — that's your fight response. And when you, "she said, turning to me, "feel attacked, you shut down and go silent — that's your freeze response. Her fight provokes your freeze, which provokes more of her fight, which provokes more of your freeze. Round and Round you go, feeling more and more alone and desperate with every rotation."

It was like the lights suddenly went on in a dark room, where I had been stumbling around for decades. It wasn't that this was all my problem, or all of her problem. It was how our survival responses were colliding, forging a dance neither of us understood we were doing but could not seem to escape.

It was the first sign of a massive change in my perspective on relationships. I realized that simply spotting my own survival patterns wasn't sufficient: I needed to know how mine intersected and clashed with the ones of those around me. And I wanted to understand how those crashes formed predictable cycles that, if left to the unconscious, would repeat indefinitely, the relationship version of Groundhog Day, mentioned earlier.

It's the dance of survival — the complicated, sometimes painful choreography that results when two different trauma responses collide, when they touch. This dance is an important one to know if we want to break unhealthy relationship patterns, and create relationships based on mutuality, healing, and not retraumatization.

When Survival Solutions Conflict

In the previous chapters, we have examined each of the four survival responses, fight, flight, freeze, and fawn, as stand-alone forms. But in actual relationships, these types of reactions seldom occur in vacuums. Instead, the vibrations interact with one another to create potential complex dynamics that can either keep partners trapped in repeat scenarios of triggering and retraumatization, or when conscious cooperation is caught, bring the relationship an opportunity for deep healing.

Below are some of the most common types of Survival Collisions:

- Fight + Fight: If both parties knee-jerk to the fight response, conflicts will escalate rapidly as they each attempt to dominate or self-defend via aggression. Each doesn't feel safe enough to share some of their vulnerability so the conversation becomes a fight to win a point, but the "win" doesn't score connection.
- Fight-Flight: One partner moves into conflict with criticism or demands, while the other disconnects either physically, emotionally or both. The more the partner who fights pushes, the more the partner who flees withdraws, leaving behind a pursue-withdraw cycle that leaves both feeling rejected, but in opposite ways.
- Fight + Freeze: As with fight + flight, but instead of actively retreating, the freeze-dominant partner emotionally shuts down while physically staying put. To the fight-prone partner, this stonewalling feels like provocation, and can lead to more aggressive attempts to force a response.
- Fight + Fawn: The fight-dominant partner shows anger or criticism, and the fawn-dominant partner quickly offers appeasement and self-reproach. This leads to a situation where one of the partners is more and more dominant and the other one becomes more and more submissive.
- Flight + Flight: In a situation where both are wired to flee, issues are never resolved because it takes little to prompt the other to leave the room. On the surface, it may look like a peaceful relationship, but

beneath there is no real intimacy or connection because it's missing the vulnerability of shared difficult emotions and needs.
- Flight + Freeze: This mix is particularly devastating, with one partner going out of their way to avoid connection, and the other shutting down emotionally. Communication falters, and the relationship is on hold.
- Escape + Fawn: When the flight-dominant avoids and the fawn-dominant becomes afraid of being abandoned and cranks up their people-pleasing, striving to keep their partner close. As a result, you have one person who feels crowded and the other who feels chronically abandoned.
- Freeze + Freeze: Two freezes and the relationship falls on ice. There are unresolved issues that haven't been aired, feelings that haven't been expressed, hungers that haven't been satisfied, but neither the lover nor the beloved has the initiative to make anything happen, and so there is a feeling then of being trapped together… in an igloo.
- Freeze + Fawn: The freeze-dominant partner's emotional detachment induces desperate bids for connection from the fawn-dominant partner, who will engage in increasingly dramatic and sacrificial acts of people-pleasing to elicit a response. For the freeze partner, role-player it's a self-esteem boost, as the freeze partner will feel yet more guilty and withdraw further while the fawn partner will feel ever more worthless.
- Fawn + Fawn: If both partners give the other the preference over themselves, the relationship may be peaceful but not real. Neither individual in question is any the wiser for they have not even seen it all. Beneath that outward agreement, resentment festers.

In my own relationships, I've encountered all of these collision patterns. With my first wife, it was fight + fight — two young people with unprocessed trauma trying to build safety through control in an unstable and unsustainable relationship that burned hot and quickly flamed out, primarily because of my father-like persona, who was extremely abusive at the time. And hats off to her for leaving the sick mind I had, and the abusive self I was demonstrating.

In a couple of later marriages, it was fight + freeze — however, my partner would criticize me or make demands (fight), and I would shut down emotionally (freeze), which would lead to even more criticism, which prompted a deeper shutdown.

Round and around we'd go, both of us feeling more and more alone and unheard.

In another former marriage, it was mostly fight +fawn: wife complains or expresses anger, I rush to reassure, I own her feelings, I sacrifice my needs and wants, harmony restored. This built a very unbalanced relationship where I lost sight of the person I truly am.

The point of acknowledging these patterns of collision is not to blame or pathologize either party's response. These are all normal, adaptive strategies that have helped us to survive previous traumas. The issue is not that we have these responses—it's that we are unaware of their intertwined nature, and how they set us up for cycles that keep us mired in disconnection.

The Pursue-Withdraw Dance: A Deeper View

Of all the styles of collision, the pursue-withdraw pattern (fight + flight or fight + freeze) is perhaps the most pervasive and damaging in intimate partnerships. It's important to parse that pattern out because understanding it can be the key to breaking free of one of the most painful and frustrating cycles that relationships can fall into.

What usually happens, in this pattern:

- The pursuer is feeling somewhat disconnected or has a need they want meet
- They approach their partner, sometimes with criticism or demands (fight)
- From the withdrawer's perspective, they feel criticized and attacked or overpowered
- They either physically or emotionally distance themselves (flight or freeze response)
- This withdrawal is experienced by the pursuer as rejection or abandonment
- They chase harder as a result, often in a critical or demanding way

The demander, on the other hand, feels even more overwhelmed, and the withdrawer withdraws more. This vicious cycle continues, each partner setting off the other's deepest fears.

I spent decades living this practice without even realizing it. It was especially pronounced in my second, third, and fourth marriages. My wives would feel this distance and approach me with what I interpreted as criticism: "You never share anything worthwhile," or "Why are you distant all the time?"

I would respond to these tactics with my freeze response, going numb, cut off from my thoughts or feelings, there in body but not in emotion. This would spook and piss them off, prompting an ever more zealous pursuit: "See? You're doing it right now! All you're doing is checking out here!"

The more she prodded, the *icier* I turned. The colder I got, the harder she tried. We were pouring salt in each other's deepest attachment wounds — her fear of being abandoned, my fear of being controlled or invaded — and contributing to a cycle of hopelessness that had us feeling more and more discouraged about our ability to actually connect.

What makes this pattern so toxic is that both partners don't want to be alone, and yet, both of their attempts at connection only lead to more distance. The pursuer pursues because they want closeness; the withdrawer withdraws because they don't feel safe in the presence of the pursuit and believe they need space to feel secure again. Both of you are attempting to get your attachment needs met with strategies that preclude having those needs met by your partner.

Both partners need to own their part in the dance and cultivate an ability to respond differently when triggered if we want to end this dance. The pursuer must know how to state needs and feelings without criticism or demands. The withdrawer must learn how to remain connected and engaged even when they feel upset.

Each has to realize that the other person's conduct is not a personal attack, but a survival response sparked by perceived danger. None of this easy. It's a lot of work.

The Triangle of Victim, Persecutor and Rescuer

Another collision pattern that is prevalent in relationships is one that the psychologists refer to as the "drama triangle" or the "victim-persecutor-rescuer triangle." This process includes the three roles, which partners cycle through (and relate to) which parallel our responses to survival:

- Victim (frequently freeze or fawn): "Poor me, this is happening to me, I can't do anything about it."
- Persecutor (repeatedly battle): "This is all your fault, you're the problem, it's all up to you to change."
- Rescuer (often fawn) "Let me do this for you, let me take care of you."

In a healthy relationship, these roles should be interchangeable and temporary. We all sometimes feel like victims, sometimes get mad, sometimes want to help. The issue occurs when these roles harden into unconscious roles, in which a toxic dance of routine rotations through these roles take place between partners.

For instance, in one of my marriages, I used to play out of my fawn-mode (rescuer stance), carrying the burden of responsibility for my wife's emotions and attempting to fix whatever was a worrying her. When my attempts were unsuccessful (as they would always be, no one can really be responsible for another person's emotions, after all) I'd move into the victim role (freeze response) and feel powerless and unheard. This would cause my wife to go into the persecutor role (aggressive, attacking behavior) and yell at me, telling me what a terrible husband I was. Then the criticisms would then shock me back into rescuing ("I know you're right… I should try harder!") or into becoming a persecutor myself ("Nothing is ever good enough for you!").

Round and round we would go, one role reversal after another, until we were both caught in a swirling dervish of blame, self-pity and codependence that only left us more fatigued and even less connected.

To become free of the drama triangle we must increase our capacity to:

- Identify if you are in one of these roles

- Own your own feelings and needs, instead of blaming or assuming others are responsible for your feelings
- Speak your truth in the first person, rather than manipulating in the process of victimhood and blame and rescuing
- Keep boundaries that lets each partner to have their own experiences

That's not easy to do, especially when these patterns are well-worn after years or decades. But the drama triangle is the first place to start if you plan on moving away from it and building healthier ways of relating.

Attachment Style and Survival Response

The patterns of colliding we have been discussing are closely related to what psychologists refer to as "attachment styles": models of how we relate to others in close relationships that we develop in early childhood in response to our experiences of our caregivers.

__There are four major styles of attachment:__

1. Secure: Comfortable with interdependence and independence while being able to manage emotions well in relationships.
2. Preoccupied: Afraid of being abandoned or rejected, needs high levels of closeness and reassurance.
3. Avoidant: Feared engulfment and loss of control, prioritized self-sufficiency and independence over connection.
4. Disorganized: Afraid of both abandonment and smothering, has inconsistent behavior in relationships.

Such attachment styles also strongly correlate with the innate responses for survival:

1. An anxious attachment frequently shows up as fight or fawn reactions

2. People with an avoidant attachment may bolt or shut down.
3. Unresolved disorganized attachment can cycle through all four categories rapidly

Knowing your attachment style and how it is connected to your survival responses, may give you some good clues about why you love the way you do! It can be a way to understand why specific things that your partners have done have provoked deep reactions within you, and why you keep falling into the same destructive patterns in spite of yourself.

My own attachment style is largely disorganized — the result of being raised by an abusive, unpredictable father, and of the trauma of sexual abuse. I switch flight-fight-freeze-survival responses and relationships patterns depending on the situation and trigger, which ends up being on and off, and sometimes contradictory.

With hung-up or controlling partners, I would often freeze or flee. If I was with a distant or rejecting partner, I'd generally fight or fawn. What these responses had in common was that they were automatic, unconscious reactions to perceived threat and not thoughtful decisions in relation to the present situation, at least not that day.

Resolve ineffective and harmful attachment wounds and develop a more secure pattern of relating, but it does take:

- Knowing your attachment style and the survival responses it induces

- Understanding that your attachment triggers are mostly related to past events rather than current ones
- Learning to NOT respond to automatic thinking, or conditioning, or programming when it is triggered.

- Slowly creating new experiences of safety in relationship
- Sometimes working with a good trauma/attachment specialist therapist

Breaking the Pattern: Unconscious reaction to Conscious Response

So, how do we escape these damaging crash cycles? How do we turn the dance of survival into a dance of connection?

It is a matter of moving beyond the unconscious reactivity to which most of us are prone-to a level of conscious response: to actually get beyond just being driven by survival beliefs to actually being helpful to ourselves and our desire for relationship.

Here are some of the strategies that have helped me, and countless other people, change relationship dynamics:

Acknowledge Your Role in the Dance

The very first thing is to know your default survival response and how it meets up with your partners. This awareness isn't about blaming yourself — it's about understanding that relationship dynamics are co-created, and you play a role in the patterns that continue to recycle.

Ask yourself:

- When I feel threatened in relationships, what is my 'go-to'?
- How does my reaction activate or increase my partner's survival response?
- What is it I'm afraid of, or what is it I believe that's causing this reaction?
- What am I afraid of?
-

For me, being aware of my pattern of defensively shutting down when I was criticized and realizing that was inviting further criticism from my partners was a pivotal realization. It helped me see what I was reading as attacks were often desperate grasps for connection from partners who felt abandoned by my emotional absence.

Identify Your Triggers

Become a student of your activation. If I haven't already stated this, you should want to make it a Life Goal to master you; you should want to be first and foremost, an expert on you.

Observe the certain events, words, tones of voice or actions that throw you into a fight-or-flight state. Some frequent relationship triggers are:

- Criticism or feeling judged
- The tone of voice is reminding you of the abusive parent
- Feeling ignored or dismissed
- Feeling withdrawal or distancing
- Unexpected changes of plans
- Feeling controlled or loss of choice
- Discord or angry words

My triggers include being criticized directly (and I go into freeze), feeling controlled (and I fight or flee) and esp in the form of withdrawal, and I fawn. Understanding these triggers helps me understand when I'm being activated prior to getting totally hijacked by a survival response.

Introduce a Timeout Between Stimulus and Response

When you become aware that you are being triggered, do your best to press the pause button between the initiating event and your reaction to it. It is at this pause that choice can happen.

Here are some effective ways to slow down the moment:

- Take three deep breaths
- Take a step back physically or distance yourself
- Try "I need to think about that."
- Concentrate on how it feels in your body
- Mentally label your feelings

The pause won't fix the problem, but it stops you from compounding the problem by reacting reflexively. It allows your prefrontal cortex — your thinking brain — to come back online.

Discuss Patterns of Communication, Not Just Content

Most couples argue about content — about specific issues, like money, sex, parenting, chores. But the real issues are typically in the patterns — the how of communication, not the what.

Learning to meta-communicate — to talk about how you're talking — can help you break destructive cycles. This sounds like:

- "I find I'm bracing myself in this moment. Can we take a breath and slow this conversation down?"
- I think that that pursue-withdraw cycle is back. I feel you are complaining and I am withdrawing, and I can see it makes you feel abandoned."
- "I'm realizing I'm in fix-it mode at the moment, trying to fix your feelings rather than hearing them out!"

This type of communication takes the emphasis away from finger pointing and into co-ownership for what's going on, therefore enabling break the patterns before they intensify. And yes, I realize that many of these strategies, where you will need to employ these logical, verbal responses probably sound *corny*, and most of this is foreign to many of us because we haven't wired our subconscious with these beliefs and strategies. It takes time.

Find Out Your Partner's Attachment Language

Just as all of us have different love languages, we all have different attachment languages — ways that we express our longing for connection and security. The more you're able to identify and respond to your partner's attachment bids, the less pressure it puts on the triggers to wake up.

For instance, the criticism that seems like criticism ("You never talk to me about anything that matters") might really constitute an attachment bid ("I miss you and want to feel close to you"). Withdrawal signals (like "I need some space") are not always about you not being good enough; it could be that your partner is feeling overwhelmed and needs to regulate before they can connect.

Learning to listen for the attachment need under the superficial communication can change your responses to your partner and stop harmful cycles from starting in the first place.

Practice Secure Functioning

Therapists Stan Tatkin and Tracey Boldemann-Tatkin have formulated the idea of "secure functioning" in partnerships—a set of principles that foster safety and connection irrespective of attachment styles and trauma.

Secure principles of functioning are the following:

- Care for each other: Each person cares deeply about the other person and the relationship.
- Shared responsibility: They both admit to owning parts of what has happened in the relationship.
- Fast repairs: When ruptures take place, partners are quick to repair the connection.
- Transparency: Partners are truthful about what they need, feel, and intend.
- Boundaries: An agreement to maintain boundaries and keep the relationship free from intruders.

While neither partner may have begun with a secure orientation to attachment, these principles are creating a container of safety which allows each to slowly heal attachment wounds, and to grow into a more secure way of relating.

Get Support

Disentangling long-standing relationship dynamics is tough going, especially if both partners are working from trauma responses. A competent couple's therapist who knows trauma, attachment, and nervous system regulation can make the difference between ongoing pain and lasting change.

Individually therapy can be helpful as well, because it enables each partner to explore their own trauma history and build more capacity to self-regulate when triggered. Working with couples and individual work together provide the strongest anchor for lasting change.

What Happens When Patterns Don't Change: The Tough Choices

No matter how much we want to transform it, certain relationship patterns seem immune to transformation. This is especially true if:

- One or both partners are not ready to take responsibility for their contribution in an unhealthy pattern
- Substance abuse or untreated mental health problems further muddy the picture
- There is active abuse or violation of core boundaries
- The attachment injuries are so profound that the trigger is chronic and overpowering.
- One or both partners are not capable of self-examination and growth

In these situations, it requires us to make hard choices as to whether or not to keep on dumping a bunch of resources into something that is causing more harm than it is contributing to good.

I cannot stress enough: usually this level of relationship breakdown cannot be handled by the two people involved. I know from experience – unfortunately – sometimes it's just not going to work out, and these relationship forks in the road need to be handled delicately between you, your partner, and a professional who will try and help you navigate the complexities.

My friend and the LMFT, (licensed marriage family therapist) Bob Hamp was kind and generous with his time to write the Foreword to this book. Bob has helped thousands of individuals and couples over the years, and if you need a safe place with a wise, licensed therapist, Bob Hamp is my highest recommendation. Please visit his website: TDacad.com for more information.

Ultimately the conclusion I came to in my previous marriage was to leave the marriage – as you know.

We did therapy, but our patterns were deeply fixed. My wife was unable to see that the dynamic was one which she played a part in and instead believed everything was my fault. Her unmanaged alcoholism led to an unpredictable and emotionally abusive environment that kept my nervous system on high-alert. At the same time, I was not only codependent, but my suitcases of undealt trauma had been regularly emptied in front of our entire household for all to see. She had a right to some of her directed anger and hostility thrown my way.

The choice to leave was excruciating. As somebody with a very strong fawn response, I was feeling a lot of guilt for prioritizing my own well-being over sustaining a relationship. I had abandonment wounds, so the fear of the pain of separation again, being divorced again, leaving a house full of step-children again, and being alone…was huge for me. But by now I'd come to realize that the relationship was stopping the healing, not enabling it — for both of us.

Sometimes, the most loving gesture we can offer to our partners, and to ourselves, is to let go of a relationship that is no longer serving as a container for growth, but a container for mutual re-traumatization. That doesn't make either party "wrong" or the love false. It is an understanding that some of the wounds of attachment, and some of the survival responses, create a relationship dynamic beyond the current ability of one, or both, of the partners to reshape.

Hope for Healing: New Dances Are Possible

It's tough, and I feel hopeful that it is possible to heal relationship patterns. I have seen incredible shifts, in my own life, as well as in the lives of those I have mentored, when both partners are dedicated to understanding their survival responses, and learning new ways of dancing together.

The most important lessons I have learned from my process are as follows:

Just the awareness changes everything: Just the awareness of your patterns and trigger points offer the possibility of choice where once only reactivity was possible.

The past is not the future: Just because you have found yourself repeating the same destructive patterns in past relationships does not mean you will continue to do so in the future.

Healing occurs in relationship: As important as individual work is, much of what we've experienced in attachment cannot be fully healed except where new experiences of safety and connection can literally rewrite old expectations.

Even the healthiest relationships are bound to still trigger a partner and fall back into old patterns at times. What separates them is how quickly they figure it out and fix the connection.

It's never too late: Even if you've been steeped in destructive patterns for a long time, if you're willing to grow and learn, you can change.

The dance of survival — the intricate choreography that results when trauma responses clash — has ruled my relationships for as long as I can remember. But I'm learning new steps now, new ways of moving with others that link rather than disconnect, heal rather than retraumatize.

You can learn new steps too. It starts by knowing your role in the dance, how your survival responses and your partner's survival responses work together – by falling in love with the difficult and tremendously rewarding work of building relationships that "trigger" you for growth rather than to keep you in the place you are hurt.

In the next chapter, we'll dive into some very practical tools for knowing when you're in survival mode and then returning to safety and connection—inside yourself, and with others.

CHAPTER THIRTEEN

MY STORY: A LIFE ON ALERT

I vividly remember, sitting in the new space all by myself in September 2023 — a 500 square foot one-bedroom. This was quite a change, and in addition to basically losing a family overnight, I suddenly felt boxed in – and in more ways than one. Our last residence was 8,300 square feet. You've heard the phrase, "a house is not a home."

For the first time in years — maybe in my life — I experienced something with a semblance of peace. But that peace was mixed with a nagging fear, an unease about where we – "we" meaning me – were going.

This time, however, things were different.

I wasn't searching for someone new to replace the spousal void.

I wasn't running to the next relationship to escape from myself.

I also knew with unnerving, but liberating, lucidity that it was time to take a real hard look in the mirror and make life-altering choices. I had to contend with myself — my broken self.

And yes, I said "broken."

There's a popular fallacy, a trending phrase that has been nourishing our culture for a while now: ***"You are not broken."***

This phrase is BS.

We break sometimes in life. In the same way that a broken bone needs to be set in a cast in order to properly heal, so too, do we sometimes suffer real brokenness of soul and spirit. The terms "brokenhearted," and "broken spirit" are even mentioned throughout the Bible. You can't cast a broken soul, a broken heart or a broken spirit, obviously, but that doesn't make the brokenness any less real, or the repair or forgiveness required of it any less true.

This toxic positivity — this idea that we're always whole, always healed, and unimpeachable in our perfect natures, never marred by anything we've been through — does far more harm than good. It denies the fact of this thing called, **trauma**. It dismisses the real pain of living through events that shatter our basic sense of safety, identity, and connection. It implies that any sense of brokenness we experience must be due to a warped, self-destructive mode of seeing ourselves, rather than an appropriate reaction to abnormal conditions.

I was broken.

My very being had been shattered as a child by my father's abuse, by my mother's absence, by my brother's violation, by fear and chaos that never went away. Other parts had been impaired in adulthood by my own choices, by relationships that replicated those early patterns, by decades of surviving, and not truly living.

Recognizing this brokenness was not an exercise in self-pity or defeat. It was honest — a first step to real healing, not the dressing of wounds or the denial that the wounds even exist.

Because for as long as I could recall, I had been living on red alert. My nervous system had been conditioned to anticipate danger when at an early age, I watched my father's face, looking for the first sign that violence was on its way. Ever since I was a six-year-old learning that even those you are supposed to trust to protect you could choose to cause harm instead, I had trained my body to anticipate harmful acts. I'd been conditioned to expect the worst since I was 10 and realized that the people who say "I love you" can negate even the most fundamental boundary of yours.

I had been in a state that neuroscientists describe as hypervigilance, which means a sustained exalted state of sensitivity of the senses, a higher readiness to trigger and a heightened awareness of the environment. But I didn't need a sophisticated scientific term to tell me how it felt. I felt that I was never really resting, even in my sleep.

I learned early on to read the micro-expressions on people's faces that others couldn't even see.

It was like knowing who was angry before they were, feeling the air change when someone was in a bad mood, knowing there was danger before any was visible.

It felt like living a life as if it were the final round of a championship fight, with one wrong punch leading to knockout.

This has been my story: a life on alert.

But, if you've been reading up to this point, it's likely your story, too, or at least pieces of it.

Because as much as the specifics of our traumas are different, the ways our bodies and brains react to them are predictable.

These fight, flight, freeze and fawn responses I've been describing aren't just theories. They're the lived experience of how trauma molds us, makes us different people, changes our relationships, the very way we move.

In the coming chapters, I would like to pull together the threads of my story — and the science I have learned about trauma responses — in an attempt to demonstrate how these patterns have manifested in my own life and relationships. Not because my story is unique or special, but because in its very ordinariness, it may help you recognize and understand the patterns in how you use and relate to them, and how maybe, just maybe, they've been manifesting in yours.

Because seeing another person's dance can help you make out the steps of your own.

PART III: BREAKING THE LOOP

CHAPTER FOURTEEN

RECOGNIZING YOUR TRIGGERS:

THE FIRST STEP TO FREEDOM

It's your time now.

If you've made it this far, you already did something most of us never do in a lifetime — you confronted the uncomfortable truth that your survival mechanisms rule you more than you might even want to admit.

You've examined the patterns that have defined your relationships, your work, your identity.

You've started to see why this pattern emerged and why is has been so difficult to change.

Now it is time to go from awareness to action.

Now is the time to take what you've learned and truly apply it to actual, lasting change in your life and relationships. But before we get to those, I want to share some research you might find surprising — research that reveals just how frequently these trauma responses show up in everyday life.

The Hidden Epidemic of Trauma Beyond the Battlefield

Most people hear "PTSD" and "trauma response" and imagine combat veterans coming home from the war zone. And while our service members unquestionably deserve anything we can do for them, the reality is that far more people are impacted by trauma responses than most of us consider.

Here's what new studies show us:

3.9% of people around the world have suffered from PTSD at least once in their life, according to the world health organization. That's more than 300 million worldwide. In the U. S., approximately 13 million Americans — or about 5 percent of the population — are struggling with PTSD in any given year.

But, this is where the story takes a really interesting turn:

Those are just reported cases of full-blown PTSD. They do not take into account the much higher number of people who suffer otherwise — individuals who are now recognized to have "subthreshold PTSD," in other words, trauma responses --- when not all of the criteria of the clinical diagnoses are being met, but conditions causing significant distress and difficulty in life exist.

New research indicates that for every individual with PTSD, there are presumably at least three to four others who are experiencing subthreshold PTSD-related symptoms. Indeed, that would mean that up to 20% of the population — or one in five, which is already considered a conservative estimate here in the States — is living with severely limiting trauma responses that are impacting their relationships, their work, their health and life in general.

And it's not just for major traumatic events like combat, sexual assault or natural disasters.

A landmark 2023 study in the Journal of Traumatic Stress reported that as many as 72 percent of adults said they experience at least one "everyday trauma trigger" in a typical week — moments when their nervous system slips into survival mode in response to what might seem like minor stresses, such as criticism from a partner, a tense work meeting or even certain tones of voice and facial expressions that bring to mind past threats.

Moreover, science from the newish field of epigenetics, or the study of how environmental factors can turn our genes up or down, has shown that responses to trauma can be passed down through generations.

A study from 2024 at Mount Sinai Hospital found that children of trauma survivors have measurable differences in stress hormone regulation and amygdala reactivity, even if they themselves have never experienced major trauma. Our bodies retain the record of our ancestors' experiences, good and bad.

But one of the most surprising has been what neuroscientists have learned about how trauma can change the brain.

Employing cutting-edge imaging technology, researchers at UCLA found that even subtle, repeated stress — the kind we experience in everyday life that often serves as a motivator — can affect the structure of the prefrontal cortex, which is involved in decision-making and the regulation of emotional responses.

These changes make it even more difficult to stay grounded and make conscious choices when we're triggered, leading to a vicious cycle of reactive action.

The bottom line? If you've experienced trauma responses — fight, flight, freeze or fawn — you are not alone.

You might be feeling broken right now, but you don't have to stay that way.

You can heal.

You're not weak.

You're having a normal human reaction to some very abnormal levels of stress, whether that was delivered in the form of big, traumatic events or the steady drip, drip, drip of little stressors over time.

And here's the good news: The neuroplasticity that led to these patterns forming also makes them changeable. You can train your brain and nervous system how to respond differently. You can grow your window of tolerance for discomfort. You can build up your capability for presence and freedom in stressful situations.

But it all starts with recognition — learning to notice your triggers and catch them before they hijack your nervous system and you automatically shift into survival mode.

What Are Triggers, really?

A trigger is something, anything (externally or internally) that activates your survival response system. It might be a vision, a sound, a scent, a touch, a memory, or a dream. Something is only a trigger if it is interpreted in a certain way by your nervous system as the result of prior trauma, rather than by the thing itself.

To take just one example: A raised voice can just be a raised voice to someone who grew up in a house in which loud shows of feeling were normal and not in the least threatening. But for someone who grew up with an abusive parent who raised their voice before becoming violent, a raised voice might immediately prompt a flight, fight, freeze or fawn response — even if the current situation poses no genuine threat.

They work on the basis of a technology known as pattern matching. Your amygdala — that Amber Alert system we talked about — is always sweeping your environment for anything that looks like the bad stuff that happened before. When it finds a potential match, it doesn't wait for your thinking brain to catch up and interpret the situation at hand. It kicks on your survival instinct right out of the box to save you from the expected danger.

And it does so really, really fast – again as shared previously – from NYU's Center for Neural Science showed that the amygdala can process potential threats in just 33 milliseconds, long before your conscious mind can even comprehend what is happening. By the time you're like, "Oh, I feel triggered right now," your body's already in survival mode.

This is why just telling yourself "Don't overreact" or, "stay calm" often doesn't have much impact when you're triggered. The survival response is not conscious. There's an automatic, physical reason for it, devised to keep you alive in the face of danger. And it favors speed over accuracy — better to overreact to a false alarm than to miss a true danger.

And the change in this pattern isn't trying to become triggerless. It is about learning how to notice when you are getting triggered earlier on in the process, before you've been completely hijacked by a survival response. This process creates an opening — a moment when you can choose how you want to respond rather than simply reacting.

Common Relationship Triggers

Triggers are incredibly personal and are the result of your personal history and life experiences, but there are some triggers that tend to be especially common within relationships. When you understand these triggers, it helps you better understand why people may come across as distant, aloof, squeamish, jumpy. Some triggers include:

- Criticism or judgment: There is a high likelihood that if you grew up with critical or perfectionistic caregivers, even mild forms of criticism can elicit feelings of shame and defensiveness for you.
- Tone of voice: Some tones — usually those that bring to mind an angry parent or other authority figure — can cause survival responses, even if the words aren't threatening.
- Feeling ignored or dismissed: Ignored is the same as kicking your brain in the shin; it's an alarm telling you that you're not part of the tribe.
- Impromptu plan changes: In people whose early environments were insecure or chaotic, surprises can prompt anxiety and controlling behavior.

- Conflict or anger: Even benign disagreement can elicit survival responses in individuals who were victims or observers of violence or explosive anger in childhood.
- Feeling controlled or that choices are limited: Being bossed around or given restricted options can activate fight or flight modes, particularly for those who have grown up with authoritarian or controlling parenting.
- Physical proximity or touch: Survivors of physical or sexual abuse may be triggered into fight or freeze responses by physical proximity to, or touch from, particular others, or just by someone standing too close.
- Financial stress or its discussion: Money issues tend to provoke deep insecurity and survival fears, particularly for people who were poor or experienced financial instability in childhood.
- Can feel abandoned or rejected: As the after-effects following the abandonment wounds, the feeling of being left out, ignored, or rejected brings may cause emotional upheaval in those who carry the wounds of abandonment.
- Sexual intimacy: Different elements of sexual intimacy can invoke a scared response in people with sexual trauma backgrounds or people who have been raised with shame about sex.

In my real life, I have encountered a lot of these triggers. And as an extremely toxic and dysfunctional young adult, I did quite a bit of triggering to those with whom I was in relationship. I was a real life, *Doc Holiday* of physical, psychological and emotional conflict. TRIGGER-HAPPY.

For a period of time in my early 20s, criticizing me just put me in some kind of freeze frame where I couldn't think or respond as effectively anymore. Feeling controlled would kick off the fight responses — defensiveness, snipiness, hard boundaries. Feeling my partners pull away emotionally would trigger my fawn response, which is an anxious state of trying to please and reconnect at all costs (usually at the expense of my own needs and boundaries).

The first step in changing was understanding these patterns. But information was not in itself enough. I wanted some practical techniques for knowing when I was being triggered before I was fully hijacked by survival reactions.

The Body Will Tell You Before You Know: Physical Warning Signs of Being Triggered

One of the biggest findings in trauma research over the past 10 years is that the body responds to triggers more quickly than the mind does. This is because physical sensations are often our earliest signal that we're being activated.

Some of the physical signs of being triggered may include:

- Altered breathing: Rapid, shallow or held (brief pause)
- Tense muscles: Especially in the jaw, shoulders, chest and stomach
- Changes in heart rate: Typically rising, but sometimes dropping with freeze responses
- Digestive shifts: "Butterflies," nausea or the runs
- Temperature changes: Sensations of quickly getting too hot (fight reflex) or too cold (freeze reflex)
- Visual changes: Tunnel vision, blurriness, or increased visual clarity
- Changes in hearing: Hearing going "dull," or sounds being too sharp
- Changes in energy: Unexpected exhaustion or hyperactivity/restlessness

- Disassociation: Like being detached, not quite here, but you notice yourself from afar

- Restlessness: Sensation that you have to get out, though you do not know why; or wanting to pace or be outside of your body or close to a door

Learning to identify these physical cues within your own body is important if you want to catch triggers early. This is what neuroscientists refer to as interoception: the capacity to notice and to interpret the physiological signals that originate in the body. Studies conducted at the University of California found that interoception-based training could reduce the severity and duration of trauma responses over time.

When it comes to me, the first hints of it are a knot in my stomach, a tightening in my chest and a slight narrowing in my vision. When I start to feel these sensations, it's an indication that my nervous system is beginning to fire up, that I am starting to move into fight or flight. I'm building enough consciousness to have a moment of choice before getting hijacked into a fight, flight, freeze or fawn reaction.

It is common for triggers to lead to not only physical, but also emotional and cognitive alterations. These include:

- Emotional signs:
- Sudden mood shifts
- Sensations of emotions that feel too much for the particular situation
- Anesthetic tendency or emotional detachment

- Irritability or out-of-nowhere anger

- Unexplained anxiety or fear

- Overwhelming shame or feelings of inadequacy

- Sudden hopelessness or despair

Cognitive signs:

- Black-and-white thinking
- Catastrophizing (jumping to the worst-case scenario)
- Mind reading (that is, thinking you can read someone's mind)
- Problems with attention or following a discussion
- Crazy thoughts or mind "static"
- That thing where you have to live over and over negative experiences
- Predicting a scary future
- Difficulty making decisions

Most of these emotional and mental shifts are the byproducts of how your nervous system reacts when it goes into survival mode. When that amygdala of yours sniffs out a possible threat, it doesn't just pick up on physical responses — it also adjusts how you feel and think to get you ready for danger.

In survival mode, we lose nuance. Complicated scenarios boil down to straightforward threats. What we see in the present is often shaped by what we have learned from the past or worry about in the future. Your brain and thinking get more rigid, more black-or-white, and more focused on self-protection rather than connection or growth.

With this in mind, keeping an eye on these shifts in how you feel and think can help you know when you're being triggered, even if and when you aren't yet aware of the physical signs. The trick is learning to develop what psychologists call "metacognition" — an awareness of your own thinking processes that allows you to observe your thoughts and more objectively assess when and if nurturing them might actually be helpful (as opposed to, you know, like, dangerous).

Constructing Your Own Trigger List

There's nothing like a personal trigger inventory to facilitate awareness of your triggers, a list of the situations, interactions, sensations, and thoughts that stir your survival responses.

This list has several functions:

- It makes you notice patterns you wouldn't otherwise.
- It diminishes shame by not allowing triggers to be this amorphous, frustrating thing but instead something that takes form and shape and makes sense.
- It's empowering – these are things you can learn to work with, rather than a scary, general reactivity.

This is a stepping stone to the more profound work of healing that we will cover in future chapters.

To build your trigger inventory, you will want to keep a notebook or digital file to write down the following information every time you realize you have been triggered:

- DATE AND TIME: When was the triggering event?

- Situation: What was going on around you when you were triggered? Where were you? Who was present? What were they talking about or doing?
- External triggers: What were the exact external circumstances that might have led to your response? Words/sounds, sounds/vibrations, facial expressions/sentiments, sensations in physical bodies, environments, etc.
- Internal triggers: What had been going on inside of you before the external trigger? Was it because you were tired, hungry, stressed out about something else? Did you notice any thoughts or feelings that may have primed you to react?

- Bodily reflection: What did you feel in your body? Where on your body were you experiencing them?

- Feelings/emotions: What was I feeling? How severe were they on a scale from 1 to 10?

- Cognitive: What thoughts or beliefs did you have? What stories were you telling yourself about what was going down? What behavior did you take? How did you react outwardly?

- Survival response pattern: With all of your survival responses (fight, flight, freeze and fawn), which one overpowered the others? Or was it a combination?

- Afterward: How did you feel about it? How did the others involved respond to it? For how long did you need to recover?

- Possible associations: Does this trigger remind you of things that happened to you in the past? Does it relate to certain wounds or unaired childlike needs from childhood or past relationships?

That's a lot of information to keep in mind, but you'll get better with time at spotting and noting this info more efficiently. The goal isn't perfection of documentation — it's a greater awareness of your patterns over time.

I know this sounds a bit monotonous, but I suggest logging triggers on a daily basis for a minimum of two weeks so you can begin identifying patterns. You might be surprised by what you find. Triggers that appeared random or other people-induced, often expose underlying patterns related to your own history, your stress level at this moment or your unsatisfied needs.

Based on my own patterns of keeping track of my triggers, I learned that I was much more likely to freeze when receiving criticism if I already was feeling deficient in something else. The amount of external trigger (criticism), was compounding on top of an internal trigger (self-doubt) to create a response in greater depth than the sum of the two components.

I also realized that my fight response was likely to come not from the immediacy of something threatening me directly, but instead to witness someone else being slighted. That just went to my infant observations of abuse I could do nothing about.

The real effect of these insights was not that they immediately altered my reactions, but that they provided me with a map of that internal terrain — a first step toward navigating it more consciously.

The Window of Tolerance: Your Nervous System's Comfort Zone

As you trace your triggers, it's useful to know about the "window of tolerance" — a term coined by the psychiatrist Dr. Dan Siegel to explain the zone in which your nervous system can function in a healthy way.

You can do the following when you're within your window of tolerance:

- Feel emotions without being flooded by them
- Try to process your emotions and make decisions based on reason
- Think of ways to stay in relationship while not over-stepping your boundaries
- Invoke curiosity, creativity, and compassion
- Include experiences and knowledge from the present time period

When triggers push you out of your window of tolerance, you shift into either *hyperarousal* (fight/flight) or *hypoarousal* (freeze/fawn):

Hyperarousal feels like:

- Racing thoughts
- Anxiety or panic
- Anger or rage
- Hypervigilance
- Impulsivity
- Feeling overwhelmed
- Exaggerated startle response

Hypoarousal feels like:

- Emotional numbness

- Disconnection from others
- Mental fog or difficulties with critical thinking
- Tightness of other parts of the body or inability to move them
- Feeling "not really here"
- Inactivity or a lack of free will
- Feeling empty or dead inside

The intention of trigger awareness is not to never get out of your window of tolerance; that isn't realistic or desirable (it's in these slips that the most growth actually happens). Rather, it's to:

Learn to recognize more readily when you're leaving your window

Build tools to get back to your window if you've navigated away

Your window can slowly get bigger overtime that you can contain more emotional intensity without going out of the window.

This is very important to know when dealing with triggers. It means that self-care is not simply about feeling good but about having a greater window of tolerance so you have more room to be present and make conscious choices when you're triggered.

Recognition to Response: The Impact of the Pause

By becoming more adept at identifying your triggers and the signals that you're getting ready to fall outside your window of tolerance, you now have access to what might be one of the most powerful tools for changing your response patterns: the pause.

The pause is literally just what it sounds like — space where there's no action between a stimulus and a response. It's the room where choice can emerge.

This pause need not be long — even just a few seconds can be all the difference between an automatic reaction that reinforces the old pattern, and a conscious response that creates new possibilities.

Neuroscience helps to explain why this can be effective. When you get triggered, your amygdala hijacks a rapid response pathway that skips the prefrontal cortex (where you do your rational thinking, perspective-taking and impulse control). That's why what you say or do in a reactive moment often isn't what you actually want to have said or done — your thinking brain quite literally was not entirely available when you spoke or acted.

Back to the pause… The (pause) break is needed for your prefrontal cortex to re-engage. It breaks an automatic circuit between trigger and response and allows time for your higher brain functions to bring to bear on the situation.

There are straightforward but powerful methods of creating a pause such as:

1. Three breaths: In times of trigger, practice taking three slow, deep breaths before responding to a triggering situation. It activates your parasympathetic nervous system to counteract the sympathetic activation of the stress response.
2. Physical step back: Turn and step out of reach, putting both physical and psychological distance between you and one whom you may be in the midst of conflict. This tiny movement can disrupt that automatic response path.

Again, some of these exercises to combat these issues may sound repetitive, but I am purposely repeating them so you can remind yourself to take action.

3. Name what's happening: Identify what's happening, either silently or aloud: "I'm beginning to get defensive" or "I can feel my fight response

4. kicking in." This activates your prefrontal cortex, allows you to observer perspective.
5. Feel your feet: Concentrate on the feeling of your feet on the ground. This puts you in current physical reality, rather than the threat the brain is perceiving.
6. Express your need for time: "I need a moment to reflect on this," or "Is it possible for us to take a brief break from this conversation?" can make the room you need to control.

These strategies do not address the root problems that caused your triggers, but they disrupt the automatic reactivity cycle that keeps you locked in the old patterns. They establish the circumstances under which new choices can emerge.

Over time, I have tried all of these, but the most consistent strategy for me has been using the three-breath technique while naming what's going on. I've learned to notice when I'm getting triggered.

This is not a foolproof system, though. Sometimes the stimuli can be too much, or too fast and I respond before I can even stop myself. But with practice, I've improved at noticing earlier when triggers go off and clearing that all-important space for choice.

The Courage to Begin

Before we move on and delve into specific strategies for how to work with each of the four survival responses, I want you to remember something really crucial: This work is brave. It takes a lot of self-awareness in you to be present up until this point and just hang with me, and based on the statistics of how little we humans read these days, it should be even more revealing to you that you have a need to change, to learn, and to grow. Congratulations to you!

It is, in many ways, easier to stay unconscious about your triggers and patterns. Knowledge is responsibility. It also means you can't ever again credibly say, "I couldn't help it" or "That's who I am." It means confronting the difficult reality that although you didn't choose your trauma or the survival responses that may have come with it, you do have some degree of choice in how you relate to those responses in the present.

This isn't about blame. It's about empowerment. It's about acknowledging that you have a greater degree of agency than you may have previously believed — not limitless agency, not complete control over the play of your responses, but more choice than automatic reactivity affords.

The road that we are traveling together is not an easy one. There will be setbacks. You will be hijacked by past patterns when you don't want them to grab your attention. This is normal. It's part of the process. The aim isn't perfection — it's progress. It is growing your capacity for choice little by little.

The number of times you get triggered, the amount of time you fall back to what you were like before, isn't what matters. What counts is how fast you recognize what is going on, how capably you deal with what happens, and how kindly you treat yourself and others along the way.

In the next chapters, we will explore these strategies as they relate to the four survival responses: fight, flight, freeze, and fawn. I'll show you how to convert those automatic reactions into conscious responses that serve your higher values and goals. I will discuss how to heal the wounds that produced such patterns in the first place.

But it starts with recognition, with the willingness to authentically see your lens and the bravery to sit with that which you see. This is how you set yourself free. And you have already taken it, just by reading this, by doing the difficult work of turning your gaze, so that it's directed not only at others but at yourself, at your own responses.

<u>Again, think about that for a moment.</u> It's no small thing.

Questions for Reflection and Practice

The first time you know you are triggered, what does your body feel like? Where on your body do you notice them first?

What are your typical emotional and cognitive cues that you're moving out of your window of tolerance?

What are three to five specific situations, words or behaviors that you can count on bringing out your survival responses in relationships?

What is the breadth of your window of tolerance in these times? What broadens it or narrows it for you?

Which pause method do you feel most connected to? How can you remember to employ it when you get triggered?

What type of help do you have in terms of gaining more awareness of your triggers?

Is there anything it could offer them, such as tracking devices, therapy, practice partners or another resource?

What is one baby step you could take this week to start cultivating more awareness around your triggers and early warning signs?

And remember: Awareness is the basis for all change. The better you can see your patterns, the more choice you have in how to respond to them. This isn't about punishing yourself for having triggers — it's about gaining the tools to work with them more consciously and effectively.

This is where freedom begins.

.

CHAPTER FIFTEEN

THE NERVOUS SYSTEM KNOWS

BEFORE YOU DO

Not that long ago, I had been sitting in a coffee shop near downtown Fort Worth, attempting to write… writing this book as a matter of fact! The location off of Magnolia Street was bustling but not full-throttle — perfect ambience noise-wise for maintaining my concentration. I'd been there an hour when a man sat down on a leather chair right next to mine. Nothing unusual about that.

But moments later, moments before he had ordered anything, before he had spoken to me at all, I felt it — that familiar knot in my stomach, the very slightest narrowing of vision, my shoulders rising toward my ears.

My body was getting into that Amber Alert mode.

Consciously, however, I had not perceived anything threatening. The guy hadn't broken the law. He didn't appear to be anyone to be on guard against. He hadn't even looked at me. But something about him: the way he plopped down into the chair, his energy, some unconscious cue I couldn't identify, had triggered my nervous system.

It wasn't until he did a loud talking to his phone a few minutes later that I realized what my body already understood: that his voice was as cutting, as laced with just enough randomness, as my father's. My nervous system had experienced that connection and responded to the threat far faster than I ever could've grasped it consciously.

At this point in my life, I'm fairly confident in my ability to handle myself physically – so there's never any bit of that going on inside of my head.

Still, this is what I mean by saying the nervous system is ahead of you. Your body is constantly scanning your surroundings for threats, all while jotting down split-second calculations and adjustments, without necessarily waiting for your conscious mind to get your back. It's reading the room, feeling the vibe, picking up all those little cues that go unnoticed by your conscious mind.

And in our hyper-distracted world, we've become more separated from this intuitive intelligence of our bodies — we're constantly bombarded with notifications, deadlines, and responsibilities. We ignore the signals of our body. We ignore its warnings. We put up with fatigue and anxiety and discomfort because we have affairs to manage and other people to please and goals to chase.

But what if the way to true healing and healthier relationship actually starts with reawakening that very body wisdom? What if the secret to changing your survival responses are not more thinking, what if it's not more analyzing, more what if it's not figuring things out, but learning to listen to what your nervous system is already telling you?

The Poker Player's Edge: Reading a Room When You Don't Know What Room You're In

I play in a weekly poker game — a tournament — with 12-14 guys who have a mixed level of playing ability. Consistently, I've won about 25% of our tournaments, one of the best of two records within the group. The question I often get asked about most (privately, of course) is what my secret?

Yes, I understand pot odds.

As Kenny Rogers would say, I know when to hold 'em and when to fold 'em – although *knowing* doesn't always translate to *doing*.

The numbers don't lie, but — if I'm being honest — so much of my success boils down to something that has absolutely nothing to do with math or game theory: I've figured out how to believe what my nervous system knows about myself, first, and the other players long before my conscious mind has locked in on it.

I'll sit at the table, holding cards, and I'll sense something in my gut when I glance across at an opponent who has just raised. I've trained myself to having fine-tuned my peripheral vision, and it helps that through my profession of being a photographer/cinematographer, I have an acute observation skillset.

So, when their breaths come out in a way that feels foreign for a moment, or a micro-expression crosses their face in a hide/seek sort of game, or they shift their posture very subtly, my nervous system picks up on the message. I haven't even registered the reason why consciously, but already my body knows they're bluffing.

Other times, I'll get a warning red-light feeling — a tightening in my chest, a freeze in my extremities — when someone's getting ready to make a play with a large bet. My unconscious mind is getting danger messages that my conscious mind is not aware of at this point.

When I heed such signals and fold, I tend to find out afterward that I had a near-miss with a trap.

This isn't esoteric or mystical. It's my nervous system performing the task it evolved to do: reading subtle social cues and making snap judgments about potential threats or potential rewards. The trick is that I have learned to heed those signals, instead of overriding them with pure logic.

But what's interesting is that the same skills that help me excel at the poker table are the very ones that are capable of revolutionizing our relationships. Learning to read and control your nervous system — to know when your nervous system is signaling danger and signaling safety, and how to pendulate between these two states — is perhaps the single most important skill that you can master for both poker and life.

The Body's Early Warning System

Think of your nervous system as essentially an early warning system that keeps you alive. It's continually scanning both the environment outside you and the interior landscape of your own mind, in search not of meaning, but of whatever might concern the possibility of danger or opportunity. And it's doing this mostly beyond your conscious awareness.

This system developed over millions of years to help our ancestors survive in a world where they were under constant threat, but it was a world in which the primary threats were physical ones; a menacing stranger, a dangerous animal or a natural disaster. It wasn't made for the intricacies of the social and psychological threats that we face today — criticism from a partner, cold shoulder in a meeting, the subtle power politics of modern times.

But it reacts to those social threats with the same urgency as if they were life-threatening, because to the ancient brain, social rejection really was dangerous. Being expelled from your tribe 100,000 years ago usually meant death. Your nervous system takes the threat of being rejected or humiliated or abandoned as seriously as it would take a physical threat.

Most of us have never been taught to identify, understand, or work with these nervous system reactions, the problem is another that besieges: We do not have any idea how to recognize, understand or work with the nervous system responses. We've been trained to value our thinking mind over bodily sensations and emotions that we may find "irrational," to be "rational," to dismiss or overrule them — you ignore feelings in order to act in the world, because you don't want them dictating to you.

But recent findings from neuroscience, and particularly from the work of Dr. Stephen Porges on polyvagal theory, have shown that this is the wrong way to look at it. It's not your nervous system response that is irrational — they are pre-rational. They occur before your reasoning mind, based on patterns laid down by evolution and by your own experience.

Realizing this can be very liberating.

It means that when you react negatively, that doesn't mean you lack character or strength — it means that these are normal physiological responses to perceived threats. It means you're not broken; your body is functioning just as it's meant to. They're just doing it in a world utterly different from the one they evolved for, following patterns that served in those other times of truly real threat or trauma.

Neuroception: Your Subconscious Brain as a Looming Sensory Perception Factory

Dr. Porges invented the term "neuroception" to explain how your nervous system — without any input from your conscious brain — can detect risk in someone else's facial expressions. Whereas perception is a conscious and deliberate process of recognizing sensory signals, neuroception is an automatic, unconscious process.

Your nervous system is always asking three basic questions:

Am I safe?

Can I connect?

Do I need to defend myself?

The responses to those questions decide which branch of your autonomic nervous system gets turned on:

<u>Ventral vagal (social engagement):</u> When your "neuroception" senses safety, the ventral vagal system kicks in, allowing for connection, calm, curiosity and compassion. This is your "rest and digest" or "tend and befriend" state.

<u>Sympathetic (mobilization):</u> If you perceive challenge or threat (through your neuroception), your sympathetic system turns on your readiness for action — fight or flight. This is your "action" state.

Dorsal vagal (immobilization): If your neuroception identifies that you are truly, direly at risk or that there is no way out, your dorsal vagal inhibits — the body giving way to the shutdown, collapse or dissociation. This is your "freeze" state.

These transitions occur without your being all that conscious of them, or exercising much control over them. You don't consciously decide to jump into fight mode when someone insults you or freeze mode when you are swamped with emotional stress — your nervous system does this automatically, based on neuroception.

And here's the critical bit: Your neuroception detected not only what's happening now. It's reading the present through the past, particularly a painful past. If criticism from your partner evokes memories of criticism from an abusive parent, your nervous system will respond as though you're under threat even if you're not — for example: you're probably in no immediate danger if your partner critiques your outfit.

That's why you may find yourself reacting far out of proportion for a variety of situations — why a little argument might make you snap into full fight-or-flight response, or why a raised voice may send you into shutdown. Your nervous system is reacting not only to what happens right now, but also what is echoes from the past.

The Nervous System and the Poker Face

In poker, we speak of a good "poker face": the ability to conceal your reaction so that your opponents cannot see whether you have a strong hand or a weak one. But what many people don't understand is that a great poker face isn't just about hiding facial expressions.

It comes down to controlling your entire nervous system.

I am acutely aware when it's happening, and I can already feel my sympathetic nervous system kick in when I am dealt a monster hand — like pocket aces or kings. My heart beats faster, my pupils expand, my breathing shifts.

They are involuntary expressions of positive emotion and are automatic, but they are also "tells" that a paying-attention-opponent might notice.

Conversely, when I'm bluffing with a losing hand, my nervous system could tilt toward dorsal vagal activation — a quiet freeze response to the social threat of being found in a lie. My breathing might grow shallow, my skin a little cooler, my posture a little stiffer.

The true consistent winners are those who are not only able to calculate odds and read an opponent, but also can regulate their nervous systems when the stakes are high. I have come back from having only one chip left in our poker tournament and won, on two separate occasions. Numerous times, I have come from behind playing against others who had stacks and stacks of chips, and won.

A good, consistent poker player can keep their ventral vagal state (i.e., remaining calm and thinking clearly while engaging socially) even when they are making a big decision or their chip stack is threatened.

That very skill — regulating the nervous system under pressure — is what makes the difference between whether a conflict between you and your partner turns into a fight or is worked out in a constructive way. It's what decides whether work criticism makes you defensive or enables you to offer a thoughtful response. It's what decides whether you can be present during a difficult conversation or have to dissociate to protect yourself.

The Scattered Life: Why We Can't Make Sense of the Signals

In our contemporary era, we are more disconnected from our bodies and nervous systems than ever before. This disconnection is due to a number of factors:

Digital distraction: The average American checks his or her phone **96 times a day** — that's **once every 10 minutes**. Every check pulls us out of our bodies and into a virtual world, distracting us from the gradual course change of our nervous system.

- Chronic busyness: While we're obsessively moving from task to task, we're closing our minds to the sensations and emotional shifts that occur in our bodies. We value productivity over physical presence.
- Information overload: We are digesting more information in a day than our forebears did in an entire lifetime. This new cognitive load has little room to spare for monitoring *inner life.*
- Comfort junkies: Modern conveniences allow us to prevent discomfort in ways our ancestors could not. We can adjust our temperature as we need, eat when we're hungry, distract ourselves from boredom or loneliness. That diminishes our tolerance for discomfort and our capacity to learn from it.
- Trauma responses: Some of us have learned to detach from our bodily sensations as a survival mechanism. If getting out of your mind was painful or overwhelming early in life, you might have learned to live from the neck up — in your head rather than your body.
- Cultural messaging: Western culture tends to privilege thinking over feeling, mind over body. We are taught to "be rational," "pull yourself together," not to be "too emotional." These messages teach us to suppress or dismiss our nervous-system signals.

The unfortunate reality is that too many of us are wandering around effectually blind to what our bodies are endeavoring to tell us. We miss the first signs of stress, the subtle hint that a relationship is no longer safe, the inner murmurs telling us we're getting close to the edge. We don't tend to notice until the signals are so loud — in the form of illness, burnout, panic attacks or breakdown of relationships — they cannot be ignored.

I lived this way for decades.

As a result, I was deeply disconnected from my body's signals. I pushed through tiredness, ignored stress warning signals, overrode my intuition about people and situations that felt precarious. I practically lived inside my head, using my thinking and analysis to solve problems while they were all unfolding on the level of my nervous system. It wasn't until I began to see a therapist specializing in trauma who introduced me to somatic, or body-based approaches that I began to rediscover my body's judgment.

What I found was a revelation: my body had been signaling red flags about toxic relationships, toxic work environments, and impending burnout for years. I just hadn't been listening.

In the opening foreword of "The Body Keeps the Score: How Trauma Lives in the Nervous System," psychiatrist Bessel van der Kolk explains an important aspect of the nature of trauma.

While trauma comes in the form of verbal memories, it is predominantly crystallized in the form of physical sensations, affective responses, and habits of behavior. The body memorizes the score of our past, particularly our traumatic, experiences.

Therefore, talk-therapy alone is often insufficient to wholly heal and process trauma: even if you cognitively understand that the trigger stimulates the reaction, the actuation of the nervous system will still orientate the response more often than not to fight/flight/freeze/fawn than reasoned consideration.

Recent developments in neurocognition suggest that trauma actually changes how the brain and the nervous system works.

Disrupting Interoception: Preventing you from accurately feeling and making sense of physical sensations

These shifts aren't psychological in the usual sense — they're physiological. They occur at the level of your nervous system, outside your awareness or control. This is why, these experts explain, sheer willpower is not sufficient to change trauma responses. You can't just make up your mind not to feel triggered, any more than you can decide not to reflexively flinch when something is hurled toward your face.

But — and this is key — these alterations are not permanent. Luckily, by way of neuroplasticity — your brain's inherent capacity to reorganize itself for all of your life by building new neural connections — you can ultimately rewire these behaviors. Your nervous system can learn to feel safe. It can create new, healthier response patterns.

I repeat: it can heal.

The first part is learning to notice what's happening in your nervous system before your conscious mind catches up with it — the early signs of wear and tear that tell you you're entering survival mode.

Reading Your Nervous System: Speaking the Language of Sensation

Your nervous system is based on and communicates almost entirely through sensation – physical feelings in your body. The ability to read those sensations is like a new language, the kind of language that most of us were never taught.

This language includes:

- Tension patterns: Are there any areas of your body that tend to hold tension in stressful situations? These include the mouth, jaw, shoulders, chest, diaphragm, and pelvis both. These tension patterns are frequently a reflection of long-term nervous system (NS) states.
- Energy: Are you energized, depleted, Wired, tired, or a mix of some of these? These states carry information about your autonomic balance.
- Temperature: Are you hot or cold blooded? Do you feel that some parts of your body are warmer than others? Those temperature shifts can reflect nervous system changes.
- Urge to move: What action is your body telling you it wants to take? Advance, retreat, freeze, crumble, reach out? These urges are a product of what your nervous system wants to do.
- Breath rhythm: Are you taking short, frequent breaths or long, slow breaths? Breath is tightly linked to autonomic state and frequently changes before you are consciously aware of a trigger.
- Digestive feelings: Butterflies, knots, a vacuum, or gurgling in your stomach? Your enteric nervous system, ENS (nick-nick name: your "second brain") is very sensitive to threat and safety.
- Sensations in the heart: Is my heart pounding? Racing? Fluttering? Beating steadily? One of the most accurate measures of nervous system condition is heart rate variability.

- Feeling in the throat: Stillness, fullness, or empty? The throat is often a reflection of what you are able to express and connect with in any given moment.
- Facial tension: Does it feel tight in the forehead, around the eyes or the jaw? And facial muscles have a direct line to your social engagement system and are frequently an indication of your ability to connect.

Learning to track these feelings is not a method of analyzing or judging them — it is a method of gaining the capacity to simply notice them with curiosity. Oh, I'm clenching my jaw right now. I wonder what that's about?" "There is that feeling of shallow breathing that I am experiencing. "What could be going on in my nervous system?"

It is this type of inquisitive attention that starts forming a bridge to awareness and the unconscious nervous dynamics. It is suddenly an obvious choice where none existed before but automatic reaction.

The Advantage of the Poker Player - Mastery Over the Nervous System

At the poker table, this superpower to read my own nervous system gives me a huge advantage.

When I find myself getting fluttery inside my chest as I look down at my cards, I know I need to pay attention to my breathing so as not to give away how good my hand is.

When I see the tension coming into my shoulders as someone bets big against me, I can notice that my system is going into defense and make a more conscious decision regarding whether to call or fold.

But the true edge is being able to read the nervous systems of other players.

And yet most people have no idea how much information they're emitting on the basis of tiny bodily phenomena. Even a player who's bluffing may keep a straight poker face, but his or her breathing betrays that tension. The punter with the monster hand, maybe he can look all casual, but his pupils dilate a little bit.

These are the *tells* that they exhibit.

I'm **not** right all the time, of course.

I might get my read of a person's nervous system signals incorrect, or I might misinterpret what I am picking up. That's why, knowing the above, I add to it a dash of calculated odds and strategic thought. It's the combination of these two acts — of bodily wisdom and analysis working together — that makes for a winning strategy.

The same integration is possible in our relationships.

It is not substituting thinking for feeling or analysis for intuition, but in partnership where they inform one another.

Your thinking mind doesn't have the wisdom of your nervous system, and your nervous system doesn't have the capacities of your thinking mind. Working together is how you have access to your full intelligence.

The Poker Table and the Dance of the Nervous System

In poker, I can usually cue into what kind of nervous system state other players are in by watching their betting trends. Other players are stuck in the sympathetic arousal — they are playing too aggressively, betting too impulsively, and having a hard time folding even when the odds are against them.

Others will drop to dorsal vagal under pressure — growing timid, missing bet opportunities with strong hands, or folding too easily to resistance.

The ones who win are the ones who can keep their ventral vagal systems engaged in the face of a challenge — who can stay calm, think clearly and read social cues accurately even while exposed to stress. They're not free from sympathetic activation or dorsal vagal responses, but they are capable of shifting among these states as necessary and returning to ventral vagal when the pressure has passed.

This same flexibility in the nervous system is also the key to our capacity for healthy relationships.

Couples who can notice when they are shifting into the sympathetic or dorsal vagal states, can communicate about these shifts and help each other return to ventral vagal connection have a major leg up. They can also avoid getting stuck in destructive patterns, rebound more quickly from ruptures and stay connected even when times are tough.

Patterns in Relationships Nervous System

Our nervous systems were created in relationship, and they are healed in relationship. Since we were born, our nervous systems are modeled by our encounters with caregivers.

Did they respond to our cries?

Did they mirror our emotions?

Were they there for us, in our distress?

These early experiences lay down the blueprint for how we form adult relationships.

With the people we date as adults, our nervous systems are constantly talking to each other. That occurs through a process known as co-regulation — the way two nervous systems affect and regulate each other by exchanging minute signals such as facial expression, tone of voice, posture and touch.

When this process is working well, partners co-regulate each other's nervous systems, bringing each other back to ventral vagal safety when one is triggered. But when partners both have unhealed trauma or insecure attachment, they can stimulate one another into survival states instead and initiate destructive cycles neither fully comprehends. "When" is a guarantee; it will happen.

Typical neuronic relationships interact as follows:

- Pursue-withdraw: Sympathetic activation of one partner
- Fight-fight: in which both partners enter sympathetic activation, which tends to increase the conflict, with neither feeling heard or understood.
- Freeze-freeze: Both partners collapse into dorsal vagal shutdown, resulting in a withdrawal-based relationship marked with emotional distance, lack of intimacy and refusal to engage in conflict.
- Fawn-dominate: one partner's dorsal vagal fawn response (people-pleasing, self-sacrifice) allows the other's sympathetic dominance, leading to more skewed power dynamics.

These patterns are not consciously chosen — they are <u>automatic</u> nervous system responses that occur between two people whose systems are reading the other's cues, and responding based on past conditioning.

I've seen all of these patterns in my own relationships at some point.

In my previous relationship, it was the pursue-withdraw cycle of an anxious-avoidant relationship (my wife would nit-pick something in me, causing me to freeze up, which in turn caused her to lean in and pursue more, and so on and so on in a cycle that was so unpleasant neither of us understood at the time).

Knowing these patterns doesn't necessarily shift them, but it opens up the possibility of interrupting them. When you notice "Oh, my nervous system is moving into sympathetic arousal and my partner's is moving into dorsal vagal shutdown," then you can start to work with these states instead of acting from them.

4 Reclaiming Your Nervous System: An Introduction to the Work of Interoception

So, where do we start in regaining our relationship with our nervous system?

How do we retrain ourselves to hear what our bodies have been trying to tell us all along?

The secret is to cultivate interoception — the sense that allows you to know and feel what's going on inside your body. Interoception is how you know if you're hungry, thirsty, tired or in pain. It's also how you feel more-subtle states, like tension, activation or shutdown in your nervous system.

Most of us have such a poor sense of internal awareness due to trauma, chronic stress or simply never being taught in a culture that values external more than internal awareness strategies. But interoception can be enhanced and strengthened through regular practice.

Here are some steps that can help:

- Body scanning: Several times throughout the day, take a few minutes to mentally scan through your body from head to toe, focusing on areas and sensations without trying to change them. What is the

- temperature, texture, weight, sensation, movement, or energy in each area?
- Focus on your breath: Just be aware of the breath without attempting to manipulate it. Where are your feeling it in your body? How is the quality of it — deep or shallow, smooth or confined, fast or slow? Directly linked to our autonomic state, the breath has a lot to teach us about our nervous system.
- Emotional location: When you experience an emotion, feel where it is located in your body. Anger might be heat in the chest, anxiety might be some fluttering in the stomach, and joy might be some expansion in the heart area. This ensures that we link emotional awareness with physical sensation.
- Mindful movement: Exercises such as yoga, tai chi, or even simple stretching, done with attention, will help you develop a richer awareness of your body in space and of your inner sensations.
- Pendulation: Observe how your nervous system naturally moves between activation and settling. Once you notice activation (one sign might be an increased heart rate and muscle tension) intentionally notice places on your body where you feel more settled or neutral. This also helps your system realize that not everything is enabled all at once.
- Follow tracking triggers: When you're triggered, stop and acknowledge the sensations you feel when triggered. As you practice over time, you will become aware of your early warning signs before you are completely hijacked by a survival response.

Resourcing: Develop short mental lists of sensations, memories or images that help your nervous system to feel safe and intentionally recall these to mind when you feel activation. This trains your system to recognize that it can go back to safety.

These are not practices of controlling your nervous system — that's neither possible nor necessarily desirable. They're about building a relationship with it, figuring out its language, and making it possible for it to discover how to regulate itself.

The point is not to never become activated empathically or end up in an actual dorsal vagal state — these are normal responses and appropriate sometimes, when there's real threat. The idea is to cultivate enough awareness and flexibility so that you're not trapped in these states when they are not serving you.

The Poker Player's Practice: Interoception at the Table

My poker game improved dramatically when I began to utilize these interoception practices on the table.

I take a moment to check in with my body before I try to make any big decisions. What am I feeling in my gut? What's going on with my breathing? Is there stress anywhere that might indicate fear or excitement?

This short check-in allows me to separate intuition ("something feels off about this bet") from fear ("I'm scared to lose"). It also enables me to notice when I'm tilting — when emotions from a prior hand are affecting my present decision-making. It can only help me stay grounded when up against a big bluff and when pondering whether to make one.

But more importantly still, it's a way for me to maintain access to my ventral vagal state—the open, connected, socially-state in which I can think forward, read players accurately, and make decisions from the whole spectrum of data available to myself, not from the pull of fight, flight or freeze.

The technique is one that you can use to be successful within relationships, too.

Pausing to do a cursory body scan before responding to an upsetting text message, or throughout a challenging conversation, helps me catch myself, as I shift into survival mode. This consciousness sets up the possibility of choice — of making conscious responses rather than automatic reactions based on past habits.

Creating Space for Awareness of the Nervous System in a World of Distractions

To cultivate this kind of nervous system awareness, we need something that is becoming more and more rare in our modern world: space. Gap between stimulus and response. Space between activities. Space to just be with what is, without instantaneously trying to fix, alter or escape what it is.

Building that room in a world designed to harvest and monetize your attention is a radical act. It involves deliberate decisions that may fly in the face of things our increasingly material culture prizes and encourages. Here are some habits which could help:

Digital fences: Set specific times when you are off limits to digital distraction. This could entail no phones at meals, no screens for the first or last hour of the day, or setting a consistent digital sabbatical, where you disconnect entirely for a day or weekend.

- Transition rituals: Develop small rituals to help you transition between activities — take three mindful breaths before you enter your home, have a moment of silence before you start your car, a 30-second stretch before you sit down at your desk. These pauses give your nervous system (and circulation) time to register the change and reset.
- Check in regularly: Schedule alarms to sound off throughout the day and check in with and become aware of what state your nervous system

is in. What sensations are present? Where are you—ventral vagal, sympathetic, or dorsal vagal? There's nothing to do, nothing to shift, just observe.

- Nature time: Exposure to the natural environment has been demonstrated to facilitate regulation of the nervous system. The stimuli of nature cue the parasympathetic pathways socially, taking us out of sympathetic activation and into more ventral vagal states.

- Moving: Regular activity helps discharge extra sympathetic energy and stops tension from just building up, leading to dorsal vagal collapse. Even short movement breaks can contribute to nervous system flexibility.

- Sensory consciousness: Actively use your senses throughout the day. What is it you see, hear, smell, taste, and feel at this very moment? This engages you in present-moment consciousness and will pull you out of rumination, which is a common initiator of dysregulation.

- Allow yourself to feel: When emotions crop up, allow yourself to feel them instead of instantly trying to change, fix or escape them. Emotions are messages from your nervous system and learning to listen to them is part of learning how to listen to your body's wisdom.

The point is not to become perfect, peaceful and perpetually untriggered. They're about creating a different relationship with your nervous system —one based on listening, rather than overriding, on cooperation, not coercion.

The body knows: Trusting the Nervous System

As you cultivate more awareness to your nervous system, you'll also start to see something surprising: Your body often has a sense of what you need before your thinking brain does.

Your nervous system has wisdom that your conscious thinking mind may not always have access to.

This wisdom manifests in various ways:

- Gut feelings about people: You know that unshakable certainty someone just ain't safe even if they're saying and doing all the right things.
- Physical resistance to situations: The heavy or closed feeling you get when thinking about a choice that doesn't align with your deeper values.
- Spontaneous relaxation: The way your body will just release and settle when you make a choice that is right for you, even when hard.
- Energy shifts: The sudden spike of energy and motivation when you are doing something that benefits your growth.
- Messages from your dreams: The symbolic messages sent to you from your unconscious, often containing ideas or wisdom your conscious mind hasn't grasped.
- Synchronicities: Quick Signposts may be meaningful coincidences that lead you in a direction or away from one.

Trusting in this body wisdom isn't always something that comes easy, particularly if you've been taught to overrule it or been through trauma that may have interfered with your connection to it. But with some practice, you can learn to start accessing this intrinsic guidance system.

That is not to say that we should listen to every urge or sensation blindly. It means using your rational mind and intellectual thought processes in partnership with your body wisdom rather than in conflict with it. It's taking a moment to ask yourself, "What is this sensation trying to tell me?" as opposed to "How do I get rid of this unpleasant feeling?"

For me personally, learning to trust the wisdom of my nervous system has been life-changing. It's enabled me to make better decisions about relationships, work and self-care. It has helped me to realize when I'm heading toward burnout and to notice it before I actually get there.

It's helped me figure out which people and places nourish my healing and which ones don't.

Most importantly, it's got me to cultivate a new relationship with myself — one of listening and teamwork instead of control and override. Rather than fighting my trauma responses, I've found ways to see them as data from a system doing its best to keep me safe.

The Poker Player's Wisdom: Knowing When to Hold 'Em and When to Fold 'Em

In poker as in life, there's a fine line between trusting your gut and making an informed decision. And sometimes the odds are one thing and my gut is another. I know from experience when to believe each of the information sources.

If the numbers say it's a virtual certainty that something is the right play, but the warning lights on my nervous system are flashing, I've become adept at pausing to look further. Occasionally I will be sensing tells from an opponent in ways that I'm not conscious of.

In other instances, my own nerves may be responding to patterns from hands long gone instead of to the reality of the moment.

The solution then, is not to treat one type of knowledge as always already superseding the other, but to make the two debatable. "The math says that I should call here, but my intuition says fold."

"What could be my nervous system responding to that my computations are not picking up on?"

And this is the same approach that serves us in relationships.

When a person looks good on paper, but my body is telling me that the energy is off, I have trained myself to take that seriously. And if, on the other hand, my nervous system is beginning to freak out in the presence of someone who is objectively safe, I might investigate what past patterns are being reactivated rather than take the alarm personally.

The point isn't that you should always trust your gut over your head or your head over your gut. It's to animate a partnership among these multiple kinds of intelligence that they may inform and interact in a mutual way.

Reflective and Practice Exercises

When was the last time you sensed your nervous system reacting to something before you even knew what was happening? What sensations did you feel?

Which of the three states of the nervous system, ventral vagal (safety), sympathetic (danger) and dorsal vagal (life threat), are you most frequently in? What does this mean for your relationships and your everyday life?

What activities bring you closer to your body and nervous system? What prevents this of alignment?

Can you recognize patterns in your relationships where your nervous system, and your partner's, appear to prompt one another predictably?

How would your life be different if you trusted more fully the wisdom of your nervous system? What would you do in a different way? What might you stop doing?

What could you do to make nervous system awareness more space in your day? Over the next two weeks, what would be one finite small step you could do?

What is a time when your body tried to tell you something important, and you ignored it? What happened as a result? What could you have done if you had listened?

Back to the Man in the Coffee Shop

So, you may have been wondering: whatever happened with the man you met in the coffee shop? I'm so glad you remembered! After he finished his phone call, I leaned in and said, "I didn't mean to eavesdrop on your conversation…but it sounded like you had to have a hard conversation with someone."

"Aww yeah – I had to show a little 'tough love' with one of my kids" – he replied.

"I get that!" – I said.

We chatted for a few minutes and exchanged pleasantries.

For too many years prior, I would have likely exited the scene while he was on the phone. This was an excellent opportunity for me to work at rewiring my nervous system in the moment, and I was glad I took advantage of the opportunity to do so.

Keep in mind that it is a practice – not a destination – to become aware of your nervous system. It's a process of slowly reattaching to a connection that may have been severed due to trauma, cultural conditioning or just the speed and demands of modern life.

You'll need to be patient with yourself.

This nervous system that you have, it has been growing over the entirety of your life — it takes time to reconfigure your relationship with it.

The next chapter will cover specific methods for dealing with the fight response – change your fight from shielding carapace into a wolfish howling strength. But in the meantime, I'd invite you to just start observing.

Notice what's happening in your body as you read these words.

Pay attention to your nervous system throughout your day; take notice of how you respond to different people, environments and situations.

Have that *observation time* rather than trying to fix or change it right away.

The sentence is the foundation of all that is to come. It's a step that will open the door to a new kind of relationship between you and yourself — one based on listening to the wisdom your body has been trying to communicate all along.

CHAPTER SIXTEEN

REWIRING YOUR NERVOUS SYSTEM

FROM SURVIVAL TO SAFETY

The first taste of what it means to re-wire my nervous system: I can still remember when it happened. I was in my therapist's office explaining the latest blowup. I'd been seeing someone for a couple of months, and it was going nicely…until she canceled our plans last minute – for the third time in two weeks.

I completely lost it.

Not on the outside, but inside; I was in attack mode.

I had a million thoughts going through my head, accusing and assuming. I got that heat in my chest again, the jaw clenching and the narrowing of vision. That night, I broke up with her via text, assuming she didn't respect me and was probably seeing someone else.

My therapist listened, absorbing it, and then said a asked a simple question: "What happened to you in your body when she canceled?"

I began to explain my reasoning — all the reasons why it was O. K. for me to be angry right then — but she gently steered me off-course. "Not what you thought. What you felt…in your body?"

I realized I had no idea. I had been so swept up in the story my mind was narrating that I had entirely missed the sensations that preceded the thoughts.

And when I came up for air and slowed down and thought about it, well, I understood that my response was not really about this woman. The physical sensations I experienced when she canceled — the rejection sensation in my gut, the constriction in my throat, the mild dizziness — were the same as what I'd felt as a child when my mother said she'd come and pick me up for visitation and then didn't.

My nervous system was reacting to an original, familiar threat pattern. It was not distinguishing between my girlfriend canceling dinner and my mother abandoning me emotionally. To my nervous system, the pattern was the same: someone important was not showing up when they said they would.

Danger.

Protect yourself.

That was the start of a different kind of relationship with my nervous system. Not a quick fix — I was going to continue to overreact to perceived abandonment by others for years to come before I could even get a handle on it — but the beginning of understanding that the way I reacted to negative stimuli wasn't the result of some character flaw that proved I was broken beyond salvation. They were ordinary physiological reactions to perceived dangers ingrained deep in me.

And if these responses were not simply psychological, but also physiological, that meant they could be altered by physiological mechanisms. My nervous system could learn new ways. It could be rewired.

This is what that rewiring looks like — how you can help your nervous system go from a default that's just survival mode on repeat, to something more permeable, something that has a chance at (contingent, unreliable, necessary) safety. This isn't about getting rid of your survival responses; those are vital and can be incredibly useful when there actually is a legitimate threat! It's about having more choice in how you respond, increasing your capacity to remain present even when you are triggered, and learning how to return more rapidly to safety when you do get activated.

"The Brain that Changes Itself" vs. The Fixed or Malleable Brain: You've Got the Capacity to Change

For decades, scientists believed that the adult brain was a relatively fixed organ, and that when it reached it peak of growth around age 25, you couldn't change its structure or function for the better. We now know this isn't true.

Because of neuroplasticity — your brain's ability to reorganize itself by forming new neural connections — you can shape the structure of your nervous system at any age.

This doesn't mean it's easy.

Whichever footsteps you've taken over decades have beaten down a path that's as hard to leave as it is to hike right back in there: Your neural pathways are like well-trodden trails through a forest — the routes your brain takes because it's the easiest path and requires the least energy.

New trails have to be blazed day after day. Think of these neural pathways…these "trails" as a path in the snow: the more you walk the same path the more pronounced it becomes. You can rewire, and learning how neuroplasticity operates may allow you to go about this rewiring process with some extra patience and self-compassion.

Below are some of the fundamental principles of neuroplasticity that matter when you are looking to rewire your nervous system:

Neurons that fire together wire together: Two neurons that fire simultaneously form a stronger connection. That's how all learning occurs, including emotional learning. Your brain will be more likely to form a stronger connection between those situations and your fear response if you continue to feel fear in a particular set of situations. But you can also forge new links by experiencing safety over and over again.

Use it or lose it: Neural pathways that are not frequently used grow weaker. That's why staying away from triggers feels safer in the short term but doesn't help rewire your responses in the long term. Exposure to triggers at a slower pace is done in a regulated environment which is why it's beneficial as it creates new pathways in the brain.

The stronger the experience, the more we encode and retain. This is also, however, precisely why trauma has such a lasting and powerful effect on the nervous system: because the experience is so intense it is easy to trigger the same neural pathways in the future. But the positive can also be reinforced to become strong through mindful attention, which helps reinforce new, healthier pathways.

New fosters plasticity: The new (new experience) finds the plastic (brain) appealing. That is why travel, the acquisition of new skills or even just shaking up your normal routine can help disrupt settled habits. The new paths toward old triggers can help develop new neural responses.

Sleep consolidates learning: Your brain processes and consolidates new learning, including emotional learning, while you sleep. Good sleep hygiene comes first in enabling the brain to rewire itself. I've said in an earlier chapter, I had a lot more sleep time after I left my last marriage – and it was definitely beneficial to my need to learn, re-learn, unlearn, and heal.

Stress is anti-plastic: Chronic stress impairs neuroplasticity by flooding the brain with cortisol, which disrupts formation of new neural connections. Being able to manage stress is an important part of the rewiring.

Age influences the speed though not the chance of change — the younger the brain, the more plastic it is — but adult brains cannot only change, they are constantly remodeling themselves, throughout the course of life. It might take longer as you get older, but you're never too old to rewire your nervous system.

Knowing the principles can shed light on why shifting ingrained trauma responses is not as easy as deciding to respond differently.

You're literally rewiring neural pathways that have been heavily fortified over years or decades.

It takes time, lots of repetition and usually support from others.

But it also accounts for why change can nevertheless occur, even in the face of generations of being stuck in old survival patterns. You have a plastic brain all your life.

With the correct techniques, you could lay those new neural pathways down to support safety, connection and choice rather than automatic survival reactions.

The Window of Tolerance: Where your Nervous System is Happy

One of the handiest ideas in the world to make sense of how your nervous system is regulated is the "Window of Tolerance," coined by psychiatrist Dr. Dan Siegel.

This is the zone where we aren't too activated, (sympathetic) or too shut down (dorsal vagal). Inside your window of tolerance, you can think clearly, feel your emotions without losing control over them, relate to other people, and deal with whatever challenge comes your way.

When you are outside your window — whether over-aroused (anxious, angry, panicky) or under-aroused (dull, numb, shut down) — your rational brain, emotional brain and social brain are barely connecting at all. You're in survival mode, and under such duress you can't rely on the part of your brain that thinks at the highest level — your prefrontal cortex, which takes care of your planning, decision-making, impulse control and empathy.

Traumatized individuals tend to operate with a more restricted window of tolerance. It takes them less to push them into hyper- or hypo-arousal, and they remain within these states for longer periods. This isn't some character weakness or flaw — it is a natural adaptation to environments where threat was all too common, or inescapable.

The good news is you can increase your window through practice. That's not to say you'll never be triggered, or activated — you will — along with everyone else. But it does mean you can:

- Allow yourself to stay regulated while in contexts that would previously have caused "dysregulation"
- Catching on earlier when you begin to drift from your window
- Return to your window faster when you do get triggered
- Tap into even more of your subconscious assets when partially activated

Expanding your window of tolerance is one of the main aspirations for nervous system re-wire. It offers greater flexibility and capacity to respond to challenges, to remain present in the tough moments of life, and to keep connection even amid conflict or stress.

The Poker Player's Window: Getting in The Zone Under Pressure

On the poker table I've seen my performance be directly tied to my window of tolerance.

When I'm inside my window — alert but calm, engaged but not overinvested in outcomes — I make the best decisions. I'm a good player, can keep odds in my head; I am a great reading-player, and can think under pressure.

But, when I go outside my window, due to a bad beat (a loss on a hand that I statistically should have won), a run of terrible cards or sometimes things that have nothing to do with the game, it becomes immediately evident I am playing at far less than my best.

If I slip into hyper-arousal and start playing over-aggressively, I could end up making poor decisions, betting or calling when I do not have the odds. When I do drift into hypo-arousal I tend to play too passively, not betting when I should with my strong hands or giving up too easily to aggression.

What's interesting is that I see this exact pattern play through all of my previous relationships. When I remain inside my window of tolerance, I'm able to listen to criticism without immediately becoming defensive. I can say what I need or what I'm uncomfortable with without being aggressive. During conflicts, I can maintain a connection with my partner.

But – when I am pushed out my window — by the sound of someone's voice that sounds like it belonged to my father, by a perceived rejection that harks back to getting left as a child, by accumulated stress that has nothing to do with my relationship — my ability to be healthily connected dramatically drops. Fight (get critical, defensive, controlling) or flight (emotional withdrawal, avoiding difficult conversations) or freeze (getting numb, dissociating, shutting down).

Learning how to expand my window of tolerance has changed my experience at the poker table and in my relationships. It's afforded me more choice in how I respond to triggers, as well as more capacity to stay present during difficulty, and more ease in repairing quickly when I do get dysregulated.

Practical Methods to Regulate the Nervous System

So how do you actually rewire your nervous system? How do you widen that window of tolerance and increase flexibility in your responses? Here are some practical strategies that are evidence-based and which I have found useful in my own recovery:

Bottom-Up Regulation: What the Body Can Do for Us

Conventional talk therapy works from the top down, with cognitive understanding dictating emotional reaction. This can do good, yet with nervous

System dysregulation due to trauma, bottom-up approaches that begin with the body are often more effective. These include:

- Breathwork: Your breath is so wired up to your autonomic nervous system and it is a powerful way to help regulate. Lengthening your exhale stimulates your parasympathetic nervous system, which promotes relaxation in response to sympathetic arousal. Practices like box breathing (inhale for 4, hold for 4, exhale for 6, hold for 2) or basic 4-7-8 breathing (inhale for 4, hold for 7, exhale for 8) can help regulate your system when you're activated, as Ms. Barabara Frederickson has taught.
- Exercise: Getting exercise is helpful for burning off extra energy from sympathetic dominance and keep from shutting down the dorsal vagal. This doesn't necessarily need to be high-octane physical activity, such as a brisk evening walk or a vigorous vinyasa yoga class; even some gentle stretching or simply shaking your hands and arms can help get energy flowing through your system. Notice what kind of movement your body may be asking for — sometimes it requires vigorous activity to dissipate energy, sometimes it needs slow, gentle movement to feel safe.
- Cold exposure: Brief exposure to cold — via cold showers or splashing your face with cold water, while holding your breath, or holding ice — activates the vagus nerve, and might help move you out of sympathetic arousal. This is mediated by the mammalian diving reflex, with instantaneous and parasympathetic response.
- Weighted: A frequently heard term in the autism community, weighted goods like blankets and vests or even something as simple as pressure from a heavy object on the person's body can engage the individual's parasympathetic nervous system as it activates deep pressure

stimulation. This can be particularly helpful when trying to shift out of bursting or supporting regulation with stress.
- Rhythm and sound: Drumming, dancing to music with a good beat or even just tapping your hands on your legs can get your nervous system in order. Some sound frequencies, especially those inherent in nature or certain forms of music, may also aid in regulation. If you don't believe this works, ask Danny Carey – the drummer for the band, Tool.
- Sensory grounding: Using your sensory faculties can help bring you back to the present moment when you're triggered into past trauma responses. The 5-4-3-2-1 method involves listing: 5 things you can see, 4 things you can touch, 3 things you can hear, 2 things you can smell, and 1 thing you can taste.
- Bilateral stimulation: When alternating the left and right sides of the body is stimulated (through activities like walking, tapping, or even eye movements), the left and right hemispheres of the brain integrate and the intensity of traumatic memories or triggers can be decreased. It's one reason EMDR (Eye Movement Desensitization and Reprocessing) therapy works.

These bottom-up approaches go straight to your physiology instead of attempting to think your way out of dysregulation. They can be particularly useful when you are too activated for cognitive approaches to work.

Window of tolerance and not overworking yourself into overwhelm

This involves:

- Pendulation: Shifting attention back and forth between activation (in areas of pain, discomfort, or distress in your body) and resource (areas that feel neutral, or even nice). This helps train your nervous system

that it has the capacity to move between activation and regulation rather than getting stuck in one or the other.
- Micro-movements: Engaging in extremely small movement toward a trigger of dysregulation, staying regulated, then pulling back before dysregulation would occur. And along the way, this helps increase the ways that you can cope with a trigger within your window of tolerance.
- Desensitization: Gradual exposure in a controlled, supported way, over time subjecting yourself to increasingly triggering kinds of exposures. This helps your nervous system learn new reactions to old triggers.
- Pausing and monitoring: Taking a look at how activated you are, and taking steps to reduce that level of activation before you get overwhelmed. This aids in developing your ability to know early when your system is breaking down.

Finding this balance usually takes a lot of guidance from a competent therapist, especially when working with heavy-duty trauma. But you can apply the principles of titration to daily life by becoming aware of when you're starting to get activated and making small shifts to support regulation while still addressing the challenge in front of you.

Co-Regulation: Relationship as the Place of Healing

Our nervous systems evolved in relationship and heal in relationship. One way trauma responses are rewired is through co-regulation, when one person's regulated nervous system helps another regulate. This can happen through:

- Safe physical presence: Just being in the physical presence of someone whose autonomic nervous system is regulated can help regulate your
-

system as well, since we unconsciously mirror each other's breathing, heart rate and other physiological cues.
- Touch: Safe touch in appropriate and welcome circumstances — holding hands, hugging, a hand on the shoulder — can stimulate the parasympathetic nervous system by releasing oxytocin and other calming neurotransmitters. A pad on the back helps us at times!
- Vocal tone: A gentle, warm vocal tone can signal safety to the nervous system, whether the content is soothing or not. It's why the "how" of something is usually more important than the what, when someone is dysregulated.
- Facial expression: We read others' expression through motor neurons and respond automatically to them. A relaxed, open facial expression from another person can help communicate safety to your nervous system.
- Attunement: If someone can accurately reflect your feelings without getting dysregulated themselves, it helps your nervous system learn to manage your emotions and tells you that you are not alone with them.
- Relationship rupture and repair: When there is a rupture in our relationship caused by conflict or disconnection followed by a return to connection and resolution, this helps your nervous system organize around the belief that you can have conflicts, moments of disconnection and then return safely to the relationship ultimately strengthening the bond and come to believe that it can tolerate stress.

Co-regulation is not about relying on others to regulate your emotions for you. It is about using the social engagement system — the most evolved part of your autonomic nervous system — to assist you in self-regulation. With practice over time, co-regulatory experiences will help you build stronger self-regulatory resources.

This is why healing from trauma is so very hard to do all by yourself. It is in experiences of safety and connection with others that we can rewire patterns that were established in relationship. By "connection" – I don't necessarily mean a person we seek out for a romantic relationship: co-regulation can occur with friends, family members, therapists, support groups — even with pets. The point is that there is something real that makes your nervous system feel safe.

Cognitive Responses: Reframing the Story

Bottom-up strategies are typically much more effective at initial regulation, but cognitive-based strategies can assist in maintaining regulation and constructing new meaning of those experiences.

These include:

- Cognitive Reframing: Finding your negative thoughts and beliefs that are contributing to your dysregulation and challenge them. For instance, refocusing "I'm broken" to "My nervous system is doing what it learned to do to keep me safe."
- Psychoeducation: Gaining understanding of how trauma impacts the brain and nervous system. When you understand the neural basis for your reactions, shame and self-blame fall, and self-compassion rises.
- Story work: Constructing a narrative of what happened to you that is understandable, and both recognizes how hard it was and how strong you are to have made it out of that. This assists in piecing together dissociated traumatic memories and integrating them with an enhanced self-narrative.
- Parts work: Understanding that various "parts" of you may have different trauma responses, and learning how to collaborate with these

parts rather than battle against them. Approaches like, *Internal Family Systems* therapy give a structure for this sort of work.
- Redefining: Making sense or finding purpose in your experiences, not in the sense that trauma was "meant to happen," but in recognizing how you grown or what you learned as a result of your healing journey.

These cognitive strategies are most effective when used in concert with the bottom-up, somatic approaches rather than in place of them. Uniting an intellectual grasp with a physical experience is what alters the wiring of your nervous system.

The Poker Player's Regulation Toolkit

At the poker table, I've created a toolbox of my own personal regulations that allow me to have maintained access to my ventral vagal even when the pressure is on. In preparation for a tournament, I'm always sure to:

- Put my body in check: I sleep a lot, eat well. I don't drink alcohol, so this helps. When you've got a body that discombobulates itself, nervous system regulation is more difficult.
- I arrive early: The rush to head to a game triggers sympathetic activation before it even begins. Having ample time to arrive allows my nervous system to calm down. I typically (take a guess) sit down at the cigar lounge where the game is happening, and arrive an hour or so beforehand to relax and get myself into the right mental frame.
- I set intentions early in the day: I remind myself whether I am playing (for challenge, enjoyment, etc., not just to win) and set intentions around how I want to play the game, regardless of the outcome. My buddies will likely tell you: "Phillip is there to win."

In the course of play, I employ these same regulatory mechanisms:

- Breathing: I consistently monitor my breathing especially after a big hand (won or lost). If I realize it's shallow or fast, I take a few deliberate, deeper breaths with longer exhales. Arguably for you, non-smokers, cigar smoking takes an active role since it involves a lot of deep breathing.
- Getting Grounded: I will notice the sensation of the floor under my feet, and my chair beneath my sitting bones. This serves to ground me in the present rather than becoming entangled in thoughts of a past hand or future result.
- Micro-breaks: After hands, I take short mental breaks—look away from the table, focus on something non-meaningful, or even close my eyes for a fleeting moment. These tiny breaks can stave off mounting tension.
- Hydration: I'm constantly sipping on water. Dehydration may mimic or compound sympathetic surge.
- Movement: If I'm not currently involved in a hand, I'll stretch my fingers, rotate my shoulders, or find a way to do something that will prevent me from becoming tense.

If I see I'm getting dysregulated—either too activated after a bad beat, or shut down after a string of poor cards—I use specific reset practices:

- Take a walk: I'll get up, do a quick walk around, or sometimes I'll go to the bathroom if I feel like I need to reset, even to the point that sometimes my fellow players fold my hand if I'm away from the table. They think they know what I'm doing in the bathroom! (LOL)

- Hand warming: If I find that my hands are cold (a sign of sympathetic activation), I warm them under hot water in the bathroom.
- Bilateral tapping: This is a clandestine one under the table, but I'll tap on my left and right legs alternately to help regulate my nervous system. Often times, I'm wearing earpods and listening to music.

These same regulatory tools are the ones that allow me to do well in relationships. When I notice my alarm going off during a challenging conversation, I can use some of these same techniques — feeling my feet on the floor, extending my exhale, perhaps taking a break if I need to — in order to help myself stay accessible to my well-regulated ventral vagal state, where clear thinking and connection are available to me.

The point isn't to never get activated — it's to gain enough awareness and skill to notice activation in the very first instance so that you can take steps to regulate before you get fully hijacked by a survival system.

Grounding Yourself in Your Body: A Daily Ritual

Rewiring your nervous system isn't something you do once and then you're all fixed. It's this continual practice of being able to create safety in your body day to day, moment to moment. Here's a framework for a daily practice that can help support this rewiring process:

- Morning: Set the Tone
- Body scan: Spend a few minutes when you wake up each day scanning your body. Notice any physical tightness, activation or lack of sensation without trying to do anything about it. Tracking your nervous system throughout the day; your baseline is affecting how you experience any given moment.

- Conscious breathing: Start your day with a few minutes of intentional breathing — perhaps lengthening your exhale, breathing into your belly, or whatever pattern helps your particular system feel regulated.
- Movement: Incorporate some kind of movement that contributes to your body feeling alive and integrated — stretching, yoga, walking, and, for example, more vigorous exercise if that works for your system.
- Intention: Decide how you want to relate to the nervous system today. This can be something as basic as "I plan to pay attention to when I'm getting activated" or "I plan to stop before reacting when triggered."

Creating Safety: The Essential Element of Healing Relationships

While individual practices are vital, so many of our oldest nervous system patterns were developed in relationship and can only fully heal **in relationship**. You cannot stay in your own bubble. Building safety and a sense of safety in your relationships — with new partners, friends or family members and, yes, even a new therapist or "helper," are all integral to the rewiring process.

Here are some rules for establishing relational safety:

- Name the patterns: Name the nervous system patterns you observe with trusted others in your system. "I realize I kind of close down a little when your voice gets raised" or "I can feel my fight response coming online with criticism." This naming opens the door for unconscious patterns and forces into conscious awareness so that they can be engaged and worked with.
- Co-create a safety "signal": Create a common language or signal that will help you and your loved ones identify when one of you is starting to become dysregulated. That word, gesture or phrase could be

something that says "I'm getting activated" without softening, blaming or judging.
- Honor nervous system needs: Understand that different nervous systems respond well to different levels of stimulation, rest, connection and solitude. This respects those differences instead of taking them personally and sensations like that being "offensive," and contributes to creating safety for various nervous system types.
- Practice co-regulation: Understand what helps each other regulate — that may involve physical touch, verbal reassurance, space or something else — and provide that support when needed and wanted.
- Repair work: Every relationship has ruptures. What is important for the healing of the nervous system is that these ruptures are met with repair—reconnection, understanding and resolution. Repeated repair serves as your nervous system's lesson that things can return to safety after a tough time.
- Create boundaries and adhere to them: Structured consistent boundaries create predictability and therefore safety which in turn support nervous system regulation. Teaching one of your children to respect others boundaries and when to set and maintain their own boundaries, is a very valuable relational safety lesson.
- Slow the pace of interactions: Intentionally slowing the pace of interaction — taking turns speaking; waiting a few seconds before responding; or a brief pause — can help keep the level of interaction from escalating, as well as support regulation.
- Celebrate regulation successes: Recognize and celebrate times that you or your loved ones do successfully in the face of triggers, or come back to regulation after becoming activated. This positive reinforcement aids new neural circuits in developing.

Making a relationship safe does not mean eliminating conflict or distressing emotions. It entails cultivating the climate in which these challenges can be managed without engendering the survival responses that harm attachment. It is about developing relationships that are supportive of regulation instead of persistently evoking dysregulation.

The Journey of Rewiring: Patience, Self-Compassion, Hope

It isn't a quick fix, nor is it a linear progression. It's a long process with gains and losses, moments of breakthrough and of inertia. There has to be a lot of patience, self-compassion and hope.

Patience: Neural connections do not form overnight. Habits that have come to define decades do not vanish overnight. Incremental gains measures over time and beat occasional big bangs every time. Believe in the process and welcome small changes rather than waiting for an overnight transformation.

- Self-compassion: You will get triggered. Old ways will sometimes respond. This is not to say that you're failing, or that the process isn't working. It means you're human and you have a nervous system doing its best to keep you safe from threats it learned about long ago. Treat these occasions with compassion rather than criticism.
- Hope: Your nervous system can change even in old age. No matter how long you've been entrenched in a survival pattern, your brain is still able to create new neural pathways at any stage of your life. And your biology is designed to change. You are not forever defined by what happened to you or how your nervous system learned to handle it.

On my path of needing to rewire my nervous system, I've gone through all the highs and lows that it takes to do that. I have had those breakthrough moments in which I broke an old trigger and felt the freedom of breaking it. There have been heart-breaking slip-ups where I've caught myself responding from that archaic layer, even though there has been all this work, where progress has plateaued and then suddenly catapulted.

And through it all, I've known that this journey is not about achieving some perfect state of permanent regulation where I never get triggered again. It's learning to relate to my nervous system in another way—one of comprehension, partnership, and trust, instead of fear, coercion, or separation.

This changed relationship allows for more distance between stimulus and response, more likely of returning to regulation when I do get activated, more capacity for staying connected to myself and others even in the midst of hard things. It doesn't get me out of the difficulties, but it changes how I navigate them.

And that's, in the end, what freedom looks like — not a life without triggers or hard feelings, but the possibility of choosing the way you respond to them. Not a life free from the challenges, but the ability to face them from regulation, rather than from survival. Not absolute domination over your nervous system, but a partnership with it, honoring both its wisdom as well as its limitations.

You have this freedom – even when you think you were abused and even if you have always lived this way. Your nervous system can learn or relearn how to feel safe. It can cultivate new, healthier response patterns. It can be rewired.

The route to this healing is not always easy or clear. It takes courage to sit with what you've been running from, humility to allow help when you need it, and stamina to stick with it even when the process is slow. But it is possible. And you don't need to do it alone.

In the following chapter, you'll read about strategies to rewire the fight response—opening a channel for its energy to guard your relationships, rather than destroy them. For now, though, I invite you to just hold this possibility: your nervous system can change. You are not your past or your patterns – forever. The good news is that there's a way to more freedom, and you've already started the process of beginning by reading these words and contemplating a different relationship with your nervous system.

Remember, the name of the game isn't perfection. It's progress. Every time you observe the state of your nervous system, every time you take even a small action toward regulation, every time you respond instead of react to a trigger — you're strengthening new neural pathways. All of these little moments add up, and over time they rewire your nervous system to be stronger, more flexible, and better able to make choices.

CHAPTER SEVENTEEN

THE PRACTICE OF PRESENCE

I was in my therapist's office sometime in the fall of 1997 with Dr. Ruffin, talking through another relationship meltdown.

This one began with an instant message (America Online for those of you who never experienced it) from my wife, whom I had married maybe five months before. "I need some space to think about things," she had written.

Eight words. And that's all it took to set me spiraling.

In a matter of seconds, my body was in full fight-flight-freeze mode — racing heart, clenched stomach, spinning catastrophic thoughts. I'd jumped to the conclusion that she was breaking up with me, that I did something wrong, that I was being abandoned all over again. I felt indignant, and returned a defensive text, and then several increasingly desperate ones when she didn't text me back immediately.

I'd already talked myself into the prospect that the marriage could be over by the time she called me the next day over lunch to tell me she'd just needed a night to process a work situation that had turned difficult.

I responded entirely based on the wounds from my past and the idea of "…need some space."

Dr. Ruffin heard my story and then posed a question that would turn everything around:

"Where were you during all this?"

I didn't understand. "At work, at my desk."

"No," he said gently. "Where were you? Not your body. You."

I stared at him blankly.

"Where was your awareness when that text came in and you went into a spin? Did you show up with what was really going on then, or were you ahead of the time and traveling in the future?"

This question gave me pause. But I hadn't actually shown up at all. The second I read the phrase "I need some space," I wasn't at my desk anymore — at least not in my mind. I was in my **childhood home** gain, gripped by the familiar pain of abandonment. I was in my head, back in my first marriage, kind of re-living the moment that my first wife said to me that she was going to leave. I was everywhere but the present moment — where my 2nd wife, who I cared about, was asking for just a little night to herself after a hard day at work.

That's what happens when we don't show up.

We never experience what is really happening now; we only experience what happened then.

Our bodies are responding not to what is happening now, but to past traumas being stirred up.

Our relationships tank not due to the actual words we say or what we do, but from the meaning our trauma-informed nervous systems bring to those words or actions.

This practice of presence — learning to remain all the way here, right now, particularly in response to stressors —is quite possibly the most potent antidote to all four stress responses. It puts a gap between action and reaction, so we can act consciously rather than react automatically. It assists us in telling the difference between actual and previously experienced-type threats. It allows us to see others for who they are, not as projections of our past.

This chapter is about cultivating that practice — not as some grand spiritual ideal, but as a real, minute-by-minute choice that can change your relationships and change your life.

The Time-Traveling Mind: Why We Struggle to Be in the Here and Now

The truth, however, is that most of our time is spent not in the here and now. We are never <u>not</u> time traveling; our minds are perpetually revisiting the past, or projecting into the future. This bias is healthy, and even has an evolutionary advantage. Because reminding ourselves of past dangers is what keeps us safe from similar threats in the future. By thinking forward we can prepare for difficulties before they arrive.

But – for those of us with trauma histories, this kind of mind time-traveling can be extreme, even automatic. Our nervous systems are wired to spot forms that remind us of past threats, and when they do, they project us back into the emotional and physiological state we felt at our most threatened. And this is happening unconsciously and out of our control — all of a sudden, we are adults in the present, and then all of a sudden, we are children again back in the past.

This time travel comes in a few forms:

- Flashbacks: Intense sensory experiences during which it feels like the trauma is being replayed right here, right now. They can be clear-cut, even dramatic. They can also be fine-grained: Sensory flashes and emotional crushes that arise and disappear fast.
- Emotional flashbacks: Sudden feelings of unbearable fear, shame and despair that may last for a few moments or hours. You may be experiencing intense guilt, fear, or anger that feels disproportionate to what's actually happening at the moment.
- Activation of procedural memory: Your body automatically goes into the same defense postures or movement patterns that it used during trauma in the past. You may even react by tensing, freezing, or getting ready to run with no thought at all.
- How you are thinking: Your thoughts will simply go where they automatically went during or after trauma. You are probably engaging in absolute thinking (I am always left in the end), catastrophic thinking (this relationship is over), and personalization (it is all my fault).

These kinds of time travel occur because trauma isn't held in the psyche so much as in the body, not so much as a narrative, coherent memory, but in broken pieces and in sensory sensations, affective states, neurobiological responses.

When something in the present reminds you of something about past trauma — a look on someone's face, a tone of voice, even a looming relationship dynamic — it can trigger those fragments of trauma, putting you into an instant elsewhere in time, pulling you out of present-moment awareness and back to a past that feels like your present, even though it isn't.

That's why it's so hard to stay present, particularly when you face something that triggers you. <u>Your nervous system is designed to keep you safe by noticing patterns that look like old threats.</u> When it finds one, it doesn't need your conscious mind to weigh in — it immediately deploys the survival response that it thinks will keep you safe, based on what has worked for you in the past.

The practice of presence doesn't resist this mechanism — that's pointless. Rather, it partners with you by helping you to notice when you've become drawn into the past and gently escorting you back to the present moment. It teaches your nervous system to discern between then and now, between real threat and echoes of the past.

The Poker Player's Presence: Read the Room, Not the Past

When it comes to poker, it's all about presence. Because if I am thinking about the hand I lost an hour ago, or what's going to happen in the next game, I'm not completely involved in what's going on at the table right now. I don't notice what might have been a subtle "tell" from my opponents, miss vital patterns in the betting, or fail to accurately compute the odds from what's happening at that moment.

The best technically are not necessarily the best winners. They're the ones who are able to keep their presence when they are under pressure — who are able to be "in the now" with what's happening in this hand at this moment, whatever has just happened, whatever other rubbish there is or whatever's going to happen next.

The same sense of presence is why some relationships are healthy and others are unhealthy.

With my partner sitting in front of me, if I'm 100 percent present, I'm responding to who they are now and what they're saying or doing now, not to who my father was or what my ex-wife did or to what I'm scared might happen in the future.

<u>I should be reading the room, not the history books</u>.

This is not to say that we should forget history, or refuse to learn from experience. It means sorting through wisdom from experience and trauma reactions of pattern-matching. It's the ability to say, "This feels reminiscent of a past pain, but it is not the same situation, not the same person who hurt me."

Presence enables us to witness and see the truth of what's actually occurring, as opposed to perceiving the present through the warped lens of past trauma. It provides access for us to choose, rather than react. And it permits us to respond to the person looking us in the eye rather than the ghosts of our past.

The Mindfulness Revolution: Leading Psychologists, Scientists, Artists, and Meditation Teachers on the Power of Mindfulness in Our Lives

The idea of presence, or mindfulness, is not a new one. Practices for training moment-to-moment awareness have been taught in contemplative traditions for thousands of years. What is new is that they are now backed by science and have been incorporated into conventional psychology and trauma treatments.

Recent research has shown that mindfulness practices:

- Decrease amygdala reactivity: Mindfulness practice has been proven to reduce activity in the amygdala (previously mentioned), that center in the brain that serves as its alarm system, thus making you less reactive to potential threats.
- Boost prefrontal cortex functioning: Mindfulness enhances activity in the prefrontal cortex, which is critical to executive functions such as planning, decision-making and impulse control.
- Enhance Interoception: Mindfulness improves your ability to correctly perceive and interpret the body's signals; this is a prerequisite for nervous system regulation.
- Boost heart rate variability: Mindfulness can increase heart rate variability, a measure of autonomic nervous system flexibility and resilience.
- Decrease inflammation: The body is inflamed when you're chronically stressed or traumatized. Mindfulness has also been demonstrated to lower inflammation markers, possibly alleviating physical health effects of trauma.

These results help to elucidate why mindfulness-based practices can be so powerful for trauma recovery and relationship repair. It's not that they're just helping you feel temporarily better — these things are actually rewiring your brain and nervous system, creating lasting shifts in how you even respond to triggers and stressors.

But there's a big fat caveat: traditional mindfulness practices don't always magically work for survivors of trauma, especially in the early stages of healing. Practices of sitting still and focusing inward can be activating or lead to dissociation for those with trauma histories.

This is why we've developed trauma-sensitive mindfulness methods, which we cover later in the chapter.

The Gap Between Stimulus and Response: That's Where Freedom Lives

Viktor Frankl, psychiatrist and Holocaust survivor, replied: "Between stimulus and response, there is a space. Between those spaces lies our ability to choose our response. That's where our growth lies, and our freedom awaits."

This gap between stimulus and response is what presence generates. Without presence it goes like this:

Trigger >> Automatic survival response

With presence it looks like this:

Stimulus → Awareness → Choice → Response in consciousness

That moment of consciousness — the point at which you notice "I'm being triggered right now" — is a space within which choice becomes possible. Not that you won't feel the activation in your body, or the pull toward old patterns. It means that you can feel those sensations and impulses without having an automatic need to act on them.

At first, this space may be only a fraction of a second. You might not even know you were triggered until after you've already reacted. That's okay. Even retrospection is valuable — it allows you to catalogue the idiosyncratic triggers and patterns you will need to learn to change.

Because with practice, that space gets bigger and bigger. Little by little, you find yourself catching yourself earlier in the process — perhaps as you're about to react, rather than after you have. At some point, you may then notice the very early signs of activation, that first whisper of your nervous system dropping into survival mode.

This early awareness provides you the most opportunity for choice.

But even a little is much. Any second during or after a triggered response an insta-have click can alter the course of interaction. It may be the difference between making a conflict worse or better, between undermining trust or supporting it, or between failing to support a new pattern and sustaining an old one.

Trauma-Sensitive Mindfulness: Practices for Safe and Transformative Healing

Traditional mindfulness instructions often focus on sitting still, closing your eyes and bringing your attention inside to observe your thoughts, emotions and sensations. These methods can cause greater activation (or can elicit dissociation) rather than supporting regulation for most individuals who have PTSD.

This is not to say mindfulness isn't effective for trauma recovery — it is, and we have hundreds of studies proving it. It just means the approach has to be modified to work with trauma, not against it. Some principles of trauma-sensitive mindfulness include the following:

- Begin where you are: If sitting still with your eyes closed feels threatening to your nervous system, don't push it. You might start by sitting with open eyes in a posture that feels secure (for example, standing or walking rather than sitting), and with attention directed to external objects rather than internal experience.

- Use anchors: Identify safe anchors that help root you in the here and now — the sensation of your breath moving in your belly or the feel of your body on a chair, or something visually meaningful in your presence. And go back to these anchors whenever you begin to feel overwhelmed.
- Pendulate: Shift your attention between activation (any place in your experience that feels uncomfortable or distressing) and resource (any place that feels neutral or pleasant). This prevents overwhelm and slowly develops your free capacity to be with difficult experiences.
- Respect dissociation: If you begin to dissociate (feeling disconnected, not there, or numb), don't resist it. Your nervous system is doing this to protect you. Instead, softly ground by noticing the physical environment, the support under you, your sense impressions, anything that can guide you back to right here in the now.
- Move when necessary: If remaining still triggers more activation, add a little bit of gentle movement to your practice. These could be subtle movements, such as gently rotating your wrists or shoulders, or something more active, like walking meditation or gentle stretching.

Be gentle with yourself: Treat your situation with kindness, not criticism. If you space out, become triggered, or dissociate, be kind to yourself in a way you would support a friend or child who is struggling.

These adaptations don't water down the practice of mindfulness — they render it accessible and efficacious for those whose nervous systems have been sculpted by trauma. The point isn't to cram yourself in some idealized state of calm detachment. It's about being with yourself exactly where you are, and slowly increasing your ability to be present with your experience, no matter what that experience is.

It's not about transcending, staying present 24/7, which frankly, isn't realistic and it's not really the goal. It's to build enough presence that you can see when you've been sucked into automatic patterns and gently, without self-judgment, bring yourself back to the moment. It's in order to stretch out the moments of choice between trigger and response, and eventually build new habits based on present reality not past conditioning.

Self-Regulation vs. Co-Regulation: What is the Difference? The Power of Being Present Together

Although self-regulatory competences are critical, humans are social by nature. Our nervous systems evolved in relationship and they calm in relationship. This is where self- and co-regulation make their difference.

Self-regulation is your capacity to manage your own state of the nervous system, so you calm yourself down when you get activated, you stimulate yourself or energize yourself when you are shut down — our nervous system has a gas pedal and a brake — and you bring yourself back to a regulated state after disruption. This ability is built through regular practice of the skills we've been talking about.

Co-regulation is what occurs when two nervous systems help regulate one another, mostly through subtle physiological cues like facial expression, tone of voice, body posture and touch. When one person is regulated, their state can regulate the other person whose system is activated.

Co-regulation is very valuable, but can be even more powerful and effective, particularly when you are activated, as in your example. This is because:

- Your social nervous system is built to connect: The most highly developed part of your autonomic nervous system — the ventral vagal

complex — is designed with the high-tech capacity for interpersonal connection and co-regulation.
- Regulation is quicker, via relationship: A regulated person can help move your nervous system state faster than you can often move it yourself, especially if you're highly activated.
- Co-regulation strengthens self-regulation: Consistent experiences of co-regulation over time actually increase your ability to self-regulate. Each process will enhance the other.
- Healing happens in the environment where wounding happened: Since most trauma takes place <u>in a relationship healing must also take place in relationship.</u> Co-regulation also gives us experiences of safety and connection where once were experienced danger and disconnection.

This isn't to say that we should become reliant on others to "handle" our emotions. It means understanding that humans are inherently interdependent, and that healthy relationships co-regulate — both parties get back to regulation much quicker with the help of the other, when one is activated.

As you do the hard, important work of healing your own nervous system, the very best thing you can do to fortify it is to become a "safe person" for others — someone whose being and presence helps others feel seen, heard, regulated instead of judged, dismissed or further activated.

This isn't about doing it perfectly, or never getting triggered yourself. It's about gaining enough self-awareness and regulation skills such that you can generally maintain your own regulation while in relationship with others, even when they're activated.

Following are some of the characteristics that make somebody a "safe person" for nervous system healing:

- Regulated presence: A capacity for living in a regulated state most of the time, and for returning to a regulated state relatively quickly if provoked.
- Non-judgment: The ability to approach others' stories with curiosity and compassion, not judgment, or the need to provide a solution.
- Attunement: Empathic attunement is the capacity to sense the other person's feelings and to respond with appropriate warmth and concern without losing your own sense of self.
- Boundaries: Clear, consistent boundaries that establish predictability and safety, not rigidity and control.
- Repair: The interest and ability to take responsibility and repair when you make mistakes or cause harm.
- Emotional literacy: The skill of being able to identify, name and challenge a broad spectrum of emotion in yourself and others.
- Differentiation: The ability to hold on to your own sense of self in close relation to others while neither being overwhelmed by their experience nor losing contact with that experience.

Building these virtues is not about turning into some perfected ideal person. It's about expanding your capacity to be with yourself and others in a way that facilitates healing, not one that re-enforces the traumatic patterns.

And here's the beautiful paradox: When you become a safe person for others, it helps heal your own nervous system. The more you get into the habit of regulating in the company of someone else's activation, the more capacity you have to maintain regulation in those situations during school that you would likely prefer not to be there at all. As you offer others the compassion or presence you wish you'd been offered, you become an inhabitant of the very compassion and presence you offer.

That doesn't mean taking responsibility for others' healing or becoming a caretaker at the expense of your own needs. It's knowing that your presence — your steady, loving, boundary-honoring presence — is one of the greatest gifts you can give yourself and anyone else you care about.

Presence is the Antidote to All Four Stress Response States

The gift of presence becomes a powerful antidote to all four stress responses and helps us turn reactive patterns into conscious choices:

- To the fight response: Presence allows you to tune into the early warning signs that trigger anger or defensiveness in your body so you don't act on them. It opens up space to channel the protective energy of fight in useful as opposed to harmful ways — say, setting clear boundaries, or speaking truth with compassion, or taking principled action instead of lashing out, complaining or criticizing.
- For the flight response: Presence facilitates you catching the impulse to withdraw, avoid or escape before you automatically do so. It creates gap to differentiate what is real space and need to withdraw and what is a habitual withdrawal. It enables you to communicate that you need some space, instead of just disappearing, and to return to the connection of it when you are regulated.
- For freeze: Being here enables you to notice when you are shutting down or zoning out before you are entirely frozen. It leaves room to take tiny steps to avoid complete paralysis: uttering a simple fact, moving out of drift, reaching out for help. It anchors you to your body and to your agency, especially when part of you just wants to vanish.

- For the fawn response: Being present helps you notice when you're abandoning your needs or boundaries to take care of someone else's feelings. It provides room to distinguish your true yes from your conditioned, automatic people-pleasing responses. It's the ability to stay connected to others without losing connection to yourself.

In either case, the presence doesn't cancel out the survival response—these responses are natural and helpful in situations of actual danger. What presence gives you is the ability to differentiate between actual threats and perceived ones, between the responses that benefit you in the current moment and the automatic patterns that have been reinforced from the past.

This *distinction* is the basis of free will. It enables you to remain responsive, not freezing in a fixed one-size-fits-all survival mode. It does this by allowing you to tap into the protective wisdom of your survival responses while not being hijacked by those more extreme or automatic expressions of them.

The practice of presence isn't just a means to an end — a way to resolve problems or strengthen relationships, though it does help with both. It's a way of being that enhances all elements of our life with more presence, choice and connection in each moment.

This possibility is open to you no matter what your story may be or what may seem to be true at the moment.

You have an inborn capacity for presence; it is not a skill you have to develop, but an ability that you simply have to tap into and build up. It may be buried under layers of survival but it is still whole and intact, ready to be absorbed back.

The road to that reclaiming isn't always smooth or direct. It takes courage to stand before the thing you've been avoiding, humility to admit when you've been sucked back into old areas of life, and persistence to continue the practice when it seems like tiny steps. But it is possible. And you don't want to do it alone.

In the next chapter we will look at how these principles of presence and nervous system regulation can be applied to your relationships with others so that you can build connections that support healing rather than re-traumatization. But for now, I'd like you to just stay with the idea that you can learn to be with whatever happens within your YOU-niverse.

You are able to develop a gap between reaction and response. You can act, rather than react. And that, my friend, is the freedom you actually desire.

Topics for Reflection and Development

When is it hardest for you to stay present?

Which circumstances, people or internal states prompt you to react from habit in response to them, as opposed to responding consciously?

How do you know when it's happening to you, when you're falling out your own presence and into the history of your reactions?

What things do you notice in your body, thinking or doing that resemble your canary in the coal mine?

What presence practices are most powerful to you? Which ones can you realistically apply into your life right now, today?

What would be possible for your relations if you no longer were triggered when they are triggered?

Which exact interactions would proceed differently?

Who are <u>your people</u> in your life, who keep you in the presence of other safe people? And what is it about them which you'd actually want to regulate?

How are you already a "safe person" for people? What elements of presence do you already possess, even if you do them poorly?

What's one small thing you could do today to invite a greater degree of presence into a challenging relationship or situation in your life?

And don't forget that the objective is not perfection. It's progress. Each moment of presence, however fleeting, is reinforcing new neural pathways. Every time you become aware that you have been triggered and bring yourself back to present, you are rewiring your default reactions. It's those little practices that accumulate over time and transform your relationship with yourself, with others, and with your life.

PART IV: HEALING THE CONNECTION

CHAPTER EIGHTEEN

PARENTING WITHOUT PASSING THE PANIC

Never did I think I would be writing a chapter on parenting. For the better part of my adult life, I was convinced I would never be a good father. How could I be a good father, after all, when my own childhood was so chaotic? The idea of inflicting my trauma responses on an unsuspecting child scared me more than any UFC fighter ever had.

But life has a way of being very unexpected. Though I have biological children of my own, I have also been a stepfather on several occasions over the course of my marriages. And in those situations — some directly applicable, many painful — I've picked up vital lessons about the way trauma responses are passed down to the next generation, and, perhaps most important, how to end that kind of cycle.

If you are a parent, step-parent, grandparent, teacher, coach or an individual who is around kids, then this chapter is for you. Because, you see, we are all contributing to multigenerational trauma — or multigenerational healing for that matter, whether we know it or not.

The Inheritance We Never Wanted

It was my first time in a father figure role… the first time I heard myself sounding just like my father; I remember it like it was yesterday, though it was 25 years ago.

I was arguing with my stepson, who was probably twelve at the time, about something silly. He'd left his bike in the driveway again after I nagged him several times to put it up. It just wasn't a big deal, not really. But something in me snapped. My voice went deeper, hit that terrifying timbre I grew up with. What I spoke weren't just words that came from me; they were my father's.

"What's wrong with you? Are you just stupid or trying to make me angry?"

As soon as the words were out, I felt nauseous. The look of fear flashed across my stepson's face — the same fear I had felt so many times as a child. At that moment, I realized that not only was I acting like my father, I was continuing the very chain of trauma that I had vowed never to perpetuate.

This is how trauma is passed through the generations. Not through DNA, but early research in the field of epigenetics has found that trauma can, in fact, influence gene expression. But mainly by behavior, by relationship patterns, by the unconscious transmission of nervous system states from parent to child.

Kids are exquisitely tuned in to their caregivers' nervous systems. Before they can make meaning of your behavior, before they can understand language, before they're able to process it through that part of their brain, the kids will know when a parent is regulated or dysregulated. Their immature nervous systems co-regulate with the adult nervous systems surrounding them. If a parent is chronically parenting from a place of fight, flight, freeze or fawn, a child's nervous system adjusts, too.

This isn't about blame. My father didn't consciously decide to traumatize me any more than I consciously decided to speak harshly to my stepson. He was functioning from his own unhealed trauma, his own survival strategies. Just as I was with my stepson in that moment, he was parenting from his limbic system, not his prefrontal cortex.

That doesn't make harmful behavior excusable, but it does make it explicable. And explanation is the prerequisite for transformation.

The Four Fs of Parenting: How the Brain Reacts to Parenthood

All four survival responses express themselves in different parenting styles. By acknowledging these patterns, you can help yourself break the cycle.

The Fight Parent: Control and Criticism

Parents who are fight-dominant tend to have an authoritarian style of parenting, that is to say, they have strict rules, use discipline that is severe and have high demands. They can become domineering, negative, and sometimes even verbally or physically abusive when provoked.

I observed this example in my dad very clearly. It was the fight of his life if there was any hint of disobedience or disrespect. His face and body language would take on a menacing appearance, his voice deep into that scary tone, and all of the sudden the smallest act of disobedience turned into a major confrontation.

There will be two strategies that kids adapted into, who were raised by a fight-dominant parent: one where they become fight-dominant also, they learn aggression as a way of getting needs met and of getting boundaries recognized, and another where they actually ended up with a high freeze or fawn profile because that was the strategy that protected them against what should have been the natural parent.

The Flight Parent: Emotionally or Physically Gone

Flight-dominant parents can be either emotionally or physically unavailable. They could overwork, become distracted or even when in body, not be present. When those triggers escalate because they are parents experiencing the daily push and pull and messiness of parenting, they escape.

When my father was physically abusive, my step-mother was there, but emotionally absent. Clobbered by her own trauma and his volatility, she would turn inward, unavailable when I needed to have the shelter of my feelings hidden and comforted.

Frequent-flying parents tend to raise flight-anxious kids. They learn that connection is tenuous, and that their needs might be what causes people to leave. They, in turn, can become clingy, [or] they can develop a flight response of their own, learning to be independent and emotionally detached.

The Freeze Parent: Emotionally Frozen and Indecisive

These are just 2 examples. 4) Freeze-dominant parents; it is like "we're just here to be." Nothing is proactive or even indecisive, converse to the flight responses. They may have difficulty with establishing and maintaining boundaries, talking around the issue rather than facing conflict, or appear "flat" or emotionally distant. Once in this place, reactive parents are paralysed and cannot respond to meet their child's real needs.

I have felt this phenomenon as a stepparent. There were moments when I felt I should step in — when boundaries needed to be set or guidance given — and yet I'd cower as my body seized up. The fear of being wrong or hurting someone would stop me in my tracks.

Freeze-dominant parents raise children who have very little sense of safety or constancy. They do not learn how to self-regulate in the absence of firm limits and consistent consequences. They will feel they either need to parentify, take on things above their years, or develop their own freeze response, becoming passive when they want to flight.

<u>The Fawn Parent:</u> Enabling and Enmeshment

Parents who are fawn-dominant are more likely to be permissive in style. They find it difficult to create the boundaries that are required, because they're afraid of the child's anger or rejection. They value being liked over structuring and setting limits.

I've fallen into that trap myself, especially when I was a new stepparent. Desperate to be accepted and liked by my stepchildren, I avoided doing things like setting boundaries or imposing consequences. I'd find myself saying yes to things I'd wanted to say no to, just to avoid a conflict or rejection.

Fawn-dominant parents' children generally have poor entitlement and discipline. With no experience of appropriate limits, they fail to develop frustration tolerance or an understanding of limits. They can also learn to emotionally manipulate in order to manipulate their way into getting what they need, because they've learned that their parent's boundaries are flimsy.

The Dance of the Nervous System: Co-regulations and Dysregulations

Parenting is, at heart, a dance of the nervous systems between parent and child. This dance actually starts at birth and carries on through childhood and adolescence.

As a parent's nervous system is regulated — in ventral vagal state and feeling safe and connected — they may help to co-regulate their child's nervous system. They can meet distress with a soothing presence rather than mirroring the child's dysregulation with their own. They can establish limits with people in a firm and kind way rather than through a cruel or indulgent manner. They can understand challenging behavior as communication instead of taking it personally.

But when a parent's nervous system is chronically dysregulated — either stuck in sympathetic arousal (fight/flight) or dorsal vagal shutdown (freeze) — they cannot provide this co-regulation. Rather, the parents escalate the child's dysregulation with their own reactivity or they don't do enough of the engaging and attuning.

I've been on the other side of this dance as well. Moments when, activated by a stepchild's behavior, I would respond from my own dysregulation—a response harsh, withdrawn, frozen, or giving in. And when I was doing my own healing work, I had moments where I could stay regulated enough to respond instead of react, to co-regulate instead of escalate.

There was nothing different about the child's behavior. <u>I was</u> in my nervous system. <u>I was</u> parenting from my trauma when I was operating out of my survival brain. I could parent from my values and intentions when I was working from my regulated state.

Breaking the Cycle: Parenting from Regulation, not Reaction

Rising above generational trauma is not about being the perfect parent. It's simply about developing enough consciousness and regulation capacity to catch yourself in the act when you're triggered and make different choices from your caregivers.

Here are a few practices that have helped me and many others interrupt the default transfer of responses to trauma:

Develop Trigger Awareness: The first step is identifying your own parenting triggers—those behavioral patterns, situations and dynamics that trigger your survival mechanisms. These buttons are often linked to your own childhood.

Disrespect would send me right over the edge. After spending my childhood tiptoeing around my father's volatile temper, I'd developed a hypervigilance for perceived signs of disrespect. If a stepchild rolled his eyes, used a sarcastic tone or ignored a request, that would activate my fight reflex immediately.

Recognize when you are activated before you react on autopilot Even better, by knowing your precise triggers, you will begin to grow aware of when you are activated before you react automatically. This is what opens up a space for choice.

Build a Pause Practice: When activated, the most important skill is simply the ability to pause before speaking. This might mean:

- Taking a deep breath
- Silently counting to ten
- Respond with "I need a minute to consider this."
- Shifting positions slightly, even apply some of that "physical separation" if you need to

This pause interrupts the reflex survival response, and it gives your prefrontal cortex time to reset. In this gap is where you get to pick your response based on your values, not your trauma.

One evening, I recall, my stepson came home without calling and he was quite late for his curfew. I trembled with fury and fear, knowing I needed to send a strong message, but instead of responding right away, I closed my eyes and took a few deep breaths. I reminded myself that my aim was not to punish, but to preserve connection while establishing crucial guidelines. And that pause gave me the ability to answer to the issue, but not with the fury of my initial reaction.

Use Self-Regulation Techniques: The best thing you can do to support your children: You're modelling your own regulation. This might include:

- Regular mindfulness practice
- Physical exercise
- Time in nature
- Breathwork
- Embodiment regulatory methods
- Therapy or support groups

The more regulated you can have your own nervous system, the more co-regulation you can provide your children and, in turn, the less often you parent from your trauma responses.

For me personally, time alone was more than necessary — to maintain physical health, yes, but also to regulate my nervous system. I notice that if I've had adequate time alone, I'm able to stay much better regulated – including during my parenting challenges.

Repair When You Miss the Mark: You will get triggered. Your survival brain will take over sometimes. Repair is necessary when this occurs.

Repair involves acknowledging the impact of your behavior, taking responsibility without shame-spiraling, recommitting to your values and intentions. It might sound like:

"I'm sorry I yelled earlier. I was scared, and I was overwhelmed, but that's no excuse for the way I talked to you. You should be treated with respect even if there's a problem we need to solve. Can we revisit the conversation once again?"

These instances of repair are not failures — they are in fact powerful opportunities for dismantling generational patterns. When you repair with your child, you're modeling accountability, emotional truth telling and the fact that relationships can recover from ruptures. This is probably very different from the household you grew up in (or, is it?).

The next day, I sat with my stepson after talking to him the night before with my father's voice. I expressly apologized for my words and tone, spoke to the fear I'd seen flicker across his face and communicated that in age-appropriate terms, I was working on not acting from places echoed in my childhood. That conversation didn't negate it, but turned it from the reiterating of trauma to an occasion for new learning for both of us.

Write a Parenting Philosophy Statement of Values: Spend some time identifying your values as a parent or caregiver. What kind of relationship do you want with the young people in your life? How do you want to be? What is it you want them to learn from you about relationships, feelings, conflict?

Having this values statement, written down or clearly held in mind, gives you a north star to navigate by when you're "triggered." It gets you back in touch with your intentions rather than being on automatic pilot.

Safety (in all forms: physical and emotional), respect, honesty and growth. In those moments of provocation, I would try to retrieve that compass: "What would respect look like in this instance? How do I stay honest and safe in this conversation?"

Build Your Support System: Parenting from trauma history is hard work. You need and deserve support. This might include:

- Individual therapy
- Parenting support groups
- Reliable friends who understand trauma
- Trauma-specific parenting classes or supports
- If co-parenting, counseling if necessary

No one heals alone, and no one parents perfectly by themselves. When you are struggling, having a community of support means you have resources beyond your own.

I know I found regular visits to Dr. Ruffin invaluable in my most intense stepparenting years. Being able to process my triggers, fears and challenges had enabled me to show up more regulated and intentional for my stepchildren.

The Poker Player's Parenting: Read the Table, Not Just Your Hand

In poker, you see, winners don't merely play their hands: They read other players around the table. They read the patterns, the tells, the bigger game.

And yet, so is trauma-informed parenting. Not only do you need to manage your own responses (and that's a big part of it). It's in reading the larger patterns and context:

- What's happening underneath your child's behavior in his or her nervous system?
- What are they trying to tell you through difficult behavior?
- What may be the environmental determinants of dysregulation?
- What styles of how you relate to each other could be in the mix for you both?

When my stepson would act defiant or disrespectful, my first read was usually personal: "He's testing my authority" or "he doesn't respect me." But when I could steer away from my childhood living room and read the room he was sitting in, I'd often see something different: a child whose nervous system was swimming in chaos, from school pressures to peer dynamics to the complicated emotions of blended family life.

This more inclusive reading let me to be able to address what was underneath the behavior instead of reacting to the behavior. Rather than engaging in power struggles that would push both of our buttons around "the fight," I might be able to regulate or meet the underlying dysregulation or need.

The UFC Fighter s Discipline Training for the Parenting Octagon

UFC fighters don't simply come out on fight night and wish for the best. They practice all the time so that they have the skills and strength and stamina to perform under pressure.

Trauma-informed parenting should be no different. "It's not how you can do perfectly in the moment, it's what it looks like day in and day out, throughout the week, that prepares you for those moments:

- Nervous System Regulating Ability of Routine Exercises
- Continued education on child development and trauma
- Regular self-reflection of your parenting styles
- Conscious training of new surroundings and old cues

As with a fighter who builds muscle memory through repeated practice, you can build new patterns in parenting through repetition. The more we cultivate this fresh perspective, the more naturally it comes, and the less effort we have to make to keep it in place.

How Healing can Happen from Raising Children: Parenting as Healing

Maybe the deepest lesson I've learned from my stepparenting roles is that parenting, at its best, is not only a channel through which trauma passes from one generation to another, but also one through which it can be mended.

When you consciously parent, understanding what you do and why, you're not just breaking the cycle for the next generation. You're actually rewiring your own nervous system and your own childhood traumas.

And I realized that when I was able to stay regulated with my stepchildren somehow during those moments that would have triggered rage or shutdown in my parents, I wasn't just providing them with something different, I was also providing myself with something different. I was teaching my inner child that there is another way.

Healing Through Repair

When you repair ruptures with a child — when you acknowledge impact, take responsibility, reconnect — you are not only teaching that child how to be in relationship. You're giving yourself the experience of repair you likely never had in your own childhood.

Assimilation by Explanation

When you help a child understand their emotions and behaviors with trauma-informed eyes, you often make sense of your own childhood experiences in new ways.

So, when I could get better at interpreting these scary, big emotions for my stepchildren — when we cried things through together, or I held them while they broke down — I was also teaching myself to interpret my own emotional reactions with more kindness, and with more clarity. What I explained to them became what I could explain to myself.

Vicarious Resilience

When you see that a child can not only heal but grow through their darkest days, it gives you more faith in the capacity for growth and resilience in us all.

Witnessing my children bounce back from disappointment, a blunder, and become more emotionally regulated with age helped me believe in myself that I could also grow/heel further. Their strength made me resilient.

The Impact of Conscious Parenting

When you interrupt the cycle of generational trauma with conscious parenting, the effects ripple through families, communities, and across generations. When you're raising children who feel safe in their bodies, who are able to regulate their emotions, who know what a healthy boundary feels like and what an authentic connection feels like, you're contributing to the healing of collective trauma.

These same children grow into adults who can have healthier relationships, parent their own children with greater attunement and carry their regulated nervous systems into every relationship/place/space they enter—classrooms, workplaces, intimate partnerships.

This may be one of the most significant bits of legacy that we can offer: that we not only cease to transmit trauma down our own lineages, but that we participate in a more resourced, connected and compassionate world for the generations that follow.

You may be a biological parent as I am, you may be a stepparent as I have also been, or maybe you are a grandparent, a teacher or a coach or, as I say, a person who comes in contact with kids in any way, but you have the opportunity to do that. Each encounter is an opportunity to either react in the same old ways or to build something new. Each moment of regulation you give to a dysregulated child ripples outward in glimmering particles that you likely will never fully see, but which alter the very celestial fabric of our common future.

This isn't easy work. It takes courage, dedication and a lot of practice. It's an invitation to look at our own injuries so that we don't unwittingly hand them down to the next generation. But it may be the most important work that we do — for the children in our lives and also for ourselves and the world.

In looking back at my stepparenting experiences — the mistakes, the repairs, the times when true connection was possible, the hard-won wisdom, as well as the things I enacted and said that I wish I hadn't — I also feel a deep sense of gratitude for the possibility they've given me to break cycles that have run through my family for generations. I wasn't always there and I had my failures, plenty of them, when my own trauma responses took over, but I know I offered something different than what I received. It is in this difference that the possibility of healing — not just for one child or one family, but for the collective nervous system we all inhabit — can be found.

CHAPTER NINETEEN

CREATING NEW NEURONS:

LIFE AFTER SURVIVAL

It's been nearly two years since that awful September day in 2023, when I walked away with nothing but a backpack and nine hundred bucks to my name. Now I'm sitting at my desk, running my marketing company, writing books, co-parenting my 9-yr old son, and at the same time, getting to know my inner-child. I'm also trying to help as many of the people around me as humanly possible. The life I have pieced together seems as if it is a world away from the craziness and suffering that characterized so much of my life.

Am I completely healed? No. Do I still have times where I get triggered and feel myself slipping back into the survival modes of old? Absolutely!

But the thing is: Those moments don't define or shape my life any longer. They are more like weather as it sweeps through, sometimes stormy, sometimes mild, but they never stay. I read them, call them out, bring my tools on hand to work with them (all of which I've shared with you throughout this book), and come right back to the present moment, to the life I am consciously creating and not just the one my trauma response would create for me by default.

What I would love for you to experience — not some perfect life where you aren't triggered or pushed or poked, but a life where you are no longer at the mercy to your survival responses. One where you can live a life of the full spectrum of human emotions without being hijacked by them. A life where your relationships are a product of your intentions, not your instincts. A life beyond mere survival.

In this last chapter before the epilogue, I'd like to consider what this life beyond surviving actually looks like and how we can go about forging the neural pathways that make it possible.

The Evolution of the Poker Player: From Surviving to Thriving

In poker, there is a world of difference between people who are just not losing and those who are actively winning. The first group is thinking, on some level, from a defensive shortage mentality — guard the chips, play it safe, steer clear of danger. There are plenty of players like that, and in fact, they fill most of the seats at most poker tables. The other group are playing from abundance — taking risk, focusing on the long game rather than the hand in front of them (and) seeing opportunity rather than just getting trapped in their fears and losing that lens.

There's my poker nemesis and good friend, Sid. When we began playing together years ago, I was the more tentative, mistake-averse player. Sid had played a self-assured and strategically aggressive game. As we have pushed each other, I've changed my game over the years. I still respect the risks, but I'm not playing scared anymore. We have a near-even record "heads-up"; that's one-on-one for you, non-poker players.

The same development occurs in life, as we graduate from survival to thriving:

Survival Mode:

- There are decisions made which are fueled by fear and avoidance
- Relationships guarded and protected
- Success, as not failing or incurring harm
- Identities have revolved around wounds and adaptations
- Focus on surviving the day or the crisis
- Chronic nervousness

Thriving Mode:

- Values and desire-driven decisions
- Relationships with an open and honest approach
- Sometimes, perfection often means growth and connection worth having
- Identity focused on calling and true self
- Draw your attention to build and contribute.

Thriving Mode isn't the sort of change that happens overnight. It's not a eureka moment, but a gradual rewiring through daily practice and conscious decisions. Like the hundreds of poker hands Sid and I have played together, each one tweaking my game ever so slightly, you'll need to run through these loops in hundreds if not thousands of tiny moments before it becomes your new default.

When the Octagon Door Closes: UFC Fighters in Retirement

It's not easy transitioning out of fighting for many UFC fighters. If they were someone who based their identity on being able to fight and win in the octagon, they are now lost and have no idea who they are anymore. Those who succeed in retirement are the ones who can apply the discipline, focus, and resilience they acquired as fighters to new arenas of life.

This is similar to the struggle to transcend a modality of identity grounded in trauma. When you have lived decades identifying yourself with your survival adaptations — "I'm the responsible one," "I'm the peacemaker," "I'm the strong one who never needs help" — it can feel like losing yourself to let go of those identities, even if they are no longer serving you.

The secret is to realizing that those very raw strengths you developed in trauma can be applied — twisted, if you will — and put you on a path of thriving not just surviving:

The hypervigilance that kept you safe can be transformed into heightened awareness to notice beauty and opportunity.

The self-reliance that enabled you to survive when others could not be relied on, can mature into healthy autonomy within interdependent relationships.

The emotional awareness that enabled the navigating of tumultuous waters may be transformed into empathy and emotional intelligence when experiences are healthy.

The perfectionism that once served as a shield against criticism can be transformed into a value-driven pursuit of excellence.

These strengths don't vanish with healing; they evolve. Like a former prize fighter who begins to mentor others, you can turn your survival adaptations into conscious abilities to enhance your life and your relationships.

The New Normal for the Nervous System: It's All About Regulation

There's an ebbing away of your nervous system that you will experience as you journey with the application of what you've taken away from this book. Through consistent practice of the regulation skills we've discussed, what once required effort becomes second nature.

This transition happened slowly and gradually over the past several years of my healing process. There was no one moment when I suddenly felt safe in my body, or in the world. Instead, I had thousands of small moments of choosing regulation over reactivity, presence over dissociation and connection over isolation. As I gradually made these changes, they physically rewired my nervous system.

The hypothesis is supported by neuroscience, with the idea of neuroplasticity, which is the brain's capacity to reorganize itself throughout life, by forming new neural connections. When you are repeatedly practicing regulation skills and new response patterns, you're not simply changing your behavior, you're also restructuring your nervous system and brain.

That does not mean you will never get triggered or dysregulated. I still do, as I alluded to previously. But three things change:

1. You get triggered less frequently, and your nervous system is less reactive to threats.
2. The emotional activation is less intense You are still triggered, but when triggered, it is never as overwhelming as before.

3. The recovery time is reduced: You can return to regulation sooner after activation, and you are less likely to get trapped in survival states for long periods.

These changes form a positive feedback loop. The better your nervous system is at regulation, the more flexible you are in terms of being able to process challenges without getting dysregulated, which in turn builds up your capacity to regulate. It's kind of like compound interest for your nervous system — little investments pay off in exponential ways over time.

Identity Beyond Trauma: Who am I When I'm Not Surviving?

One of the hardest parts of recovering from trauma is the identity shift it necessitates. Once you've built your identity around survival adaptations — as the strong one, the caretaker, the achiever, the invisible one — who are you when those familiar patterns are not at play?

I was confronted with this question with great intensity when I left my most recent marriage. For so long I had defined myself in terms of my relationships, as a husband, a parent, a provider, a solver of problems. When that identity blew up, I had to face the dreadful question: Who am I now?

For so many years I made every role in my life a component of my identity rather than viewing the roles as components *because* of my identity. In other words, focus on becoming the most healthy man or woman possible, every day, and you will offer your greatest contribution to everyone in your life, and in real-time.

That's the identity question that arises often when you're healing and it can temporarily exacerbate symptoms while your psyche resists being in the not-knowing-what-the-hell-it's-becoming. This is normal, and in fact necessary:

The old identity must be partially deconstructed and maybe even completely demolished before a new, truer one can begin to take shape.

Below are a few practices that worked for me in navigating this identity shift:

- Values Clarification
- Identifying your core values gives a strong beginning to creating a sense of self around what actually matters to you, not what kept you safe.

   Ask yourself:

- What do I appreciate most in a person?
- When do I most feel alive, aligned?
- If I were not afraid, what would I stand for?
- What do I want to be known for when I die?

For me, this investigation unearthed a set of basic values: authenticity, growth, connection, and contribution — four potential value centers that had been repeatedly squelched by my survival-mode self, but that could now become the basis of a new being.

Experimentation and Play

To heal often means to be willing to practice new ways of being even when we don't know how they are going to turn out. This is an experiment best embarked upon in the spirit of curiosity and play, rather than pressure to do it right.

I was experimenting with new things, sharing thoughts that had stayed locked away, drawing lines in the sand I had never braved to draw and showing vulnerabilities I had always buried. There were some experiences that felt weird or uncomfortable at the outset, but revealed parts of myself that had been dulled under survival adaptations.

Grieving What Wasn't

Encompassing a true identity often requires <u>grieving the childhood you never had</u>, the person you were unable to be when in fight or flight, and even the adaptive or coping identities that shielded you in ways that were limiting and limiting your life. This was a very long and difficult process for me that spanned many years – and it is still ongoing.

This sadness is not a reflection that healing hasn't worked; it is an integral part of the process. You allow new and different possibilities to arise by making room for these losses by recognizing them and feeling them.

Finding Your Contribution

For many trauma survivors, turning their pain into service or creation serves as a potent link between identity based in trauma and burgeoning authentic self.

For me, working on this book is part of that bridge. And by using what I've learned through my own healing journey in the hopes of helping others, I am shifting my relationship with my suffering from a source of pain without point to one with purpose.

Purpose isn't your job. Purpose isn't your field of study. Purpose isn't the ladder of success you're attempting to climb, or the social circles you're in. <u>Purpose is what happens when you've deposited something of intrinsic value into the life of another, leaving an indelible mark on their existence.</u>

This doesn't mean your trauma should be at the center of your life's work. Your contribution to change does not have to have anything to do with your history of trauma. What does matter is finding the ways you create and contribute that are consistent with your true self, and not with your survival adaptations.

Because your identity and nervous system are changing, your relationships automatically do as well. This change isn't only about meeting new people (though sometimes it is); it's about relating to others differently, whether with established or new connections.

Growth Together vs. Caretaking or Dependency

Survival relationships often have roles that are unequal: one partner as the super-responsible one, the other partner as the needy one; one partner as the rock, the other as the laissez-faire, but emotionally volatile one; the one partner as the organizer, the other partner as the follower.

On this side of mere survival, relationships are marked by mutuality and reciprocity. Each party promotes their own health and wellness, while supporting the other's journey. Roles are constantly shifting rather than fixed; everyone is a potential giver and a potential receiver.

This mutuality isn't the same as perfect equality at all times; it means a balanced give and take overall, with each person contributing to and offering support in the relationship in ways that work for them and feel good to both.

The Daily Practice: Sustaining and Enhancing Your Healing

Recovery from trauma isn't a place you get to and then you're there. It's more akin to physical fitness — something you keep up with regular practice, and then take to another level (or not) in periods of intensified practice, then dial back down to the maintenance level.

Here is a sampling of practices that can help sustain and deepen healing over the long run:

Routine Nervous System Check-Ins

In the same way that you check your physical vital signs, routine check-ins with your nervous system enable you to remain cognizant of your regulation state and catch dysregulation early.

I'll do it for a couple of minutes a few times a day, especially before big meetings or having difficult conversations. I do nothing other than step back, take a breath and observe: Where am I on the autonomic ladder in this moment? Which state of my arousal am I in: ventral vagal (safe and social), sympathetic (fight/flight), or dorsal vagal (freeze/shutdown)? Just this awareness already tends to move my being more towards regulation.

Systematic Policy Implementation

Similar to how the body feels when we neglect it of physical activity, without proper practice the nervous system goes out of regulation. This doesn't have to mean you go into formal practice for hours on end every day, but it does mean integrating regulation practices throughout the day.

> For me, this includes:
> - A brief morning meditation
> - Moderate physical activity around the clock
> - Awareness of breath in transitions
> - Evening reflection & nervous system settling

These practices need not be fancy or time-consuming. Even seconds of purposeful regulation that you engage in throughout the day can keep you in healing or deepen it.

Community and Connection

Healing takes place in relationship. Although most of the work is on the inside, staying connected to those who understand and support your healing journey is crucial for continued growth.

This might include:

- Therapy or support groups
- Friends who get it about trauma and recovery
- Web communities centered around recovery
- Spiritual or religious groups that offer a sense of connection

I've discovered the community of healing in unlikely conversations among friends, like the guys from our weekly poker game. We almost never talk trauma or healing out loud, but the over and over connection, the competition, the deep sense of belonging are all contributing to my mental, emotional, and physical wellbeing.

The magic of healing is that as you heal something miraculous happens - your transformation becomes contagious to those in your life. What you may not know is that this ripple gets tossed bigger and wider than your circle, and joins the ripple of collective healing in ways you may never fully see or understand.

As you become a more regulated nervous system, you naturally offer more safety for others to regulate too. This co-regulation mostly occurs outside of conscious awareness, as nervous systems adjust to each other.

Inter-generational Patterns of Trauma

In the process of working through your own trauma responses, you disrupt patterns which might otherwise endure through generations. With and without children of your own, your healing touches how you show up to the young people in all of your relationships.

As I've recently shared in the previous chapter, working with my stepchildren was part of an endeavor to break cycles that have run through my family for generations. This healing ripples on in ways I may never entirely appreciate but ripples on through the future just the same.

Helping the Collective Healing

At the highest level, your healing contributes to our collective healing as a society. And as more and more people go about this work our culture patterns around conflict, power, vulnerability, and connection slowly change.

So, the journey continues.

I'll close here by recognizing that your healing work — like the book you are reading — will continue even after you finish the last chapter. There is no finish line, no ideally healed state to arrive in. There will be ups and downs, times when rapid progress is made and times when you feel too tired to take another step, new difficulties and unexpected blessings.

It's not about arriving at some imaginary place of perfect healing. What matters is that we keep showing up for the journey with courage, compassion and a willingness to listen. The important thing is development of the new neural pathways that set you free to live them from chosen response rather than reflex, from truth rather than fitting in, from love rather than fear.

This is what I want for you. Not perfection, but possibility. Not a life without challenge, but one with choice. Not a life without triggers, but a life no longer ruled by them.

The path is your own to tread, at your own speed, in your own fashion. But understand that you are not walking alone. Millions more are on pilgrimage to do this essential work of healing their fight-flight-freeze responses and crafting lives of greater freedom, authenticity and connection.

You are in this collective healing process. Your personal journey is not important only for the fate of your own life and relationships, it is also crucial for the future of us as human beings who are all in this boat together. Every step you take toward healing your nervous system is contributing to a healing of our <u>shared</u> nervous system.

This is what your healing has left behind. This is what you give to yourself and everyone in whose life you show up. This is the power of making new circuits – neural pathways that in the end will impact not just personal transformation, but also the transformation of our world, one relationship, one interaction, one moment at a time.

The journey continues. So does the potential for change, connection and a life truly worth living — not just surviving.

EPILOGUE

―――――――――――――

I'm writing these final words on a Friday evening in May 2025. It's been an emotional week, capped off by the fact that I have missed out on what could have been the partaking in a joyful chapter that started about 24 hours ago.

A young lady who had been an important part of my life and family just got married. She is the eldest daughter of my ex-wife, but naturally it would have presented some awkwardness had I been invited and then attended the wedding. Needless to say, I have been working overtime in the *basement* of my soul, using this neuroscience-Phillip-knowledge to stay on top of the spectrum of emotions.

Today, she sent me some photos from her wedding day, and what can I say? I was moved, honored, and grateful by her thoughtfulness to share some of her (and her new husband's) moments with me.

These easy things to forget might sound trivial, but if you've spent most of your life fending for yourself, then to notice and appreciate such everyday occurrences are anything but. It's a testament to a nervous system that's regulated enough to just be here, to take in the beauty, to be present in this moment instead of being hijacked by the past or worried about the future.

It has been nearly two years since I left my marriage and left a family.

One of the hardest things I have uncovered and learned about myself is the harsh truth: I never had a <u>home</u> growing up.

I have never had a <u>home</u> in any of my marriages.

I had the illusion of what I thought was home, and the illusion was based on what my subconscious recognized, by what was *familiar*. And every time I walked away, I reaffirmed my definition of that home by recreating it, and allowing it to be recreated.

Essentially, I came to a painful truth on that September morning in 2023: I had always been <u>homeless</u>.

In the last almost two years since, I've created a new life, and the new life began when I found *home*… within.

— Don't take this with sadness.

Healing isn't something that's clean and linear, with an obvious end point.

It's more akin to negotiating a landscape that grows ever more familiar, even if it still trips you up from time to time.

The only thing that has changed is that those feelings and experiences don't own me anymore. They go through me instead of becoming part of me. They guide my decisions– they don't make them. They're weather systems in my inner landscape, not the landscape itself.

That's what I want for you — not a perfect life, free of pain or challenge, but a life where you are no longer a prisoner of your survival responses. A life in which you can be more aware of the whole range of human emotions than you are overwhelmed by them. A life in which your relationships are a reflection of a conscious choice, as opposed to unconscious patterns.

A life beyond mere survival.

The Call to Slow Down

If there is any one thing I want you to take away from this book, it's an invitation to slow down. We live in a culture that glorifies busyness, productivity, movement. We're taught to suck it up, ignore our body's protest signs and power through. This cultural programming is especially destructive for trauma survivors, whose nervous systems have, as the Sufi mystic Rumi once said, "The wound is the place where the light enters you."

Pressing the "unfriend" button will not change who you are.

There is an opposite way to heal. It involves taking a moment to slow down enough to notice what's happening in your body and in your emotions. It is about creating a gap between the trigger and the response. It takes patience for the intermittent, non-linear nature of healing.

This sense of slowing down isn't laziness or self-indulgence. It is a radical act of self-reclamation in a world whose economy thrives on your disconnection from yourself. It's the baseline that is required for any real change in your relationship track record.

In poker terms, it's a bit like: instead of just playing reactively in the moment, and taking the time to really read the table before making your play. The winners in this game are not the ones who play the fastest, but rather those who take the time to step back, observe, think and then act.

The Bravery of Becoming Conscious

Healing takes courage too—the courage to see the truth of what patterns you've been running on autopilot, the courage to feel the feelings you've been trying to avoid, the courage to make new decisions even when they feel uncomfortable or scary.

This bravery is not about being without fear. I still experience fear all the time — fear of rejection, fear of failure, fear of being hurt again. Courage is about actually experiencing these fears — and continuing anyway when doing so is consistent with your values and well-being.

The best fighters in the world are not without fear, they simply know how to use it constructively instead of being a slave to it.

The journey toward healing your fight-or-flight-freeze responses will take this kind of courage: not the absence of fear but a willingness to feel the fear and still choose to be conscious rather than automatically reactive.

Final Note: You Are Not Alone

As we near the completion of our journey together, I'd like you to take one more truth with you: You are not alone in this work.

The patterns of relating we have examined throughout this book— your fight-flight-freeze-fawn responses and how they have affected your relationships and identity—exist as universal human experiences, even when they are experienced in totally unique ways by each individual. Millions of others share our journey, struggle with our challenges and seek a similar healing.

This is not to downplay your own experience, or the actual traumas you've suffered. But it does situate them in the larger context of our common humanity. Your challenges are not proof of some deep flaw or "failed" effort; they are the predictable side effects of a nervous system doing precisely what it was built to do in the face of perceived threats.

And just as you're not alone in your pain, you don't have to be alone as you heal. Whether through professional help, close friends, another guy who is in your shoes, a support system, or just a community with mutual interests can make a world of difference to connect with others who know and support you in your particular journey.

This book is a connection in its own way — my hand reaching out to yours, down the long corridor of time and space. We may never see each other face to face, but we're bound together by these words, by the shared experience of what it is to be human, to travel the universal road from survival to flourishing.

Wherever you are in that quest today, I respect your courage in picking up this book and confronting these difficult yet liberating truths. The fact that you're reading these words means that something in you is ready for transformation, ready to release the patterns that have kept you bleeding, running, standing still, or just endlessly apologizing.

That readiness, that openness to a new way of being, is the first breath of a new life. It's the start of a journey that will assuredly have its challenges and setbacks, but that can result in freedoms and authenticity you might have never fathomed.

I know because I have walked that path. I'm still walking it. And while I can't guarantee you a life where there is no pain or struggle, I can guarantee you this: there is life outside the grip of fight-flight-freeze. A life where you're no longer living "in your trauma responses" is attainable. Life in presence, choice and true connection is all yours.

I am happier than I've ever been in my life!

I have a 9-yr old son, who has the world at his fingertips.

I now have thriving relationships based on authenticity, rather than survival patterns, and the biggest difference isn't on the outside; it is the relationship I have with myself, my body, my emotions, my past.

The journey continues. And so is the possibility of change, of connection, of a life that's actually worth living — not just one that's about survival.

Thank you for letting me come along for the ride.

This book is finished.

With deep respect and hope,

- Phillip

Neuroscience and Trauma

Porges, S. W. (2011). *The Polyvagal Theory: Neurophysiological Foundations of Emotions, Attachment, Communication, and Self-regulation*. W. W. Norton & Company.

van der Kolk, B. (2014). *The Body Keeps the Score: Brain, Mind, and Body in the Healing of Trauma*. Viking.

Levine, P. A. (2010). *In an Unspoken Voice: How the Body Releases Trauma and Restores Goodness*. North Atlantic Books.

Dana, D. (2018). *The Polyvagal Theory in Therapy: Engaging the Rhythm of Regulation*. W. W. Norton & Company.

Siegel, D. J. (2012). *The Developing Mind: How Relationships and the Brain Interact to Shape Who We Are*. Guilford Press.

Cozolino, L. (2017). *The Neuroscience of Psychotherapy: Healing the Social Brain*. W. W. Norton & Company.

Sapolsky, R. M. (2017). *Behave: The Biology of Humans at Our Best and Worst*. Penguin Press.

Maté, G. (2011). *When the Body Says No: Understanding the Stress-Disease Connection*. John Wiley & Sons.

Trauma Responses and Healing

Walker, P. (2013). *Complex PTSD: From Surviving to Thriving*. Azure Coyote.

Fisher, J. (2017). *Healing the Fragmented Selves of Trauma Survivors: Overcoming Internal Self-Alienation*. Routledge.

Herman, J. (2015). *Trauma and Recovery: The Aftermath of Violence--From Domestic Abuse to Political Terror*. Basic Books.

Rothschild, B. (2000). *The Body Remembers: The Psychophysiology of Trauma and Trauma Treatment*. W. W. Norton & Company.

Scaer, R. (2014). *The Body Bears the Burden: Trauma, Dissociation, and Disease*. Routledge.

Ogden, P., & Fisher, J. (2015). *Sensorimotor Psychotherapy: Interventions for Trauma and Attachment*. W. W. Norton & Company.

Relationships and Attachment

Johnson, S. M. (2019). *Attachment Theory in Practice: Emotionally Focused Therapy (EFT) with Individuals, Couples, and Families*. Guilford Press.

Tatkin, S. (2012). *Wired for Love: How Understanding Your Partner's Brain and Attachment Style Can Help You Defuse Conflict and Build a Secure Relationship*. New Harbinger Publications.

Levine, A., & Heller, R. (2010). *Attached: The New Science of Adult Attachment and How It Can Help You Find—and Keep—Love*. Penguin.

Real, T. (2007). *The New Rules of Marriage: What You Need to Know to Make Love Work*. Ballantine Books.

Hendrix, H., & Hunt, H. L. (2019). *Getting the Love You Want: A Guide for Couples*. St. Martin's Griffin.

Parenting and Intergenerational Trauma

Siegel, D. J., & Bryson, T. P. (2020). *The Power of Showing Up: How Parental Presence Shapes Who Our Kids Become and How Their Brains Get Wired*. Ballantine Books.

Levine, P. A., & Kline, M. (2007). *Trauma Through a Child's Eyes: Awakening the Ordinary Miracle of Healing*. North Atlantic Books.

Perry, B. D., & Szalavitz, M. (2017). *The Boy Who Was Raised as a Dog: And Other Stories from a Child Psychiatrist's Notebook*. Basic Books.

Siegel, D. J., & Hartzell, M. (2013). *Parenting from the Inside Out: How a Deeper Self-Understanding Can Help You Raise Children Who Thrive*. TarcherPerigee.

Mindfulness and Somatic Practices

Kabat-Zinn, J. (2013). *Full Catastrophe Living: Using the Wisdom of Your Body and Mind to Face Stress, Pain, and Illness*. Bantam.

Brach, T. (2013). *True Refuge: Finding Peace and Freedom in Your Own Awakened Heart*. Bantam.

Haines, S. (2019). *The Politics of Trauma: Somatics, Healing, and Social Justice*. North Atlantic Books.

Blackburn, E., & Epel, E. (2017). *The Telomere Effect: A Revolutionary Approach to Living Younger, Healthier, Longer*. Grand Central Publishing.

Journal Articles and Research Papers

Felitti, V. J., et al. (1998). "Relationship of Childhood Abuse and Household Dysfunction to Many of the Leading Causes of Death in Adults: The Adverse Childhood Experiences (ACE) Study." *American Journal of Preventive Medicine*, 14(4), 245-258.

Yehuda, R., & Lehrner, A. (2018). "Intergenerational Transmission of Trauma Effects: Putative Role of Epigenetic Mechanisms." *World Psychiatry*, 17(3), 243-257.

Porges, S. W. (2007). "The Polyvagal Perspective." *Biological Psychology*, 74(2), 116-143.

Schore, A. N. (2001). "Effects of a Secure Attachment Relationship on Right Brain Development, Affect Regulation, and Infant Mental Health." *Infant Mental Health Journal*, 22(1-2), 7-66.

Teicher, M. H., et al. (2016). "The Effects of Childhood Maltreatment on Brain Structure, Function and Connectivity." *Nature Reviews Neuroscience*, 17(10), 652-666.

Online Resources

The National Child Traumatic Stress Network. (n.d.). Retrieved from https://www.nctsn.org/

Trauma Research Foundation. (n.d.). Retrieved from https://traumaresearchfoundation.org/

The Center for Polyvagal Theory. (n.d.). Retrieved from https://www.stephenporges.com/

The Gottman Institute. (n.d.). Retrieved from https://www.gottman.com/

International Society for Traumatic Stress Studies. (n.d.). Retrieved from https://istss.org/

www.ingramcontent.com/pod-product-compliance
Lightning Source LLC
Chambersburg PA
CBHW050734010526
44107CB00010B/854